Library Services for Multicultural Patrons

Strategies to Encourage Library Use

Edited by
Carol Smallwood and Kim Becnel

THE SCARECROW PRESS, INC.
Lanham • Toronto • Plymouth, UK
2013

Published by Scarecrow Press, Inc.
A wholly owned subsidiary of The Rowman & Littlefield Publishing Group, Inc.
4501 Forbes Boulevard, Suite 200, Lanham, Maryland 20706
www.rowman.com

10 Thornbury Road, Plymouth PL6 7PP, United Kingdom

British Library Cataloguing in Publication Information Available

Library of Congress Cataloging-in-Publication Data

Library services for multicultural patrons : strategies to encourage library use / edited by Carol Smallwood, Kim Becnel.
p. cm.
Includes bibliographical references and index.
ISBN 978-0-8108-8722-0 (pbk.) — ISBN 978-0-8108-8723-7 (ebook) (print) 1. Libraries and minorities. 2. Academic libraries—Services to minorities. 3. Libraries and community. I. Smallwood, Carol, 1939- II. Becnel, Kim.
Z711.8.L5285 2013
027.6'3—dc23
2012029338

♾™ The paper used in this publication meets the minimum requirements of American National Standard for Information Sciences Permanence of Paper for Printed Library Materials, ANSI/NISO Z39.48-1992.

Printed in the United States of America

To Jon and Skeeter Pope
and the contributors

Contents

Foreword

We live in an increasingly multicultural world. The U.S. Census Bureau recently released estimates that in July 2011, for the first time, the majority (50.4%) of our nation's children under the age of one were minorities (Passel et al. 2012). In fact, according to Pew Research Center projections, by 2050 non-Hispanic whites are expected to become a minority of the nation's population (Passel et al. 2012). This diversity brings a richness and vibrancy of experience and cultural heritage to our communities.

Libraries are in a pivotal position to strengthen their communities by giving voice to the diverse members of their communities through programs, collections, and services and, most importantly, by creating environments of inclusiveness, respect, empowerment, and empathy. This timely publication, *Library Services for Multicultural Patrons: Strategies to Encourage Library Use*, is a collection of practical and personal articles written by public, school, and academic librarians who share their successful approaches to planning and delivering dynamic library programs that create such environments for their communities.

We see through these articles that librarians must start with themselves, putting aside their cultural assumptions and actively listening and engaging with those they serve. They need to be learners who are willing to study and practice other languages, ask questions and act on the expert advice given by their patrons, seek materials that satisfy multilingual needs, and do the research that is required to plan culturally authentic programming. As a result of these focused efforts, librarians are creating a context of inclusiveness and respect that deepens the understanding and empathy that community members hold for each other.

This book is organized around seven themes about serving multicultural patrons through libraries: the initial steps of getting organized and finding partners; developing library programs that reach students; establishing connections to the community; applying technology to empower individuals and extend the library into virtual services; creating initiatives of special outreach around critical issues like family literacy, health, and oral history; conducting multicultural programs and events; and refining reference services to serve multicultural patrons effectively.

Each section is replete with articles written by a rich variety of authors from multiple perspectives and all types of libraries. The authors bring a wealth of experience from their work in diverse areas of librarianship, including teen and adult services, collection development, cataloging, reference, academic library services, instructional services in academic and school libraries, programming, and library directorship. They provide examples from Australia, Canada, and all sections of the United States. Although the articles include helpful references, the focus of each one is not research but effective practice, an in-depth description of a program that has been developed, tested, and proven to be successful in serving the needs and interests of specific populations within the community.

This is an important book because it enables readers to step out of their own cultural identities and see the types of programs and services that match the needs and priorities of patrons with other cultural and ethnic identities. By reading the stories of successful programs and partnerships, librarians will start to develop cultural competence; they will be able to design programs and services that not only encourage library use among their multicultural patrons, but also provide opportunities for their community members to develop understanding and empathy for the multiple perspectives of others within their communities.

Barbara Stripling
Assistant Professor of Practice
School of Information Studies, Syracuse University
President-Elect, American Library Association (2013–2014)

WORK CITED

Passel, Jeffrey, Gretchen Livingston, and D'Vera Cohn. May 17, 2012. "Explaining Why Minority Births Now Outnumber White Births." http://www.pewsocialtrends.org/2012/05/17/explaining-why-minority-births-now-outnumber-white-births (accessed June 6, 2012).

Preface

Libraries welcome everyone regardless of gender, race, ethnicity, sexual preference, or means. We exist to serve our communities in the broadest sense. However, simply embracing this philosophy in our mission statements and even in our hearts is not enough. Librarians understand that we must take action to draw in and work hard to better serve those members of our communities who, for whatever reason, don't typically take advantage of our services. When asked to contribute to a collection of essays describing how best to do this, we heard from librarians across the nation and from around the world, librarians working in school, university, special, and public libraries as well as in faculty and management positions, who had one thing in common: they had all experimented extensively and successfully with various strategies designed to attract, serve, and retain a multicultural patron base.

This volume presents their greatest success stories and features numerous tips and techniques to help other librarians improve services to the multicultural groups in their own communities. We divided these helpful chapters into the following categories for ease of access: (1) Getting Organized and Finding Partners, (2) Reaching Students, (3) Community Connections, (4) Applying Technology, (5) Outreach Initiatives, (6) Programming and Events, and (7) Reference Services. The chapters included in these sections offer suggestions for collaborative efforts, many rich and varied programming ideas, strategies for improving library instruction and reference services to speakers of English as a second language, marketing and promotional tips, and much more.

It was an honor to have the foreword written by Barbara Stripling, assistant professor of practice at the School of Information Studies, Syracuse University, now President-Elect of the American Library Association. She has had experience serving diverse populations as a school librarian, library director, and in other positions in New York, Colorado, Arkansas, North Carolina, and Tennessee.

We hope that staff in all types of libraries will implement some of the ideas presented here, tweaking them to suit the needs of their own communities and improving them in the process. Most of all, we hope this volume offers inspiration to librarians to take creative risks and bold action to welcome the multicultural populations in their towns, cities, and schools into the library community. We'll all be richer for the effort.

Acknowledgments

Howard C. Bybee, family history librarian, Harold B. Lee Library, Brigham Young University

Brenda Lincke Fisseler, director, Friench Simpson Memorial Library, Hallettsville, Texas

Kerry A. FitzGerald, assistant director, Loutit District Library, Grand Haven, Michigan

Emily Griffin, reference/local history librarian, Crawfordsville District Public Library, Crawfordsville, Indiana; contributor, *Preserving Local Writers, Genealogy, Photographs, Newspapers, and Related Materials* (2012)

Vera Gubnitskaia, Orange County Library System, Orlando, Florida; coeditor, *How to STEM: Science, Technology, Engineering, and Math Education* (forthcoming)

Kerol Harrod, Denton Public Library; coeditor, *Marketing Your Library: Tips and Tools That Work* (2012)

Courtney L. Young, head librarian, Penn State Greater Allegheny

Part I

Getting Organized and Finding Partners

Chapter One

Becoming a Multicultural Services Library

A Guided Journey to Serving Diverse Populations

Donna Walker and Padma Polepeddi

BECOMING AN EXPLORER

Embarking on the journey to serve patrons from diverse backgrounds is an exciting adventure for those of us interested in equity of access. Our own journeys started with an awareness that led to discovery and proceeded to greater understanding, which then propelled us to action. We know that lasting impact can result from taking this personal journey. Making a personal commitment to this journey is the first step on the road to serving diverse populations. Sometimes that means being pushed out of your comfort zone, exploding obstacles in your path, and facing other adventures heretofore unimagined. Where will that commitment start for you? In this chapter, we will provide landmarks for service to help you recognize some important destinations along the path of your discovery. We will also provide skill builder activities that are intended to take you out of your comfort zone and create learning opportunities that will inform your own personal journey.

DONNA'S JOURNEY

Seven years ago, I got my dream job of managing library services to the branches that served the most ethnically, racially, and economically diverse populations in our system. At the same time, I also became the manager of

Outreach Services. My heart was ready for this exciting new work. The minute I stepped into our branch, where we primarily served Russian speakers, I had my first culture shock. Of course, I was familiar with this branch and our services. But I was taken aback by my own reaction to the unfamiliarity of the patrons, materials, and staff. What was most startling was the lack of trust on both sides around the ideas of competency and understanding. I had a long way to go to comprehend how to best serve cultures that were so different from my own. At that moment, I committed to looking at myself and others in a new way—taking my own first steps on an exciting, fruitful, and gratifying journey to developing and delivering library services to this and other special populations.

PADMA'S JOURNEY

My personal journey started several years ago from having experienced the long-lasting impact of receiving inclusive and effective service in a public library on Halsted Street in Chicago. The commitment of public libraries to provide access to all has made me a passionate advocate for serving diverse populations in a public library setting.

A growth experience for me happened more recently at the library where I am the supervisor. I was called to defend a woman who was being verbally attacked by another woman for wearing a burka in America. The verbal diatribe was upsetting not just to the woman and her family, but to the other patrons in the library as well. I had to remove the offender from the library. A lasting impact was made on me by the response of the woman in the burka. She thanked me for standing up for her and showing her children that there are public places like the library that are welcoming and where they can be treated just like everyone else.

It is difficult encounters such as these that pushed us to grow personally and professionally. They emphasized the responsibility we have as service-providing professionals to ensure that public library environments provide access to people from all backgrounds. It is such incidents that act as springboards for developing our own cultural competency. It is such personal journeys that help us become tour guides to our peers and our organizations for their journeys as well.

LANDMARK: COMMITMENT TO PERSONAL CULTURAL COMPETENCY

Building awareness of the changing demographics in communities, creating welcoming and inclusive environments in library spaces, building inclusive collections and resources, and ensuring the cultural competency of library staff serving diverse populations are initial destinations on a personal road map to serve multicultural populations. By doing so, we can be leaders in helping public libraries fulfill their mission of providing free and equal access to information for people of all languages and backgrounds.

In addition to increasing our knowledge of changing demographics, we can take steps to build our personal knowledge of cultures around the world. Such inner curiosity leads to exciting discoveries that can permeate all levels of service personnel in libraries. This results in bringing a sincerity of approach and lending an authenticity to services offered. We all start at a different place in the journey of building cultural competency. Start where you are. No matter how broad or limited your previous experiences have been, we think you will benefit from testing yourself with some very specific activities intended to stretch yourself, increase your knowledge of other cultures, and lead you to better understanding.

SKILL BUILDER: CULTURAL COMPETENCY

1. Attend a religious or social ceremony of a culture different from your own.
2. Attend a fair celebrating a culture different from your own that is hosted by that culture.
3. Seek out a spot where you are the minority and spend some time there. Blog or journal about your experience.

LANDMARK: KNOWING THE POPULATION

Good data is a prerequisite for libraries to understand the makeup of their communities. Using needs assessment helps a library design and deliver services to multicultural populations that are authentic, intentional, and high quality. As entire books are written on this topic, we will not describe the full process here. However, we think it's worth mentioning some of the steps libraries take when they strive to know their communities more fully.

Depending on the type of library system, some or all of the information they need may already be available. Libraries that serve diverse populations find a starting point that makes sense for their situation. Reviewing multiple sources helps a library decide on an approach for a needs assessment. Literature from our professional organizations and other industries are resources that libraries use to compare different strategies. Creative approaches are also developed when libraries use literature about marketing to different cultures when developing a needs assessment.

When a library takes this data-driven approach, rich information about the community is gathered. This information builds on the observations and experience of staff that also are an integral part of a full needs assessment process. When a library makes its personal experience the sum total of its data collection, it can miss key aspects of serving multicultural populations that might not have made themselves known otherwise. A library that analyzes and understands the data it has collected is in a better position to create service that meets the real needs of their population. When multiple levels of staff are involved, it can also demonstrate a level of commitment to knowing a population that permeates the organization.

SKILL BUILDER: NEEDS ASSESSMENT

1. Attend a PTO meeting at a local school. Listen for information needs. Don't ask what the library can do for them.
2. Walk the neighborhood of the area you are studying. Stop in for coffee at a locally owned establishment. Listen and learn.
3. Find an organization immersed in your target culture. Attend the meetings. Be a listener.

LANDMARK: AN AUTHENTIC COLLECTION

Quality service to target populations manifests itself in the materials a library provides. Thus, a critical destination is a discreet collection development policy based on what was learned in the needs assessment. The analysis from the needs assessment informs a library's choices when it begins to formulate a plan for a special collection.

Depending on the target population, it is not much of a leap then for a library to find sources for collection development policies that already exist. Many library systems, businesses, and organizations have long-standing services to multicultural and special populations. Using the work of a successful organization as a template can be a best practice for a library just starting to develop these services. Even when targeting a population that hasn't been served well to date, templates used by others are helpful starting points.

Using the same collection development policy template for a special collection as the other collection development policies in a library validates it. It also serves as a guidepost when training staff to help them understand the core values of the larger organization. Using this template also helps a library think about what formats make sense for a population and what formats are less successful. It can also be used to articulate a library's reasons for selection, deselection, inclusion, and exclusion. Once materials have been purchased, a library is sometimes challenged about its choices. Staff who are knowledgeable about why selection decisions have been made are front-line advocates for the collection and related services as well.

LANDMARK: INTENTIONAL STAFFING FOR MULTICULTURAL SERVICES

This brings us to another important landmark on the journey to serving diverse populations, which is having a staffing model that supports these services. For example, once the collection development policy is in place, it is ideal when staff from the targeted population do the selection of the materials. In addition, having someone from that population on the floor every open hour creates access points to the collection that are optimal. Taking this intentional step creates a pathway to authenticity. We realize that staffing for multicultural services takes time and advocacy. There are ways that libraries make progress in creating this environment until their staffing fully meets the needs of the community. For example, a library might have trusted people from the community review the material selection periodically or at least do spot checks of the virtual and physical shelves and report their opinions back to staff. Sometimes, libraries take creative detours to get to our desired destinations.

One way to determine that a library has reached this destination is by using hard measures like circulation and turnover figures. Another hard measure is whether a library has phone and floor coverage by staff from that population every open hour. When an organization sets target goals like this, evaluating success and discovering opportunities comes more easily. Retention of staff in this area is another measure of success that a library with well-developed services will use to evaluate its progress.

SKILL BUILDER: COLLECTION AND STAFFING ACTIVITIES

1. Call a library that serves a population similar to the one you are targeting. Ask them what they do best.
2. Visit the website of a library that is well known for serving multicultural populations. What features do they use to make that population feel welcome to the site? What barriers do you see?
3. Visit a library in person that claims to serve a particular population. Do you see staff of that culture in the library? Do you see patrons of that culture in the library? Where are the materials to serve that population located?

LANDMARK: REACHING YOUR TARGET POPULATION

Effective outreach to the targeted population is another important marker on the road to creating authentic, intentional, and quality services. As with collections, the analysis of the needs assessment leads to better outcomes, as does a fully developed outreach plan.

One way libraries create an environment for effective outreach is by developing a vision statement at the outset as a way to visualize outcomes. Many plans include goals, objectives, and specific action steps as well. An example of a goal for outreach might read something like this: bring in new library users, or assist new immigrants in integrating into U.S. society. Once these important elements are in place, outreach venues start to come into focus.

Of course, outreach venues depend on the target population. One common venue is through newspapers, radio, or other media. Success in this area is achieved when a library takes the time to discover what media a population uses and focuses their efforts on that first. For example, a Russian-speaking population might be reached best through the local Russian newspaper, and a Spanish-speaking population might be best reached through radio. Media outlets that focus on special populations often seek out and welcome partnerships with libraries.

Other outreach venues are as varied as the populations, but there are common areas in which libraries have had success. Involvement with the chamber of commerce or consulate creates immediate opportunities. Conversations with day cares and senior centers can also lead to ideas for services. Partnerships with other organizations including but not limited to those serving new immigrants and refugees are often fruitful, especially when the partners share a common customer. Festivals and events have organizers who often welcome participation from libraries. Some populations have special camps supporting adoptive children from a particular country or youth of a particular ethnicity. These are especially rich connections. Churches, mosques, or other religious organizations also offer excellent outreach opportunities. Visits to local markets also bring results. Libraries and library staff who write articles, join organizations, and are visible in the places that their diverse populations use for sources of information, entertainment, business, or socializing are libraries that have effective outreach. The more the library is involved in the target community outside the library walls, the more effective their outreach efforts demonstrate themselves to be.

SKILL BUILDER: STRETCHING YOUR OUTREACH

1. Go to an international food market or a restaurant that serves a specific multicultural cuisine. Don't cheat by going to a Chinese fast food place.
2. Show up at a cultural event in a local church or mosque. What are people wearing? Find out why.
3. Visit an institution or organization that serves a particular age group like seniors or teens. See what programming is available. Brainstorm a list of ways you think the library might serve this special population.
4. Share ideas with peers at library and information science conferences.

LANDMARK: WELCOMING AND INCLUSIVE LIBRARY ENVIRONMENTS

Creating welcoming and inclusive library environments is one of the most effective visual landmarks in the journey to serve all populations. The hallmark of welcoming and inclusive library environments is where the commitment to diversity does not stand out but is integrated into the flow and movement of library service. Walking into a library and finding patrons talking to their friends or relatives on Skype in various languages by taking advantage of the free WiFi in the library is a great way of showcasing to patrons the welcoming nature of the library.

Providing welcome signage in languages that reflects the composition of the library community can be done as naturally as providing bike stands to the public. Universal graphics used to indicate basic amenities like restrooms, information kiosks, book drops, trash, recycle bins, and so on helps in removing any language barriers. As much as special displays to commemorate special celebrations like Martin Luther King Day or Cinco de

Mayo promote targeted outreach, the concept of inclusion can be worked into day-to-day merchandising of library resources too. Using bilingual signage for language collections and resources provides access to all collections.

This inclusive environment can also extend to digital spaces like the library website and catalog. Integrating exciting graphics and moving away from text-heavy websites also draws in diverse users. Having more than one language portal on the website indicates the demographics of language users using the library. Having a catalog in multiple languages takes a real commitment to being inclusive. Successful libraries map out a plan to create this important access point. It is an important indicator of an inclusive environment.

SKILL BUILDER: BEING WELCOMING AND INCLUSIVE

1. Challenge yourself to learn common phrases like "hello and "good-bye" in the different languages used by your library community. Use them.
2. Use a foreign language–learning software from your local library, as that will develop an appreciation for the effort involved in grasping the basic concepts for communicating in a different language.
3. Go to places like international food markets and take note of the signage, the service extended by the cashiers, and the body language of the people using the food market, as well as the people at the cash registers and other service personnel.
4. Attend an ESL class in session at a local elementary school, a local library, or a local community college.

LANDMARK: QUALITY LIBRARY PROGRAMS

Offering multicultural library programs is a key indicator that a library is providing authentic service. Programs such as these draw in large numbers of residents and also fuel the interest of the community in learning about themselves, their society, and the larger world. Ensuring that cultural sensitivity components are built into the design and delivery of programs is the key to making all populations feel welcome and having them actively participate. Use of resources and tools for developing library programs that reflect inclusion of diverse populations results in meaningful service provision. For example, a diversity calendar featuring celebrations around the world is a handy resource for planning library programs. The delivery of "celebrations around the world" programs is most successful when everyone in the community has the opportunity to learn and participate in the celebration, not just the ethnic group that is familiar with the celebration. When a staff member delivering the program prefaces the presentation by introducing its significance followed by interactive activities, learning happens. Program evaluation and program feedback forms available in more than one language invite dialogue from all groups attending and indicate a sincere desire to hear from everyone.

Bilingual delivery of important programs like storytimes, computer classes, and book clubs ensures access to important literacy and skill-building resources. Delivering programs in the home language is another way a library signals its commitment to serving a particular population. Having a program delivered in the nondominant language sometimes creates tension in a library community. Successful libraries develop their staff so that they understand the philosophy around such decisions and are ready to explain them if challenged. Informed staff create opportunities for building bridges to understanding.

SKILL BUILDER: PROGRAMMING FOR DIVERSE COMMUNITIES

1. Participate in the Cinco de Mayo celebrations or any cultural celebration hosted by your local government. Take note of the event highlights and the makeup of the audience. Go a step further and make inquires as to who coordinates these cultural events and express interest in meeting with the person.
2. Take time to talk to non-English speakers and their children attending cultural events in your library and ask them what they liked about the program.
3. Attend a cultural celebration put out annually by a specific ethnic group, like the Japanese festival or Festival of the Dragons. Observe how people interact with each other and what draws them to attend.

NEXT STEPS ON YOUR JOURNEY: USING YOUR NEW COMPETENCE TO GUIDE YOUR ORGANIZATION

We hope you have gained some new understanding about the ongoing nature of building cultural competency in yourself and your organization and the landmarks of success to watch for along the way. The essence of serving multicultural populations is understanding that it is a continuous journey with many twists and turns. When library strategic initiatives incorporate the awareness and inclusion of the multicultural populations using the libraries, it shows the library's commitment and sincerity to provide service to all community members. It also encourages nonusers to become users. Setting newer challenges for our own personal growth and understanding of the changing global community needs to be part of our daily experience as well as our strategic planning. Just as explorers have always looked for new ways to old destinations and new destinations too, we want to challenge the standard routes to serving multicultural populations. We want to find innovative and exhilarating ways to engage with our community. Further, our services to multicultural populations can be a springboard to engage with global communities on a larger scale. The more we seek out newer and creative collaborations and partnerships, the more authentic services we can provide.

ARE YOU READY?

When thinking about the future of libraries, we cannot help but think about how serving diverse, multicultural populations opens a whole new avenue of opportunity for expanded use and access. Exciting new vistas in library service are out there waiting for champions like you to embrace the opportunities in serving these populations. As we challenge ourselves, we challenge you to create expansive, inclusive library service that is an authentic reflection of the communities in which we live and serve.

Chapter Two

No Surprise, Community Engagement Works

Theresa Beaulieu

A well-worn plot in television sitcoms is the surprise party. Imagine it is your birthday, and some friends at work decide to throw you a surprise party. The tension builds—and not just from keeping a secret—but because they do not really know if you would like a surprise party or if you loathe surprise parties and do not even want to think about getting older.

This surprise-party scenario is the same as creating multicultural programming at the library without involving the intended audience in the planning. In most cases, if you plan multicultural programming without involving the target audience, you do not know enough about the intended audience to ensure success. Without engaging the multicultural community, you cannot be sure if they would be more interested in a course on estate planning, in listening to a speaker who survived the Holocaust, or in hearing about the causes of childhood asthma. Consequently, when you hold a surprise-party event at the library, you may get a less-than-spectacular response.

An events planner may have a couple of common responses to this lack of community participation. Librarians and staff may respond by deciding that nine participants is a pretty good turnout for a first try. They may even blame the intended audience for not appreciating their efforts. However, a more effective long-term solution involves giving up on the surprise-party approach and working with the multicultural community to see what they are interested in and what needs they actually have for library services. By giving up the surprise-party approach to multicultural events planning, you are free to use the community engagement approach, which will deliver much better results for your library.

Broadly speaking, community engagement requires relationship building. It requires you to get out from behind the desk and into the multicultural community to meet with, to interact with, and to network with others. Since this article is concerned specifically with multicultural partnerships, for our purposes community engagement is collaborating with multicultural organizations in mutually beneficial partnerships to achieve common goals. Both partners—the library and the multicultural community—bring their skills, knowledge, and abilities to the table and work together from a place of shared goals. Community engagement is also a long-term proposition, not a one-shot deal. In fact, if what you are looking for is a one-time grant partner, community engagement is probably not for you. Community engagement is much more like developing and maintaining a mutual friendship, or like growing old with a partner—one you know so well that you are sure whether or not your partner likes surprise parties.

There are several elements of community engagement to keep in mind when working to establish such a relationship:

- Think user-centered. Focus on what you can do for the community group, not just what the group can do for your library. For example, improving your library's gate count or increasing other library statistics will most likely have no benefit for the community group, if they are not interested in the events held at your library or if the resources in your building are not relevant to them.
- Be open and flexible. You may be learning to do things in new ways, but you will also be serving new patrons. Since this may be a new venture for your library, you may also need to agree to perform new services, to collect different types of resources from those you are used to, or to communicate in different ways.
- Establish lines of communication. Open and frequent conversations, discussions, and communications will go a long way toward creating a good relationship. Try to establish formal and informal means of communicating with your new partner. A potential difficulty here may be actually getting out of the library building, especially if your institutional policies do not make it easy to be away from the physical library. Community engagement really does require spending time in the community.
- Show mutual respect. Learn about your new partner, and let your partner know about you and the library you work for. You may discover that each of you has different knowledge, abilities, and ways of doing things. Respect those differences, rather than trying to change them.

- Create a shared vision. You will be planning as a part of the group, not apart from the group. "Two heads are better than one" is not just a cliché. Besides bringing extra brainpower to a project, though, creating a shared vision puts you both on the same team. Building from that position is powerful.

These are handy starting points, but they just scratch the surface of community engagement. Unless applied consistently, your endeavor can start to unravel. For example, a local library had a long-standing information literacy class for multicultural students that suddenly experienced a decrease in the number of participants. Calls to one teacher confirmed that the school and the students were very interested in the class, but still the numbers lagged. Further contact with the teacher revealed that the teachers and students were interested in participating, but budget cuts had eliminated funds for the field trips, so they could not come. Though the lines of communication had not been open consistently, the situation could be fixed with some persistence, flexibility, and new thinking. A little brainstorming by both parties exposed several potential solutions:

- The students could pay for the field trip bus.
- The students could come on a Saturday and take their own transportation to the library.
- The library's friends group could pay for the bus.
- The library visit could be done in conjunction with another visit to the area.
- The library service could be delivered at the high school.
- The library could create remote access for the students.

Fortunately there were several potential ways to address the problem. However, simply coming up with a list of solutions to existing problems will not create a relationship with any community. In order to understand which solution is viable, a successful librarian will not only know the elements of community engagement, but also will have a deep understanding of the culture of the community. This culture is reflected in the social context of the community.

Understanding the social context of the community and careful consideration of that context, along with the basic elements of community engagement, will help you create a successful long-term partnership. There are several loosely defined steps to understanding the social context of a community and to effectively engaging with it. While these steps are essential, they are not necessarily sequential, and they may indeed be recursive: (1) conduct background research about the diverse community you wish to engage; (2)

know what you want to accomplish and select potential partners; (3) establish a relationship with the partners; (4) find common ground with your partners; and (5) continue to maintain the relationships.

1. Start with some background research on your own and become knowledgeable about the diverse community you wish to engage. The strengths and resources you begin to identify are potential places you can build on. Besides research, this requires a lot of observation. This is much more of a hands-on type of learning than reading a list of stereotypes, which can be found in many books or workshops. Discover for yourself what the situation is for a particular community rather than relying on someone else's perceptions. Taking notes or journaling may help with the process. This is also the start of mutual respect.

    *   What assets does the community have? These may include a community center, archival collections, strong networks, and community groups. In order to keep current with the groups, sign up for newsletters if available; read related blogs; and friend organizational or personal Facebook pages as appropriate.
    *   Visit the local community center or communal gathering spot. You may notice things that are unfamiliar to you. Take note; these perceptions will help you later, when you imagine what it is like for a member of that community to enter your library.
    *   How does change take place in the community? Is there one person or group identified as a community leader? Identify the key stakeholders who are essential for your success.
    *   How does the community feel about the initiatives that your library has done in the past? Did the community perceive these events as successful or not? If the community views the past actions of your library as unreliable, it may take longer to build a solid relationship. Unfortunately, for whatever reasons, unreliable partners do exist, and their actions have impacted how the community perceives them. In one case, the population statistics of an American Indian tribal community were used to apply for funding for a county library, and though the funding came in and remained in place, the bookmobile that was to provide service to the American Indian tribal community was short-lived. This experience put a tangible strain on the relationship between the tribe and the county.
    *   Ensure your own cultural competence; no one else can ensure this for you. Basically, this requires an expanded understanding of others, and it requires that you understand how your own cultural view impacts your perceptions, in order for you to develop the competen-

cy and comfort required to engage with the intended community. If deep down you dislike or are uncomfortable working with people outside of your own group, it will be apparent to others.

2. Know what you want to accomplish in a partnership, so it does not get forgotten in the process of working together. Review what the community groups focus their resources on to see which will best match your goals, and select the best potential partners for engagement.

   - Review your institutional goals to ensure that any list you come up with will be in alignment with them.
   - Create a list of the things you hope to accomplish from any potential partnership. If you have specific requirements, perhaps due to grant funding, try to frame these broadly and at the outcome level, rather than as specific activities. By doing so, you are freer to look at alternative ways of achieving the same outcome. For example, if you use the following output measure as a goal you will have little flexibility: "Five students will attend a class in the library on information literacy." However, if you think in terms of broad outcomes, you will have more flexibility as to how to achieve your goal: "Students will evaluate Internet sites for reliability." Do not box yourself in. If you do not have specific requirements to begin with, you can enjoy the flexibility.
   - Find the groups that have shared values with your library. This will make it easier for you to find common ground. For example, if the community center runs an after-school program, holds adult education classes, or features public speakers, it is a good indication that the community center shares values with your library.
   - Meet with key parties whose values align with those of your library and those interested in library services to determine if they would be a good fit and if they are interested in working together.

3. Begin to establish a relationship with the community partner or organization. These relationships are key to moving forward, and even the intervening casual conversations you have with the community may reveal much about how the community has interacted with your library in the past and how they perceive it, which will help you gain a big-picture view of your target audience.

   - Get involved with the various community groups you see as potential partners. You have started by finding some background information. Next, attend meetings of the potential partners.

- Begin establishing lines of communication. Ensure groups have your contact information or business card. Talk with them about your library. Get an informal sense of their take on the library.
- Participate in the community. You can bring refreshments to meetings or anecdotes to share. Volunteer to help where you have the expertise or resources. Nothing shows good faith and friendship like helping with a problem.
- Build trust. Meet with community groups in their areas, instead of having them travel to the library. Be aware that past breaches of trust by others may make your job more difficult. Transparency, honesty, good will, and patience are your allies.
- Practice mutual respect. Imagine how someone feels coming into your library; what is there that would make them feel at home? Check the artwork in your library. Is your potential audience represented in a way that would be perceived as positive by them? Are there resources and exhibits that reflect their interests? Do you have resources and signage in your audience's language? This can be more of a long-term process, as you do not want to have a superficial transformation. Just be aware that the audience may not feel automatically at ease.

4. Develop a shared vision by staying open and flexible. Work together to develop a project you both are interested in that meets shared goals. Keep the target user in mind, and ensure their voices are heard and respected.

- Ask what types of things they are already doing, what they would like to accomplish, and what things they have in place already to accomplish their goals.
- Ask what are the community's needs for library services and partnership. It may not be initially apparent to the stakeholders that your resources can be of use to them. You could hold future community meetings in your library to familiarize the community with your resources and to demonstrate some of the services you offer in order to get the community's reaction to the services, the collections, and the building.
- Survey or interview community members to supplement the knowledge you have gained by observation or direct involvement. Community members can be enlisted to help create the questions, which may generate more interest in the survey. In lieu of interviews, questions can be posited with focus groups or talking circles, depending on what works best for the community you are working with.

- Be sure you have the community review the results of your survey or focus group. This will provoke more discussion, clarification, and prompt more ideas, as well as provide depth to the final report. Share the final report in multiple venues: in public meetings, online posts, and so forth.
- Establish incentives for participation. Incentives could include access to library information resources, the use of library physical space, or research time.
- Work together to figure out how your goals complement each other. You have heard what the group is doing, and you have data from the surveys or interviews. Brainstorm ways to combine your efforts. If brainstorming is slow going, a list of the types of activities the library can do or already does for other groups may help, though do not let the list of services limit your thinking.
- Be willing to negotiate, take risks, and say yes. Grab hold of a good idea when you hear it. Support the enthusiasm of others. Recognize, though, that this can be an interesting balancing act, as the nuts and bolts of implementation are down the road, so do not overpromise.
- Formalize your agreement to work together with a memorandum of understanding or another mechanism that works for your group.

5. Since the focus of community engagement is on the library's relationship with the community, continued attention to the relationship is essential. This step entails more than maintaining a line of communication with your partner. It involves developing your relationship at a more significant level and celebrating the successes of your shared vision.

- Ensure you have the contact information of the people you meet with, as well as the information for the person who is the administrative liaison. Send your thanks for any meetings, interviews, and so on.
- Keep the community informed. Send information, such as potential grant opportunities, programming ideas that you run across, or even current events at the library that the community may be genuinely interested in. Find out if it is possible to link your Internet sites. If your new partner has signed on to be a grant partner with you, send copies of the progress reports and the final grant report to your partner.
- Find ways for the community organization to take part in your library's continued development. This may involve community inclusion on library committees, invitations to speak as a guest speaker, or participating as partners in creating library exhibits. Addition-

ally, you could create an input mechanism on your library's home page, so the community has a clear way to make comments and suggestions without risking that the comments get misdirected.

- Find ways for your library's volunteer groups, friends groups, and staff to participate with the community. These could be reciprocal to the events above: inclusion on local committees, speaking engagements, or creating materials for the community.
- Recognize what you and your partner have achieved. Such recognition could include an awards ceremony, a year-end celebration, and newsletter or social media announcements. Additionally, local media outlets can be sent press releases to announce your partnership and your success.

Finally, there is a great deal of community engagement that cannot be confined to bullet points. That is because while working with others can be described so it may appear to be as easy as following directions, applying it is actually more of an art. It takes time to develop an understanding of your partner's culture. There will be things that you miss, because they are invisible from your perspective, and you will need your best judgment and people skills to overcome them. Working with multicultural community partners and engaging with them involves the same give and take, love and caring, and time that working successfully with your family and friends takes. When you reach that level of engagement, you will know whether or not they like surprise parties.

Chapter Three

International Advisory Committee at the Charlotte Mecklenburg Library

Meryle A. Leonard

In an ideal community, the library staff would reflect the diversity of the community it serves. A diverse library staff could help overcome language and cultural barriers that may prevent the international population from becoming regular library patrons. As libraries across the country face drastic budget cuts, diverse staffing may not be an option, but establishing an International Advisory Committee for your library can be a free and creative method to serve and reach the international members of your community.

PURPOSE

Charlotte Mecklenburg Library always recognized the need to address the diversity in the community, and the commitment became part of the 2009–2012 Strategic Plan. In 2009, our executive staff and board of trustees created specific goals to create cultural and global awareness. They were committed to library services, programs, and collections that reflected the increasing diversity of the community. This commitment continues and was restated in the new and current 2012 Strategic Plan.

To better provide access to information and resources, as well as meet the needs of our diverse population, Charlotte Mecklenburg Library solicited assistance from community volunteers and formed an International Advisory Committee. The advisory committee serves as a benchmark for the library. The committee asks the following question: "Is the library meeting the needs of the international community with our collections and services?" The committee then responds with three different strategies: advising, advocacy, and specific projects.

The committee advises the library on services, programs, and collections that reflect global awareness and the diversity of cultures represented in the community. They offer feedback on services and programs and facilitate networking opportunities between the library and our international community. For example, the committee was instrumental in recognizing the need for the library to have programs and services honoring Native American History Month, and with their assistance, we offered community and branch programs. Committee member Barbara Locklear, a member of the American Indian Lumbee Tribe of North Carolina, provided branch and community programs that increased participants' understanding and appreciation of Native American history and culture. Additionally, members of the International Advisory Committee have successfully volunteered their time, talent, and resources to support specific library projects. Committee members have participated in Charlotte Mecklenburg Library's annual Día de los Niños/Día de los Libros celebration, Asian American History Month programs, Con A de Arte (a celebration of Latino artists), and our Global Family Story Festival.

The committee is comprised of informed volunteers who are aware of the library's vision, goals, and key messages. By advocating for the library, they highlight and promote Charlotte Mecklenburg Library's services and programs. Our committee was particularly effective in communicating with stakeholders during a very critical funding process. Committee members were present and spoke on behalf of the library during the board of county commissioners' budget meetings. Mecklenburg County is the library's largest funder. Since committee members worked with the library and they had knowledge of library services, especially in regard to our growing international community, they were the ideal candidates to speak on the library's behalf.

Advocacy is also an ideal opportunity for volunteers who are strong library supporters but have limited time. Supporters who may not have time to attend meetings or volunteer at branches and programs can be informed citizens and share the library's key messages with funders, partners, community members, and other stakeholders. Advocates can help community members understand the value of the library in the community. Advocates can detail the role the library plays in education, literacy, and workforce development, not to mention their ability to promote the foreign language collections and other resources appealing to and needed by people who may not speak English as their first language. This information is not only necessary for stakeholders, especially funders, but for patrons who are new to the community and culture.

FORMING THE COMMITTEE

At the time this committee was formed, Charlotte Mecklenburg Library was already actively participating in international organizations in the community. Library staff participated and had membership in local international organizations such as the Charlotte Asian Chamber of Commerce and Latin American Organizations. From these organizations, we began recruiting committee members, making sure we had a team that represented the diversity in our community. Library staff members and community organizations such as Charlotte International House also had representation on the committee. The committee has four formal meetings per year. A twelve-month plan is created during the first meeting of the fiscal year. During each meeting, committee members are brought up to date on all library activities and policy and staff changes.

COMMITTEE BENEFITS AND OPPORTUNITIES

Irania Patterson is an employee at Charlotte Mecklenburg Library. A native of Venezuela, she participates on the International Advisory Committee. Irania believes that "the International Advisory Committee provides excellent insight and represents the communities that we serve. The committee allows us to serve the international community with authenticity. Our committee members know the culture, traditions, and educational needs of the international community." Mrs. Patterson's duties on the committee include recommending adult Spanish language books for the library's foreign language collection. Her recommendations are based on the comments and feedback she receives from patrons throughout our county.

Sharadi Gullapali is a library volunteer and has been a member of the International Advisory Committee from its inception in 2009. She feels that the committee exposes the majority population to the cultures of other countries and regions. The committee gives the library access to different international communities to help identify their needs. During this year's planning meeting, Mrs. Gullapali recommended that the library offer nontraditional programs for African American history month. She suggested programs that focused on education and careers. She believed this type of program would give community members a broader understanding of African American culture.

Since 2010, the International Advisory Committee has successfully provided a library program that recognizes many cultures in our community. Over three hundred participants attended the April 2011 World Family Festival. The World Family Festival honored several cultures through literature, art, music, and dance. As a result of this festival several attendees from the international community registered for library cards, and survey results revealed that participants would return to the library and they would like the library to host more cultural activities and programs. Members of the International Advisory Committee were successful in recruiting and recommending high-quality, experienced performers from different cultures. Program attendance and positive community response has made this festival a regular library service.

CHALLENGES

Maintaining a committee that represents the diversity in the community is a challenge. Library staff constantly recruit members for the committee, especially male members. To assist with this challenge, we welcome adjunct committee members. These volunteers lend talents in areas where they are subject area experts. One committee member who works for our local school system assisted the committee by advertising our cultural programs and activities with thousands of students and teachers. He also worked on specific projects. During our annual Día de los Niños/Día de los Libros festival, he planned a "Cinderella around the World" event with guests retelling the classic fairytale from their country. This activity added value to our event, engaged several community partners, and allowed our volunteer to participate in a meaningful way that fit his schedule. Another dedicated volunteer recently relocated. She continues to support the committee by seeking grants and other funding opportunities to support the library.

GETTING STARTED

Having an International Library Committee at your library is easy to do with some planning and support. The return on investment is worth the effort. You are utilizing volunteers in a meaningful fashion, identifying and addressing community needs, and being relevant in our ever-changing community. To get started, consider the following:

- Determine community needs. Hold a focus group to identify needs and possible volunteers.
- Create a job description. Let your volunteers know exactly what they will be doing and for how long. Do not forget to include options.
- Open the opportunity to staff. Staff members who work with the public have insight on the needs of the international community.

- Collaborate with other organizations that serve the international population.
- Involve library administration. Capture library buy-in starting at the top.
- Tell your story. Use pictures, blogs, and other forms of social media to detail your work and effectiveness.
- Set measurable goals. Be able to show stakeholders the value and impact of the committee.
- Keep statistics. Track how often as well as when and where your volunteers served.
- Always thank your volunteers. They are providing a valuable service.

CONCLUSION

The International Advisory Committee is a creative, rewarding method used by Charlotte Mecklenburg Library to increase library usage by multicultural, international populations. The committee allows volunteers to have meaningful experiences and encourages members to utilize their talents and expertise. With the help of volunteers, the library can reach out to international populations, overcoming the obstacle of hiring limitations due to lack of funding. Having educated and involved volunteers has created advocates that help communicate the library's key messages and community value. The committee also connects us to other community organizations that serve the international community. The International Advisory Committee has been successful in reaching and serving our diverse population. This committee, with its dedicated informed volunteers, has been successful in reaching our ever-changing community amid these challenging economic times.

Chapter Four

The Gathering Place

A Multicultural Experience at the Joseph F. Smith Library

Zoia Adam-Falevai and Becky DeMartini

Both Laie, Hawaii, the town where Brigham Young University, Hawaii (BYUH) is located, and the university itself were established by the Church of Jesus Christ of Latter-Day Saints as a "gathering place" to bring together students and learners from throughout the Pacific Islands and Pacific Rim. Out of a student body of over 2,600 students, half are international students who have traveled from approximately seventy-six countries to attend our school. Not only is there great diversity among our students, but this is true of our faculty and staff in the library as well.

The library supports the vision of the university "in their efforts to influence the establishment of peace internationally" by fostering an environment that provides a safe, collaborative space for learning together, not only on an intellectual level but on a personal/social level as well (Brigham Young University–Hawaii 2012). While we want to encourage academic research, we realize that there is a certain amount of interaction required. In this light, we plan for fun activities that project the image of a friendly, as well as a scholarly, space.

There are many ways we attempt to lessen the cultural and language barriers that might be problematic in such a setting as this. In working with this diverse population, we here at the Joseph F. Smith Library find the following practices to be an effective way of bringing people of different cultures and backgrounds together, as well as helping all have a comfortable and enjoyable experience while using the library:

- Hiring and training
- Activities and programs
- Assessment

HIRING AND TRAINING

When hiring student employees at the Joseph F. Smith Library, there are a few things we consider in regard to serving our diverse student body population. First, we look to hire a well-rounded pool of students from a variety of cultural backgrounds. We find the majority of our library users are more comfortable in approaching their peers with similar backgrounds, especially with international students. For example, if there is a student behind the desk who speaks their language, they are more likely to approach the reference desk for help, as they are more comfortable speaking their native language. However, it is an important requirement that our student employees be able to comprehend and communicate in English effectively. Currently the students employed in the library are from various countries such as Russia, Ghana, Samoa, Taiwan, Burma, New Caledonia, Hong Kong, the United States, and more.

Second, besides looking for applicants who are dependable, honest, and responsible, we look for those who are particularly friendly, patient, and easy to approach. There are also some basic technical and educational requirements, but we find that a lot of the specifics of the job can be learned after applicants are hired. We determine these factors through the interview process as well as contacting their references. One of the questions we ask in the interview that relates to customer service is: "Share an experience when you had to deal with an upset or angry customer, coworker, or classmate, and how you dealt with it." We find that when applicants share their experiences, we get a glimpse of how they will react when dealing with communication situations that are frustrating because of the language barrier and cultural differences.

Upon employment, we hold weekly team meetings for the purpose of continually developing confidence in their reference and customer service skills. One of the recurring training topics that arise with our student employees is the need to always have patience and humility and to be sensitive when serving our students who speak English as a second language. This includes being sensitive and approachable, as well as being able to read nonverbals, facial expressions, gestures, and so on. For example, Ben Vezzani, one of our reference student workers from New Jersey, but with considerable experience living in Korea, suggested that we all need to "speak simply and slowly, and check for confirmation through facial expressions. Even if they grunt and say 'yeah,' they may not have understood, and it's usually written on their face in this case." He reminds us that it is important not only to use words, but to notice patrons' body language, which may be more telling than what is actually being said. As librarians and supervisors we need to work on the above skills just as much as our students. We notice that when we deal with issues in a positive manner and with a sense of humor, it rubs off on our students. We like to give the patron plenty of opportunity to describe the context/nature of their question.

Overall we feel that proper hiring and training of our student employees are essential in helping us create an environment in which our diverse population of library patrons feels comfortable in approaching us for the assistance they need.

ACTIVITIES AND PROGRAMS

A number of the programs that have been started at our library in recent years have really helped us get our international students involved. One example includes the introductory library tours we hold for each of the remedial English as an International Language [EIL] classes. These students are coming from very diverse library experiences, so we try to prepare them ahead of time with some basic library vocabulary terms they will be introduced to on the tour. Familiarizing them ahead of time with words such as call number, circulation, and interlibrary loan helps in diffusing potentially confusing situations during the tour and makes this introductory experience more effective and valuable.

One program that we are involved in at the university level is the New Student Orientation (NSO), which takes place on campus each semester. The library's booth in the Student Center is the first experience that many of our new students have with our library. Here they learn about many of the services we offer in the library. We find that assigning student workers from a variety of backgrounds to facilitate the booth creates a more relaxed feeling and promotes more conversation and more smiles. We also have at least one librarian there to reinforce the fact that we are here to assist them with *anything* they may need help with and hopefully be a friendly, familiar face that will come to mind quickly when they start to get their research assignments. The second part of the library's participation in the NSO includes a library tour. We recently changed our tradition of librarians leading these tours to student employees who are trained in this capacity. Students seem to have a positive reaction with peer-to-peer interaction. Barriers fall, and there is greater trust in their more experienced peers to show them how they can use the library in their future university life.

We recently started a Book-a-Librarian program, which is often utilized and deemed a success. The program is on our library website with a button that leads to a form with the following statement: "Through Book-a-Librarian you can get one-on-one help with whatever you need! Simply fill out the form below with your name, e-mail address, and the date you want to meet with a librarian and we will be glad to help you." We have been surprised at the popularity of this new program and have noticed that interestingly over 73 percent of students using this program are international students. We believe the rise in the use of Book-a-Librarian by international students is directly correlated to advertising via the web, through library research classes, and more so through students telling other students about it. We also have English and some International Language professors referring their students to this service as they need help with their research.

One of the activities the library has hosted during our annual Library Week celebration was called *Reading in Different Languages from around the World*. We invited seven different language classes, including Samoan, Tongan, Hawaiian, Maori, Chinese, French, and Spanish, to participate in this activity, where they read library literature in their native language. The students then provided an explanation in English of what they read. Through this activity we were able to promote the language resources available, as well as showcase some of the diversity existing all around us on our campus.

Another activity hosted during Library Week was a spelling bee, which turned out to be a huge success. We were extremely happy with the number and enthusiasm of the participants, who included not only native English speakers but many nonnative-English-speaking students as well. Of our four winners, three were international students, each from a different country. Because of the success and popularity of this contest we have decided to host it each semester. This activity was a great way to get students from many backgrounds to come together in our library, have fun competing, and be able to appreciate each other's talents.

Our "Lua Letter," a newsletter posted inside the door of our bathroom stalls, is a fun but practical way to educate and inform our students about library topics and current affairs. We often include messages pertaining to different aspects of the cultures and traditions of different countries. For example, we might feature different ways of celebrating Christmas or other holidays in various countries. When we include students' quotes in our Lua Letter, they experience a sense of belonging to the library community.

One principle we generally live by when planning activities is to include food. Because this is Hawaii and we're dealing with young and usually hungry college students, this seems to be a sure way of getting people to participate in our activities. We have come to the conclusion that universally, no matter what country or culture they are from, advertising and offering free food are a great way to get students from all around the world to join in. We have had a hard time finding anyone who will turn down a free hot dog or some cookies for a few minutes of their time.

In the future, one of the ways we plan to welcome our diverse population into our Joseph F. Smith Library is to greet them with a large mural of the term "welcome" in various languages as they enter our library foyer. We also have plans to create a think tank/focus group comprised of library student employees to get input from our students' point of view on how we can improve our services and create a more appealing atmosphere in the library. In general, we usually run our ideas through our student workers to get their reactions and input.

ASSESSMENT

In recent years we have adopted a culture of assessment in our library. We strive to evaluate our programs and activities and respond to the feedback we receive. Through assessment we have created new programs, discontinued programs, and made alterations to others.

For example, one item of feedback that has been received after librarians have taught bibliographic instruction classes is the request to speak more slowly in the future. This was a great reminder to us that there are many international students in these classes who have only basic English language listening skills. This feedback has helped us be mindful of the students who speak English as a second language, and we have made a sincere effort to speak slowly and pay closer attention to their facial expressions and mannerisms to judge their comprehension.

When we decided to move much of our library instruction online through video tutorials, we were again mindful of our students who speak English as a second language by speaking clearly and slowly in these tutorials. We also adopted a policy that required the inclusion of scripted captions in the creation of our video tutorials. Although it would be much simpler and a lot less time-consuming to quickly create on-the-fly videos, without using a script or captions, we have found that this is not ideal for the nonnative English-speaking population. We have found that these students are able to comprehend the content of the tutorials with audio coupled with captions.

For the past two years during each NSO, we surveyed our new students and asked them to answer the following questions:

1. What city, state, and country are you from?
2. When you needed information in the past, where have you gone? Families, friends, relatives / Internet / Library / Other

3. Are you confident in finding books / articles / websites?
4. Are you confident in evaluating information you find for your research?

The purpose in conducting this survey is to gather information regarding the research abilities, library experiences, and information-seeking preferences our students bring with them from their home countries. For the purposes of this article, we have divided the students into four groups; Hawaii, United States and Canada, Asia, and the Pacific.

Our data shows that in seeking information our students are more likely to consult the Internet first, then family and friends, followed by the library. This answer was expected, and we try to accommodate this by setting up Google Scholar to work with our proxy and databases, as well as creating website evaluation guides. We continually keep this in mind as we move forward.

Our data also shows that those from Asia, the United States, and Canada feel more confident in finding information from the Internet, while those from Hawaii and the Pacific are more confident in finding books. All are least confident in finding articles. From this we gather that we need to start with the basics when introducing articles in our bibliographic instruction and reference interviews. We also try to introduce students to articles in other ways, such as including examples in our "Lua Letters" and highlighting them on our website.

Our students' answers also revealed that all except those in Hawaii were 85 to 90 percent confident in evaluating information they gather for their research. Only 62 percent of students from Hawaii showed confidence in evaluating information. What we see in the survey and what we have experienced in the library do not necessarily match up. For example, when working with students on finding more sources, we frequently lead them from a Wikipedia entry and nonscholarly websites and articles that they believe to be reputable to peer reviewed and scholarly sources available through our library.

Although we are not entirely pleased with the questions we have included in this survey, we plan to modify them to get information that proves more useful. We do believe that cultivating a culture of assessment is extremely valuable and will help us serve each of our students to the best of our abilities.

STUDENTS' REFLECTION

Our library student employees reflect on their experiences in helping students from different countries and backgrounds. Stacie Farr from California has been working as one of our reference student employees for the past year and shared this experience with assisting an international student:

> He didn't speak English very well so I tried to talk slowly and patiently, and we eventually reached an understanding. After helping him, he thanked me for doing my job and made sure he could pronounce my name. Since then, when I see him around campus he always says "Hi" with a big smile on his face. . . . In my experience, international students are more likely to approach me and ask for help with English language assignments. I think this is because I am Caucasian and I look like I would be able to help them with their English grammar questions. I've noticed that people from a particular culture will usually feel more comfortable approaching the student worker that is closer to their culture or race, but when it comes to English questions, people are more than willing to ask me about them.

Tauva Lima, one of our most recent hires from Western Samoa, shared a tip that she uses when encountering language barrier problems. She suggests that it helps "to have them write down on a paper if the workers are having a hard time trying to understand what they want." Since it is sometimes easier to express the question in writing, this is one additional way to alleviate some of the confusion that comes with a language barrier.

One of our international students who has also been with us a year, Liang-Chieh Ko from Taiwan, shared:

> I love serving people from various cultural backgrounds. English is also my second language and, as an international student, I understand how challenging it can be to communicate in their second language. Through interacting with people with different ethnicity, I tend to be fascinated by their tacit behaviors, expression, logical thinking, and word choices. The more I work at this position, the more enjoyable my life has become.

Natalya Askhatova from Russia has been with us for three years now and says:

> I love my experience helping students from different backgrounds and cultures. Because I'm an international student myself, it is amazing how other students are interested in where I come from and usually they ask simple questions about my language and my culture and traditions. I also enjoy seeing how native speakers are patient/impatient with me when I am taking my time to explain something in English. Most of the time students are friendly and nice. I think it is all about the attitude that we have towards one another.

Natalya sums it up nicely by finishing: "Just be friendlier, smile and be patient and understanding when they are trying to say something. Encourage them to explain what they mean, and from our side try to speak slow and clear."

CONCLUSION

The techniques, services, and programs that have been outlined in this article are a few of the practical ways that the Joseph F. Smith Library family strives to lessen the cultural and languages barriers that are prevalent at our university. Many have been successful, and we continue to improve and add more services toward this goal of creating unity among our multicultural student body.

To summarize the most important points we have learned in helping such a multicultural clientele here at Brigham Young University, Hawaii: First, we prepare by hiring the right people and training them to be sensitive to cultural differences. This includes being open-minded, friendly, confident, and patient. These student employees are most often the first point of contact for those seeking help. Constant discussions with our students provide valuable feedback on how to improve our customer service and create a positive learning environment.

Second, we devise activities and programs that can be enjoyed by everyone. Some are specifically created with international student body participation in mind, for the main purpose of encouraging them to take part and be involved in the library community, as well as being comfortable and confident in approaching library employees for help.

Third, the opportunity to improve our services for our multicultural patrons is made possible through the process of assessment. Reaction and comments from the student body are always taken into consideration, as we are here to serve them to the best of our abilities.

Above all, we feel the most important trait that we cultivate and live by on our campus is the Spirit of Aloha. Our multinational environment, plus the Hawaiian Aloha Spirit, minimizes cultural differences and allows everyone to work toward the common goal of getting a university education. This Aloha Spirit encompasses acceptance, love, harmony, and the sense of *ohana*, or belonging to one big family. This, coupled with the fact that everyone is a minority here, encourages cooperation and understanding. Working in the BYU-Hawaii Library is truly a unique experience.

WORK CITED

Brigham Young University–Hawaii. "BYU–Hawaii Mission and Vision." BYU–Hawaii. http://about.byuh.edu/mission (accessed April 12, 2012).

Chapter Five

Partnerships Linking Cultures

*Multicultural Librarianship in
British Columbia's Public Libraries*

Allan Cho and Ada Con

The British Columbia Library Association (BCLA) Diversity and Multicultural Services Committee (see textbox 5.1) creates partnerships and shares resources to serve their communities. Using creative community outreach initiatives, such as programming for world cultures, sharing collection building and access concepts, and multilingual content design for websites and intercultural communication workshops, their efforts show that success in attracting new users is possible despite the challenges of managing public libraries in a booming multilingual and culturally diverse environment. This chapter is a practical guide illustrating the flavor of the work, which other libraries may use as an outline.

Textbox 5.1: Members of the BCLA Diversity and Multicultural Services Committee

Sara Amon, Vancouver Public Library
    www.vpl.ca
Ravi Basi, Surrey Public Library
    www.spl.surrey.bc.ca
Michael Burris, Public Library InterLINK
    www.interlinklibraries.ca
Barbara Buxton, Port Moody Public Library
    http://library.portmoody.ca
Allan Cho, Irving K. Barber Learning Centre

www.ikebarberlearningcentre.ubc.ca
Ada Con, Fraser Valley Regional Library
www.fvrl.bc.ca
Gillian Guilmant-Smith, Vancouver Public Library
www.vpl.ca
Wendy Jang, Richmond Public Library
www.yourlibrary.ca
Fereshteh Kashefi, North Vancouver City Library
www.cnv.org/nvcl
Roberta Summersgill, Burnaby Public Library
www.bpl.bc.ca

Acknowledgments
Sheryl Adam, University of British Columbia Library
www.library.ubc.ca
Sylvia Crooks, UBC School of Library, Archival, and Information Studies
www.library.ubc.ca
Jan Fu, Vancouver Public Library
www.vpl.ca
Miseli Jeon, UBC Asian Studies
www.library.ubc.ca
Pat Parungao, Gladstone Secondary School
www.vsb.bc.ca

Newly released census data reveals that in 2006 Canada's foreign-born population represented one in five Canadians, the highest number since the 1930s (Ethnocultural News 2011). Since 2001, immigrants from China, India, the Philippines, and Pakistan account for two-thirds (68.9%) of Canada's total population increase. Immigration trends indicate that by 2017, the visible minorities will be the majority in Canada. To demonstrate our diversity, in the Abbotsford-Mission area, 22 percent of the population is South Asian, Chinese, and Korean, while in the Vancouver metropolitan area, South Asians, Chinese, Filipino, Korean, and Southeast Asians make up 41 percent of the population (Ethnocultural News 2011). Richmond continues to have the highest total visible minority, as 65 percent of the population is of Asian heritage. Coquitlam and North and West Vancouver have the largest groups of West Asians.

The BCLA Committee, created in August 2001, has a mandate to improve services to ethnic communities and to support and advise libraries in British Columbia (BC) who share the same goals. Despite not having an operating budget other than one-time project grants, the BCLA librarians are passionate in sharing knowledge about public programming and establishing a digital presence on the BCLA website, which includes a list of suppliers of multilingual materials, a list of library staff throughout the province with language expertise that other libraries can call upon, and links to other useful sites and materials for intercultural communication training workshops.

PROGRAMS FOR THE PUBLIC

Library programming is an integral and essential element of service to any diverse population. As a vital community destination where newcomers often look for resources in recreation, culture, and education, a library is a focal point for programs that not only attract new customers but also stimulate interest in the library collection and services.

Programs for the BCLA Committee's multicultural communities are created with community partnerships. These collaborations ultimately require an ability to cater to the needs of community members and newcomers. Often program presenters have both linguistic expertise and knowledge on subjects of interest such as local information, health issues, financial planning, and daily necessities.

ACTIVITIES FOR THE FAMILY FROM TODDLERS TO SENIORS

Story Time

Story times held in other languages are desired so that newcomers feel welcomed in their home language. Parents can encourage their children to listen, practice, and retain their mother tongue.

Book Clubs

Libraries hold book clubs for adults in their home language. Richmond Public Library holds a monthly Philosopher's Café in Russian, and five Chinese Book Clubs are available in Cantonese, Mandarin, Taiwanese, Classical Chinese, and Yijing. For ESL learners, new book clubs are held at the Port Moody Public Library and at the Terry Fox Library in Port Coquitlam. Low-literacy readers are used to enable discussions on topical subjects for those practicing and learning English, while "newcomer" social gatherings with job-related "meet a mentor" sessions are held.

Conversation Circles

These English language practice groups enable newcomers to feel secure and safe in learning their new language and feeling comfortable speaking, while also making new friends. The groups become more socially active, and day-to-day activities, learning to make reservations, buying tickets, asking questions, getting directions, and shopping are practiced.

Library Displays and Exhibitions

World language collections, artwork, and cultural artifacts provide insight to the arts and culture of a diverse community. Local artists as well as newcomers share their crafts for display. Programs include making a specific craft during a special holiday, such as making "lucky red envelopes" for Chinese New Year.

Guest Speakers

Workshops and series offered in various languages are very popular. In Richmond, the partnerships with numerous health, financial, and career counseling agencies provide well-attended programs on topics such as diabetes in Cantonese or Mandarin; chronic disease self-management in Cantonese and Mandarin; and tax planning in Mandarin, Cantonese, Tagalog, Punjabi, and French.

Welcome Brochures

Libraries provide these brochures in other languages so that basic library information is provided in a language they can understand. These brochures are brief general translations of library rules and regulations covering topics such as registering for membership, due dates, and overdue fines.

Community Radio

Librarian Wendy Jang, coordinator of multilingual services, provides book talks in Cantonese on the first Saturday morning of each month on Fairchild community radio.

The "Human Library" or "Living Library"

The "Human Library" or "Living Library" has been held in several lower mainland libraries with great success. In 2002 in Denmark, youths wanting to end violence and break down cultural stereotypes collaborated with the public library in inviting people of various professions, experience, and knowledge of any subject to become "living books." This movement has gradually taken hold and spread across the world's libraries (Ashmore 2010). In Vancouver and Burnaby, a number of school libraries have held Living Libraries inviting human books to the schools. In Coquitlam, a joint program with Douglas College and Coquitlam Public Library held several events and featured a Muslim, a police officer, a geologist/anthropologist, and a stained-glass artist as their books. The Fraser Valley Regional Library's Living Library, held at Langley City Library, had nine "books," including a crossword puzzle champion, the oldest surviving cystic fibrosis carrier, and even the city mayor. At Surrey Public Library, the Living Library was inundated with volunteers willing to share their stories. Called "These Books Are Meant for Talking," these living books included Laughter Yoga instructors, a Canadian soldier, a refugee, lesbian parents and activists, a quilter, a glassblower, and a tarantula lover. Even the University of British Columbia Library held this type of event in 2010, when on-campus students and staff met a collection of fascinating figures.

COLLECTIONS

Multilingual collections are a vital part of any multicultural community. Not only do collections serve new immigrants, they also strive to provide older generations with the support needed to maintain links to their families' heritage languages. In the Vancouver Lower Mainland high schools, due to cutbacks in collections, public libraries fill an important gap in areas of multicultural collections for youths. The BCLA Diversity Committee was born after a report presented at the 2000 BCLA conference outlined that the needs of the multilingual community were not being meet in public libraries. Its mandate was to provide multilingual browsing collections to public libraries as its starting point.

   Although an action plan had been approved by the BCLA, a funding shortfall prohibited the committee from moving forward with a circulating multilingual collection for BC libraries. Instead, the committee redirected its energies to building shared resources, namely knowledge and expertise of its members, in building a topnotch website for its members. The success of this shoestring-budget approach shows the possibilities of increasing access and resources for patrons and improving their experiences in public libraries. The librarians

- Shared knowledge of the suppliers of multilingual materials, particularly jobbers, vendors, and distributors. Since public libraries in BC purchase books locally in the province, pooling their knowledge facilitated better prices and access to multilingual language books.
- Shared bibliographies.

- Created a list of library staff with language expertise in the Greater Vancouver Region.
- Created links to the BCLA website, the National Library toolkit, and other useful sites.
- Posted InterLINK's multilingual holdings list.

These resources ultimately helped the libraries develop and maintain multilingual collections and provided inspiration in the form of example libraries, online resources, and a list of resources for further reading (see textbox 5.2).

Textbox 5.2: Developing and Maintaining Multicultural and Multilingual Collections

Library and Archives Canada, Multicultural Resources and Services Toolkit
    http://www.collectionscanada.gc.ca/multicultural/005007-300-e.html
INTERlink Multilingual Holdings
    http://www.interlinklibraries.ca/services
International Children's Digital Library
    http://en.childrenslibrary.org
WorldLinQ
    http://www.worldlinq.org
Free Multilingual e-Books
    http://www.e-book.com.au/morefreebooks/freemultilingual-books.htm
Press Display
    http://www.pressdisplay.com/pressdisplay/viewer.aspx
Online Newspapers
    http://www.onlinenewspapers.com
Family Language Kit Program
    http://www.webjunction.org/canadian-libraries/articles/content/433969

WEBSITE

All of the Committee's libraries have web pages that highlight library services for new Canadians. These special web pages are dedicated information sites to assist newcomers with information on citizenship, ESL courses, and materials in other languages. Some of these websites have multilingual translation capabilities.

- Port Moody Public Library has a "Multicultural" page that provides information on their world language collections, English as a second language collection, and world newspapers online.
- Richmond Public Library provides an online "Canadian Citizenship Practice Test."
- Surrey Public Library, on their "New Canadians" page, provides information on settlement, translation websites, and health and legal information in other languages.
- North Vancouver City Library has a "Persian Language" web page that lists Persian language materials and websites.
- Vancouver Public library provides a guide called "Finding Material in Languages Other Than English in the New Catalogue," with detailed instructions on how to search the catalogue.

"MY FIRST LANGUAGE KITS"

With populations comprised of various cultures, it is important to have multilingual staff who possess relevant cultural knowledge and sensitivity and who are available to communicate in a preferred language to provide effective service. The retention of linguistic cultural identity promotes ethnic awareness. At Burnaby Public Library, special multicultural materials such as "My First Language Kits" support home language development and cultural identity in the early years. Similar to Hamilton Public Library's family language kits, the Burnaby kits contain children's picture books, a translated parent resource guide, and music CDs or VCDS and informational DVDs, if available. Burnaby also has a fantastic website titled "Embracing Diversity: Sharing Our Songs and Rhymes," which is an online community resource to inspire sharing across cultures. It features video performances of children's songs and rhymes in fifteen languages, plus resources to support the use of the material.

Surrey Public Library also has general story time kits, Aboriginal story time kits, and multifaith kits for preschool-aged children. Materials are themed and chosen to support early literacy skills and reading readiness. Kits contain picture books, a felt story, a puppet, songs and rhymes, and an idea book. The multifaith kits, featuring Judaism, Christianity, Sikhism, Hinduism, Buddhism, Baha'i, Islam, Paganism, Unitarianism, Latter-Day Saints, and First Nations Spirituality, honor the richness of diverse faith traditions. North Vancouver City Library also provides ESL Start kits for beginning adult English learners. While staff can develop culturally diverse programs and services using these kits, the public can also borrow them for home use.

INTERCULTURAL WORKSHOPS

Communication is an integral part of culture, and there are specific rules and norms for everyday social interaction. In the context of Canada's variations in cultural assumptions, perceptions, and expectations, there are often grounds for intercultural miscommunication and misunderstanding. The workshops created by the BCLA Committee are aimed at adjusting staff's communication styles to facilitate intercultural communication easily and effectively. The workshops for library staff stress that there is no recipe or formula for intercultural communication, only guidelines and common sense. The goal is to move out of one's comfort zone.

In 2005 the Committee presented a highly successful half-day intercultural communication workshop at the BCLA annual conference, which led to the Committee expanding its content to develop and implement a two-day "Train the Trainer." The goal of this workshop is to teach librarians and other library staff members how to construct an intercultural communication workshop. The following section describes the theory, philosophy, and implementation of the workshop and is highly adaptable to any library setting.

Training Objectives

The BCLA Committee workshops aim to support librarians and library personnel to build upon current experience and strategies to develop increased awareness and communication skills for working with diverse client communities through the following objectives:

- To heighten awareness of the impact that cultural differences have on expectations and interactions
- To explore the concept of culture and diversity as it pertains to library services
- To develop skills and strategies to mindfully and effectively communicate with patrons with diverse backgrounds, languages, and experience

In particular, the BCLA Committee librarians provide six key elements in the workshops that demonstrate and strengthen communications styles. Materials for the workshops can be found at the BCLA Diversity and Multicultural Services website. The following are samples of the exercises.

"The Cocktail Party"

This exercise gives participants the experience of modifying their communication style to conform to a different (and artificial) culture and is designed to raise awareness of differences in communication styles and of our assumptions and reactions to differences. Participants are divided into groups of five and asked to imagine that they are at an international library conference reception. Each group receives a set of cards, each with different communication styles and patterns of behaviors for five imaginary countries. Each participant follows the cultural rules set out on their cards and role plays. In the debriefing of the activity, participants describe each other's assumed roles in negative terms, such as painfully shy, not paying attention, pushy, loud, or slow, when in fact, the communication styles specified on the cards are described in neutral terms and are well within the range of normal in some cultures. The exercise shows how we tend to interpret difference not as an expression of a valid cultural norm, but as unacceptable behavior within our own culture.

"Stand Up, Sit Down"

"Stand Up, Sit Down" underlines the many differences in individual experiences, tastes, and personalities *within* any cultural group and demonstrates that there are similarities *across* cultural groups. To play "Stand Up, Sit Down," the leader asks the group, while seated, to stand up if they enjoy hockey, or if they were the first born in the family, or if they bus to work, for example. While the participants are standing, the facilitator asks them to note who else is in their group and then to sit down. This exercise shows that despite external differences, people share similarities in some ways.

Personal and Cultural Values Awareness— Iceberg Model of Culture

Just as an iceberg's bulk is one-tenth above the waterline and nine-tenths below, culture has some aspects that we can observe and others that we can only imagine or intuit. We can see ways of doing lifestyle, laws and customs, institutions, dress, and physical features, for example, but we cannot see ways of thinking—norms, ideologies, beliefs, philosophy, values, and tastes—or ways of being, such as roles, attitudes, desires, assumptions, expectations, and myths. Failure to understand and recognize these parts of culture and the layers that compose them, as well as how they influence each other, is the main reason misunderstandings occur.

"Comfort Zone"

Each pair of partners forms two lines facing each other, about 2.5 meters apart. While talking and moving slowly toward each other, they continue until the first member of the pair says "Stop," to indicate that any closer would be a violation of their personal space. The exercise is repeated, but as the pairs move together, the facilitator asks that one member turn sideways. Are they closer than before? How do they feel? The idea of this exercise is to challenge the perceptions of how people from all cultures typically interpret physical distance as a personal rather than a cultural trait: people who violate cultural norms are described as "aloof" (too far) or "pushy and aggressive" (too close).

Bias—Stereotypes

Librarians, as well as those in other professions and occupations, have been victims of stereotyping; think of the timid, rule-bound, "shush-ing" creature in books and onscreen, for example. In addition to occupation, characteristics such as clothing, visible racial differences, speech, perceived intelligence, physical attributes, and age all contribute to our assessment of one another. This activity challenges participants to reevaluate their own perceptions.

"Photograph Identification"

Working in small groups, participants examine a collection of photographs of people unknown to them and make their best guess of the life situation in the picture. This exercise has the most impact when the facilitator shares the real story behind the photos—the man praying in a church is a career criminal, the ragged-looking person is a professor, and so on.

In the whole group, the facilitator asks participants to consider what visible clues led us to make assumptions or judgments about the people in the photographs and asks the group to consider the following questions:

- How can we minimize snap judgments or ingrained biases?
- Is it difficult to assess your own biases?
- How do you overcome them?

These activities are gentle ways of exploring culture, values, and bias.

CONCLUSION

As Varheim argues, libraries have an important role in society, especially as spaces for social integration (Varheim 2011, 12–18).The BCLA Committee's tried, tested, and true approach to intercultural workshops, public programming, and resource sharing can also offer any library strategies for better engaging their multicultural communities. This chapter offers libraries everywhere with a multiethnic population some key strategies that do not require large budgets to attract, retain, and facilitate community integration.

WORKS CITED

Ashmore, Amy. 2010. "Alive with Knowledge: Engaging Communities through Living Libraries." *Library Student Journal* 5. http://librarystudentjournal.org/index.php/lsj/issue/view/11/showToc.

"Ethnocultural News." 2011. Statistics Canada, Census and Administrative Data 2006. Ottawa: Statistics Canada.

Varheim, Andreas. 2011. "Gracious Space: Library Programming Strategies towards Immigrants as Tools in the Creation of Social Capital." *Library and Information Science Research* 33: 12–18.

Chapter Six

The Bridge

Librarians Collaborate with the Office of Multicultural Affairs, a Division of Student Affairs

Fantasia Thorne and Kimberly Williams

If your library is adjacent to other buildings on a college campus, do you know who your neighbors are? Syracuse University's Bird Library is fortunate to be positioned next door to the Schine Student Center, but many library staff are unaware of the variety of student support offices that exist inside the center. Universities strive to serve their student population to the best of their abilities, producing successful and global citizens in society. Departments with common goals may reach more students by working together, but such unions take effort to form and determination to continue to develop. This chapter will discuss the collaboration between Syracuse University Learning Commons librarian liaison Fantasia Thorne and staff in the Office of Multicultural Affairs (OMA). It will detail the creation and continued efforts to maintain the relationship between the two departments.

It seems natural for Academic Affairs and Student Affairs departments to collaborate, but many times these relationships remain undeveloped because each department operates independently. In fact, the two are often at odds with each other because their work with students manifests in such different ways. Student Affairs practitioners are usually heavily involved in the whole development of a student, while librarians often only interact with students a few times during their time at the university. The book *Learning Reconsidered 2* (Keeling 2006) by a number of Student Affairs contributors from the American College Personnel Association (ACPA), Association of College and University Housing Officers–International (ACUHO–I), and other higher education organizations "argued for the integrated use of all higher education's resources in the education and preparation of the whole student. One of the most critical elements required to accomplish this is the creation or enhancement of strong, collaborative working relationships among academic and student affairs educators" (Keeling 2006, 69). Serving the "whole student" is a goal the Academic Affairs and Student Affairs departments both desire to accomplish, and it can take just one discussion to make a connection and begin the collaboration.

With this sentiment in mind, in 2009 Bird Library's associate dean of undergraduate education, Lisa Moeckel, began conversations with OMA's director, Dr. James Duah-Agyeman ("Dr. D."), to investigate how the two departments could form a partnership. The two new Learning Commons resident librarians were introduced to the OMA staff members, because the resident program is a diversity initiative and OMA also focuses on diversity-related programs. Fantasia Thorne (one of the original resident librarians) currently serves as the inaugural liaison between the Bird Library and OMA.

METHODS OF COLLABORATION

There are a number of ways the two departments collaborate. The library liaison attends OMA staff meetings once a month, providing an update on the latest library news and also recommendations for future projects. As a member of the Black History Month planning committee, the liaison works closely with the Coordinator of Student Engagement to plan and implement programs that serve students and staff as they celebrate Black History Month. A Black History Month display is exhibited annually in the library, containing advertisements for programs, books by and about African American authors, and educational materials and information regarding events sponsored by OMA and student organizations. Wall space near the circulation desk is also used to display large posters made by members of the Learning Commons staff. Library technicians work closely with the liaison to create posters that contribute to exposing library patrons to black history facts and traditions. As a result of the collaboration, small but impactful things have been done to enhance Black History Month. One such thing is that shelf space has been granted to this committee in the new book display area. This practice has taken place for the past two years.

Attending OMA and student group events is another way to show support and continue the growth of the relationship between the two departments. The liaison regularly attends university Black History Month celebration events, as well as a number of other program events sponsored by OMA such as the spoken word poetry program Verbal Blend, which engages students in a number of events throughout the year. By attending such events, even though they may not be specifically focused on library research, the liaison librarian becomes recognizable and familiar to students. Interacting with students in a nonacademic setting allows the liaison to seem more approachable when students are seeking research assistance in the library.

The Office of Multicultural Affairs recognizes that academic achievement is an important part of a student's development. The library liaison assists OMA staff in a variety of ways by facilitating workshops on library resources and services. Remaining flexible is important when working with students, so occasionally the liaison visits the OMA programs in spaces on campus where they meet regularly or provides instruction in the library so students become familiar with the building and its space. The young women of color in the Dimensions program have received library instruction sessions in a classroom space in the university, as well as in various locations in Bird Library. The liaison has also visited Verbal Blend in the classroom space reserved for their weekly poetry workshops. The Multicultural Empowerment Network (MEN) has also taken the time to visit the library, and the Multicultural Living Learning Community has welcomed library instruction into their workshop schedules. The students and OMA staff who have attended the workshops have appreciated the liaison's enthusiastic and interactive sessions.

SUPPORTING EACH OTHER TO SUPPORT STUDENTS

Open communication and a deep respect for one another has been a major reason the collaboration between the library liaison and OMA staff continues to prosper. OMA graciously invites the liaison to staff retreats, as well as on a visit to a multicultural center at a nearby college. The proximity of the two departments is ideal; being next-door neighbors makes visiting offices, retrieving flyers, student visits, and attending meetings incredibly convenient. OMA also visits the Learning Commons department and has contributed several sessions to the department's staff development program. Early on in our collaboration we walked the library building together, talking about resources, spaces, and programming and sharing ideas for supporting student success.

The benefits of this collaboration have varied in positive ways both professionally and personally. When opportunities arise, such as a call from the university for funding for new and innovative projects, the first thought from both departments is to find a way to work together to create a proposal. Recently, the two departments wrote a proposal to work with Syracuse area high school students. Although the project was not funded, it was another way in which the strong collaboration between the two departments was demonstrated. This article is another example of the collaboration between the two departments.

The Office of Multicultural Affairs and Bird Library have found ways to collaborate across the boundaries of academic and student affairs. This model should be used for future projects on which academic and student affairs departments wish to concentrate their efforts. Students need both units to successfully transition from high school to college and from college into the world of graduate school or employment. The article "From Services-Centered to Student-Centered: A 'Wellness Wheel' Approach to Developing the Library as an Integrative Learning Commons" (Hinchliffe and Wong 2010) describes the student college experience as a wellness wheel. The wheel is composed of "Six Dimensions of Wellness," including intellectual, emotional, physical, social, occupational, and spiritual, and it is a model used by many student affairs departments when creating programs and services for students.

As the article states: "The Wellness Wheel offers a useful approach to ensuring the holistic impact of the learning commons by presenting a framework for planning, developing, and assessing programming and identifying various campus partners" (Hinchliffe and Wong 2010, 221). Librarians can partner with a variety of student affairs departments to accomplish this goal, such as, for example, displaying materials from the counseling and health centers or holding special events such as providing massages around finals time, as it is currently done each year in Bird Library Learning Commons. Events such as these illustrate the library's efforts to serve the student as a whole, and show that the library is more than an academic building.

CONCLUSION

Learning does not only take place in the classroom or in the library; it occurs in everyday situations. We can be more intentional about the ways in which we connect students' lives in the classroom and their lives outside of it. The model described above is one way to do it. No one department can impact students alone; departmental partnerships benefit more than just the students served, but also the staff members working together to build and nurture the collaborative relationship.

WORKS CITED

Hinchliffe, Lisa J., and Melissa Autumn Wong. 2010. "From Services-Centered to Student-Centered: A 'Wellness Wheel' Approach to Developing the Library as an Integrative Learning Commons." *College and Undergraduate Libraries* 17 (2–3): 213–24. doi: 10.1080/10691316.2010.490772.

Keeling, Richard P., ed. 2006. *Learning Reconsidered 2: Implementing a Campus-Wide Focus on the Student Experience.* Washington, DC: ACPA, ACUHO-I, ACUI, NACADA, NACA, NASPA, and NIRSA.

Part II

Reaching Students

Chapter Seven

Connecting Native American Students to Cline Library

Amy Hughes and Carissa Tsosie

Statistics show that compared with other groups, a relatively small percentage of the Native American population is currently enrolled in higher education institutions. According to the most recent U.S. Census, approximately 7 percent of Native Americans are enrolled in college or graduate school in the United States, representing slightly more than 150,000 active students. And yet, despite those numbers, there is a strong possibility that you are serving Native American students at your library. According to the National Conference of State Legislatures (NCSL), in October 2011, there were 595 federally recognized tribes, spanning across thirty-three different states, and twenty-nine state-recognized tribes within twelve different states. These numbers reflect an increase in tribal status; in 2000 there were thirty-three fewer federally recognized tribes. The most recent U.S. Census shows that the overall Native American population has increased over the last ten years and is estimated to continue to grow. Additionally, the majority of Native Americans, nearly two-thirds of the population, live in urban areas.

Northern Arizona University (NAU), located just eighty miles south of the Grand Canyon, is committed to serving Native American students. Each year, NAU typically serves between a thousand and twelve hundred Native American students, representing over ninety different tribes across North America and Canada. The university provides support to Native American students in many ways, as indicated by the university's strategic plan, Goal 6: "A Commitment to Native American Students." In fact, just recently the university celebrated the grand opening of the Native American Cultural Center, a 12,650-square-foot building centrally located, near both the University Union and the Cline Library. This building serves as a central gathering place for Native American students and was constructed with Native values and design in mind. While it was built to serve as a meeting place for Native American students and tribes, it is open to all students at the university.

In support of this university goal, the library engages in instructional support and services for Native American students and hosts a public awareness event for the university and local community. For the past several years, serving Native American students at NAU's Cline Library has taken on a multi-pronged approach. Through different methods we have created opportunities to work with Native American students that have ultimately increased their use of the library. In this chapter we present our approaches for connecting with Native American students and discuss how we encourage and support their use of the library.

PROMOTING AN AWARENESS OF
NATIVE AMERICAN CULTURE

Film Series

A good way to connect and educate the community about Native American culture is through films. Several years ago Cline Library conducted focus groups to brainstorm ideas about how to support the university's Goal 6. As a result of these focus groups the library decided to host a film series focusing on Native Americans. Our intentions were to educate our audience about contemporary Native American issues and to offer a meaningful place for dialogue about those issues. The Native American and Indigenous Film Series at Cline Library, which is free and open to the public, celebrated its fourth season this year. While the attendance varies for each film, there is an average of seventy audience members attending each film screening.

The film series planning committee sought out films produced by Native American directors either at the local or national level. Through community support we have been able to bring Native American directors and documentary subjects to the library to discuss their films with the audience. We have also invited faculty to discuss films, and many faculty encourage their students to attend the film series as either a course requirement or as an extra credit opportunity. Networking with faculty has helped boost attendance, awareness, and support for the film series. Recently we selected films based on a theme, indigenous and environmental injustice, and we were able to include whole classes whose course learning outcomes were related to that theme.

The film series committee consists of three to five library staff members who commit to selecting the films, marketing, and hosting the screenings. Our marketing relies heavily on word of mouth. We also distribute fliers around campus, contact faculty and student groups, and frequently update our Facebook page. We use several websites and take suggestions from audience members for potential films to include in the next film series. In fact, we ask audience members to complete a brief, five-question survey at the end of each film to elicit feedback about the film, the film discussion, and overall improvements for the film series.

Some of our favorite websites to consult for possible films include:

Native Networks
American Indian Film Institute
Red Nation Film Festival
Izuma TV

Some of the more popular films we have shown include:

Weaving Worlds (2007), directed by Bennie Klain
Paatuwaqatsi: Water, Land, and Life (2007), directed by Victor Masayesva Jr.
Lady Warriors (2001), directed by John C. P. Goheen
Our Spirits Don't Speak English: Indian Boarding School (2008), directed by Steven R. Heape and Chip Richie
Sweet Blood (2009), directed by Shirley Cheechoo

Collection Management

Protocols for Native American Archival Materials were developed at the Colorado Plateau and Digital Archives, the special collections department at Cline Library. They were developed to guide archivists and collections managers to collect and care for Native American materials in a way that considers and is culturally sensitive to Native American tribes. The protocols encourage partnerships with tribal agencies like the Navajo Nation Museum, Library and Archive, and are available free online. We encourage you to read the protocols if you are developing and managing your collection.

We are currently reviewing our print collection and looking for materials that may be culturally inappropriate. As an example, we identified several items in our collection that were the subject of a controversy that questioned the true identity of a proclaimed Native American memoirist. In this case the author eventually admitted to having no known Native American ancestry or tribal affiliation and acknowledged that the memoirs were not true. We decided to withdraw these items from the collection because they were culturally insensitive, geographically misleading, and perpetuated negative stereotypes. Not all items will jump out as culturally inappropriate. Therefore it is helpful to be familiar with prominent Native American scholars and writers such as Ned Blackhawk, Linda Hogan, Vine Deloria Jr., Leslie Marmon Silko, Walter Echo-Hawk, Winona LaDuke, and Sherman Alexie, among many others. Additionally, the use of selection tools can further expand your knowledge on culturally appropriate resources. Relatively speaking, there are a limited number of selection tools to guide librarians in collection management in this area, and many of them are geared toward children's literature rather than institutions of higher education. However, many scholarly journals such as the *American Indian Culture and Research Journal* and *Studies in American Indian Literatures* include book reviews, and a few websites such as Oyate and the Gathering of Nations are helpful. As with any management strategy, looking for culturally appropriate and curriculum-relevant resources to collect becomes easier with experience.

In addition to managing the collection, we are looking for content gaps so that we can better reflect the diversity of Native American populations. One gap that we recognized is the availability of legal resources in print. At NAU many classes research tribal governments. When working with those classes, a useful online resource is *The Native American Constitution and Law Digitization Project*, coordinated by the University of Oklahoma Law Library and the National Indian Law Library of the Native American Rights Fund, which is available online. A key journal is the *American Indian Law Review*, and other helpful resources include Westlaw's Native Peoples Law and tribal library, Bibliography of Native North Americans (EBSCOhost), and Ethnic NewsWatch (ProQuest).

Featured Resources Room

The library partnered with the university's Multicultural Student Center to create an exhibit in celebration of Native American Heritage Month. The exhibit, *Celebrating Native American Heritage Month with Cline Library*, included books and videos on contemporary Native American issues and was located in the current reading room. The current reading room is located on the first floor directly adjacent to the reference and circulation desk of the library and was an ideal space to showcase these resources. Since the display was installed, the circulation of the resources has increased. Students are likely to feel connected when they see resources that represent their culture. Having a collection of resources on display sends a powerful message about the significance of those resources and the library's commitment to building a relevant collection. We hope to continue the partnership and in the future involve Native American students in selecting items for display as well as asking them to include book suggestions and reviews that we can post as part of the display for their peers.

CULTIVATING AN ENVIRONMENT OF RESPECT

Preparation

Academic support is an all-encompassing way to describe how we work with faculty and students. This work includes such activities as locating and providing supplemental course materials, coteaching courses with faculty, and providing research assistance to students in person and online. Allowing time to prepare for academic support is often undervalued. Yet, learning about other cultures and expanding perspectives are critical steps for creating an environment that welcomes and encourages Native American students. The more knowledge one has about Native American culture, the easier it is to refer to cultural examples and to include those examples when working with faculty and students. It is also important to be aware of contemporary issues facing tribes, including economic, social, environmental, and land issues. The easiest way to stay up-to-date is to read journals and news sources. There are several great resources available, including the *Journal of American Indian Education*, *American Indian Quarterly*, *Wicazo Sa Review*, and the American Indian Higher Education Consortium's *Tribal College Journal*. A useful website for current news is *Indian Country Today*.

Working with Faculty

Presenting at faculty meetings is a useful approach to introduce library resources and is often a good tool for networking. In past faculty meetings, it has been helpful to show examples of an online hypothetical course, created in the university's course management tool. At NAU, the course management software we use is BlackBoard Learn. A visual representation of a course helps show faculty how the library's resources can seamlessly integrate into the course and augment course content. This approach helps to highlight culturally sensitive and appropriate resources specific to a course without being overly didactic.

Working collaboratively with faculty has varying results, from very little interaction and support to librarians being well integrated into the course, often in coteaching environments. When teaching a class, regardless of the subject content, it is important to incorporate multicultural material into the instruction. This is not difficult if you allow some time to prepare. Eventually, infusing multicultural material into course instruction will become innate.

Furthermore, if there are Native American faculty members on campus, schedule a time to meet with them to ask about their teaching methods, especially if they teach research methods. You may discover a new way to present research. This was my experience when I met with an instructor to discuss how to include oral stories as resources for a history course. In this case, oral stories represented a way of knowing and were considered legitimate sources.

Working with Students

As mentioned earlier, the best way to prepare to work with students from another culture is to become knowledgeable about their culture. Knowing about cultural heritages makes it easier to include relevant references as you present information. One tip I've learned from working with Native American students is to keep the learning active. Generally this means allowing the students to work in groups to solve a real-life problem that is likely occurring at home, whether it is on or off the reservation. Using a contemporary problem makes it easy to facilitate active learning and is often engaging, especially if students can add to the conversation by sharing personal experiences. I always encourage this type of conversation if it occurs during class. Finally, how you come across to students speaks volumes about your interest in their ability to succeed. Keeping a positive attitude and offering encouragement goes a long way.

Working one-on-one with students is often the most rewarding part of the job and offers an opportunity to learn more about students and their research interests. Research consultations are a way to show students that you are invested in their success. When scheduling a research consultation it is important to make sure that the time and date are convenient for both you and the student. At NAU, several of the Native American students we meet with do not live on campus and often have a job in addition to being a student; therefore, being flexible with meeting schedules is helpful. When you do meet with students, allow some time for introductions and offer your contact information so that they can call your office or e-mail you directly. This simple gesture may become a significant connection, especially considering the lower retention rates among Native American students.

MAKING CONNECTIONS THAT COUNT

Native American Student Services

One strategy to help increase awareness about library services and resources is being involved in relevant programs and committees across campus, as well as working with different service units across campus. In the article "Native American College Students: A Population That Can No Longer Be Ignored," the author contends that in order for Native American students to succeed at the university level, student affairs offices need to participate in supporting Native American students (Maxwell 2001). The article specifically addresses the value of the ALANA (African, Latino/a, Asian, and Native American) student center. One service unit that we currently partner with is Native American Student Services (NASS).

NASS supports Native American students through financial aid and academic mentoring programs and provides a social network for students on campus. They have a special focus on Native American freshman and transfer populations, although many of their services are available to any NAU student. Several years ago, through the efforts of a former colleague who is now a librarian at the Southwestern Indian Polytechnic Institute, the library began partnering with NASS to support a scholarship program. A component of the scholarship requires students to attend a library orientation session. Although much of the literature suggests that Native American students are unfamiliar with a university library, it did not take long to discover that a generic library orientation was not very exciting for the students and was rarely helpful if the students were not actively working on a research assignment. The generic library sessions overloaded students with information that they were not able to immediately apply and were therefore not likely to remember.

We learned that in order to have more success connecting to students we needed to create a casual environment that incorporated active learning and encouraged a sense of belonging, so we changed our approach. Since the students are meeting with us as a group rather than with a class, we had to come up with a way to engage the students, make our involvement relevant, and finally assess whether or not we were being effective.

We decided to begin simulating meetings about local environmental issues and having students discuss solutions involving different stakeholders' perspectives. A student or pair of students is responsible for locating information that reflects a specific stakeholder perspective and during the discussion presents a case based on that perspective. After the simulation we discuss how different information sources are retrieved and used. We also leave some time at the end of the session to encourage students to ask questions about the library, the university, and the local community.

Finally, in order to manage the workload we distribute the instruction sessions among three people in the library and organize six different large-group sessions over the course of two days. The key component that helps make this partnership work includes a group of staff willing to provide support and spend time preparing for the instruction session.

Helping Students in the Library

Crosby (2011) identifies five factors that affect Native American students' achievement in higher education, noting that familial support and financial aid are the most significant factors. Therefore, having some knowledge of financial aid at your university is worthwhile, and if your library has an acquisitions budget, you may want to consider purchasing *Financial Aid for Native Americans, 2012–2014* by Gail A. Schlachter and R. David Weber (2011).

One challenge for Native American students that we have noticed is the lack of experience with course management software. Many classes are either a hybrid course with both face-to-face and online components or are completely online. Reminding students to read the course syllabus and take note of due dates and assignment requirements is helpful. Many of these issues may be due to the fact that Native American students do not typically ask clarifying questions of their professors. If you are meeting with students in a group setting or one-on-one, a good question to ask students might be how well they are navigating the syllabus and the course management systems.

CONCLUSION

Over the past three years we have worked to build our knowledge of Native American cultures and have reached out to Native American students across the university. Some methods have worked better than others, but above all, taking the time to get to know the students has proved to be invaluable.

We understand that no one has unlimited resources and time. However, becoming knowledgeable about Native American cultures is an inexpensive and important first step to helping Native American students feel welcome and connected to the library. If you do decide to embark on a culture knowledge quest, share what you have learned with others through informal conversations, staff development workshops, and meetings when appropriate. Equally important is ensuring that a consistent message of respect for different cultures is expressed by all departments within the library. This message of respect is necessary and helps make a lasting impression on students, and it will help them feel comfortable using the library.

WORKS CITED

Crosby, Heather. 2011. "Explaining Achievement: Factors Affecting Native American College Student Success." *Applied Research Projects, Texas State University–San Marcos*. Paper 349. http://ecommons.txstate.edu/arp/349.

Maxwell, Deanne. 2001. "Native American College Students: A Population That Can No Longer Be Ignored." http://www.uvm.edu/~vtconn/v22/maxwell.html.

Chapter Eight

Delivering Library Instruction in a Native Language

LaVentra E. Danquah and Wendy G. Wu

Asians are the leading group of international scholars, researchers, and students in the United States. Offering library services to meet the informational needs of multicultural patrons is thoroughly discussed in the literature. The discourse on language barriers and learning maintains that English-as-a-second-language (ESL) learners encounter challenges during the learning process (Blau 1990). Even Internet-savvy ESL library users needed assistance with clarifying terminology used by librarians during orientation programs (Jackson 2005). Librarians have implemented various measures to address this challenge. Some emphasize the use of multiple learning styles and vocal techniques to accommodate multicultural users. Others support conducting library tours and orientations in patrons' native language, incorporating information literacy standards with culturally competent communication practices, as well as integrating library instruction into the ESL curriculum (Barron and Strout-Dapaz 2001; Conteh-Morgan 2001; Liestman and Wu 1990). These methods only benefit multicultural patrons in providing them with a brief overview of selected library resources and services. Given that the literature well documents learning barriers experienced by ESL learners and the increasing number of patrons from Asia, instruction librarians at Wayne State University, Shiffman Medical Library, opted to teach a library workshop in a native language. The following chapter chronicles the experience of an academic medical library's initiative to teach an EndNote workshop in a Chinese language.

THE LIBRARY'S INSTRUCTION PROGRAM

Library instruction is a fundamental service at the medical library. Librarians provide bibliographic instruction, course integrated instruction, and user instruction on premier biomedical research support tools. Research and scholarship are catalysts for professional advancement; therefore, utilizing library resources that aid in these endeavors is of great benefit to our patrons. The bibliographic management program Endnote is such a resource. Faculty, researchers, and students use EndNote as a time-saving tool for capturing article citations and preparing manuscripts for publication. Initial EndNote trainings sponsored and promoted by the library were stand-alone sessions and were marginally successful. Attendance was less than expected. Consequently, instruction librarians decided to offer EndNote instruction by request only. Ironically, despite low class attendance, reference data demonstrated a steady interest from patrons to learn more about EndNote. Therefore, a team of librarians developed a collaborative relationship with the School of Medicine's Department of Faculty Affairs and Professional Development (FAPD) to provide library instruction through the department's Professional and Academic Development programs (PAD). Collaborating with the department offered several benefits: (1) PAD programs are well attended by faculty, researchers, and professional staff; (2) sharing course evaluations allowed librarians to improve instructional programs; (3) librarians had a captive audience in which to continually promote other library services and resources; and (4) whenever EndNote was promoted through PAD, classes filled quickly.

THE CASE FOR TEACHING ENDNOTE IN CHINESE

Reportedly, for newly arrived Asians in the United States, reading levels are much higher than their listening and speaking skills (Fu 1995; Preston 1992). They have difficulty fully engaging in classroom instruction, especially following the instructor, providing feedback, and participating in group discussions. Unlike Western culture, Asia's pedagogical approach focuses on knowledge consumption, observation, obedience to authority, and exercising sensitivity toward colleagues, and it discourages acts of incompetence (Zhang 2006). As such, adapting to new teaching and learning techniques requires additional instructional support. Offering library instruction to multicultural patrons is not a novel idea. Yet, conducting instruction in their native language is a value-added approach when rendering such services. It is equally important to teach on a resource that is heavily used and valued by patrons.

Previous course evaluations and anecdotal evidence suggested that Asian patrons often repeated EndNote training sessions. Learners frequently verbalized the communication and language barriers they encountered during library instruction. For these reasons, librarians constructed a plan to address language and communication barriers during instruction. First, they assessed their knowledge and skills in instructional design and culturally competent communication strategies. The instructional goal involved improving learners' comprehension and efficient use of EndNote and included the following objectives: (1) customize training and promotional material to include Chinese language characters, (2) actively promote training to potential participants, (3) conduct training in Chinese language, and (4) distribute and collect evaluations to assess learning outcomes. Theoretically, teaching the course in a native language would improve patrons' efficiency while advancing their academic, research, and scholarship objectives. Forging collegial relationships with resident librarians and increasing patrons' knowledge of other library services and resources are beneficial outcomes as well.

Garnering support from collaborators to offer EndNote workshops in Chinese was essential. Librarians met with colleagues to present their ideas and discuss program logistics. The department immediately backed the concept of providing non-English library instruction for this patron group. Everyone involved was committed to the success of the program and gave much thought as to how the training would be best promoted. The following practices were successful in promoting the course: (1) the instructing librarian formed an ad-hoc discussion group with potential participants to gather feedback on learning needs, training styles, and preferred dates, times, and locations; (2) asking professional and academic Chinese associations to share course information with members; (3) soliciting relevant campus leaders to help with promoting the course; (4) posting announcements on the library's website, listservs, and other e-mail lists; and (5) incorporating Chinese language characters on all promotional material.

TEACHING ENDNOTE IN CHINESE

Multilingual librarians who utilize their expertise to offer non-English library instruction for multicultural patrons offer several benefits. Studies show patrons are more inclined to discuss their learning needs with individuals who understand their native education system and cultural norms, and speak their language. The International Students and the American University Library study suggested that providing separate, customized sessions with individualized attention can help improve instruction for multicultural patrons (Patton 2002). Librarians might consider having one colleague conduct the training, while another librarian provides individual assistance for participants.

Teaching Environment

Many participants had never used EndNote, while others had only limited experience and came to the session with questions. The presenting librarian carefully reviewed the agenda, learning objectives, and training format. The demonstration was conducted at a slower pace to ensure learners had additional time to comprehend terminology, process information, and develop skills. The instructing librarian demonstrated features on how to import, manage, and properly cite information sources, which was followed by immediate hands-on application. Practice at the point of instruction is particularly important for technical classes. Introducing Endnote's terminology in English and explaining it in Chinese, enhanced learners' English vocabularies while helping them comprehend EndNote's functionality. Also, selected active learning techniques were employed to encourage engagement and reinforce learning. Administering a level one evaluation demonstrated that participants achieved their learning goals.

Selecting Training Materials

The presenting librarian revised existing Endnote class materials to reflect the learning needs of the group. The group preferred illustrative handouts with sequential instructions. Altogether, the handouts included an agenda briefly describing EndNote and detailed learning objectives, a learning activity that reinforced demonstrated features, a list of online learning tutorials, and librarians' contact information for additional follow-up.

CONCLUSION

Non-English library instruction is a valuable service, particularly for ESL scholars, researchers, and students. When deciding if the service will benefit your patrons, first, consider analyzing previous course evaluations, user surveys, informal communications, and anecdotal data. Take into account the library's capacity to render such services. For example, it may not be feasible to schedule multiple sessions throughout the year. Our trainings were conducted during new student and faculty orientations. Remember, over time patrons will encounter fewer communication and language barriers and will eventually adapt to traditional library instruction.

To help improve communication with multicultural patrons, librarians might also consider conversing with patrons in their native language during other library service encounters.

In our experience, participants gained a comprehensive understanding of the resource and ultimately experienced a more engaging learning environment. For example, participants asked more precise questions, established professional connections with resident librarians, and opted to utilize additional library resources and services more often. Consequently, librarians are currently exploring the creation of an EndNote tutorial in Chinese to supplement the course, in addition to teaching other library-supported resources in a native language.

WORKS CITED

Barron, Sarah, and Alexia Strout-Dapaz. 2001. "Communicating with and Empowering International Students with a Library Skills Set." *Reference Services Review* 29(4): 314–26.

Blau, Eileen K. 1990. "The Effect of Syntax, Speed, and Pauses on Listening Comprehension." *TESOL Quarterly* 24(4): 746–53.

Conteh-Morgan, Mariam E. 2001. "Empowering ESL Students: A New Model for Information Literacy Instruction." *Research Strategies* 18(1): 29–38.

Fu, Danling. 1995. *"My Trouble Is My English": Asian Students and the American Dream.* Portsmouth, NH: Heinemann.

Jackson, Pamela A. 2005. "Incoming International Students and the Library: A Survey." *Reference Services Review* 33(2): 197–209.

Liestman, Daniel, and Connie Wu. 1990. "Library Orientation for International Students in Their Native Language." *Research Strategies* 8(4): 191–96.

Patton, Beth Ann. 2002. "International Students and the American University Library." Master's thesis, Department of Education, School of Arts and Sciences, Biola.

Preston, Bonita. 1992. "Foreign Students: Lost in the Library?" In *Understanding the International Student*, edited by S. M. Kaikai and R. E. Kaikai. New York: McGraw-Hill.

Zhang, Li. 2006. "Communication in Academic Libraries: An East Asian Perspective." *Reference Services Review* 34(1): 164–76.

Chapter Nine

The Role of Teacher-Librarians in Encouraging Library Use by Multicultural Patrons

HOW TEACHER-LIBRARIANS CREATE SAFE ENVIRONMENTS FOR MULTICULTURAL PATRONS

Teacher-librarians trained in multicultural education have the power to help students of diverse cultural backgrounds wishing to learn and conduct research by creating an environment conducive to making them feel accepted and comfortable. Their feeling of acceptance and comfort will encourage them to ask questions as they feel connected to their library. The students' developing sense of belonging will in turn help them to feel inspired to learn and enhance their academic potential (Mestre 2009). Establishing an atmosphere where students feel comfortable asking for help and also see representations of themselves in the materials around them is important to creating an environment that encourages library use by multicultural patrons.

This concept of the school library bringing a sense of belonging in its patrons centers on two concepts: security and freedom (Tuan 2001). To conceptualize security and freedom in the school library as a sense of place, Johnston and Bishop (2011) state that children need a safe place at school to learn, and they also need a space to explore new ideas and for creative self-development. Moreover, Johnston and Bishop support the idea of a place as being connected to the identity of those individuals and their daily experiences, social structures, and the relationships they value (Eyles 1989). This multicultural concept of libraries as a place allows school libraries to reflect meaning in the lives of children as well as supporting the school curriculum, but a conundrum exists that has the potential of detouring the potential of school libraries of becoming educational spaces for multicultural patrons. This conundrum centers on the reality of the academic preparation of teacher-librarians during their time as candidates for both teacher certification and their Master of Library Science (MLS) degree.

TEACHER-LIBRARIANS AND THEIR PRESERVICE EXPERIENCES WITH MULTICULTURAL EDUCATION CURRICULA

Despite the plethora of multicultural education theory that exists and the literature that presents it, many teacher-librarians lack the adequate training that would create school libraries as educational spaces that promote learning in a safe environment for multicultural patrons. Currently, school librarian programs leading to the MLS degree require teacher-librarian candidates to also obtain or already possess a teacher license. However, many teacher education and library programs do not adequately prepare their candidates to retain the content knowledge to implement multicultural education throughout their careers. Segall (2002) conducted a qualitative study of the experiences of preservice teachers in various teacher-education programs, and he found that many teacher education programs may include one or two mandatory multicultural education courses that candidates must take. Moreover, Segall (2002) revealed that they had taken these courses very early in their studies and forgotten much of what they learned by the time they started their mandatory practicums. Similarly, school librarian programs may or may not require courses that involve multicultural education. In California, for instance, candidates for San Jose State University's teacher-librarian program "may select a series of elective courses outside the mandatory courses that allow for the earning of California's teacher-librarian credential such as the course Libraries for Racially Ethnic and Diverse Communities" (San Jose State University School of Library and Information Science 2012). At the University of North Carolina's School Media Specialist program, only one course, Curriculum Issues and the School Librarian, hints of multicultural education as a major component of the course (University of North Carolina at Chapel Hill School of Information and Library Science 2012). Consequently, the potential lack of preparation may well lead to teacher-librarians' developing a prejudice—any social perspective or attitude of a negative nature that is unsupported by facts (de Melendez and Beck 2010). Teacher-librarians and other educators who choose to not examine the epistemological nature of their prejudicial attitudes risk engaging in discrimination—the reinforcement, action, or behavior based on a prejudice toward a particular cultural group (Colbert-Lewis 2011).

A FOUR-PHASE PROCESS THAT HELPS TEACHER-LIBRARIANS GAIN MULTICULTURAL COMPETENCY

Teacher-librarians who realize that their academic education did not prepare them to work with multicultural patrons still have a chance to become competent in multicultural education. A four-phase theoretical process exists that the researchers of this study have applied in the training of teacher-candidates and licensed teachers with little to no competency in multicultural education (Colbert-Lewis 2011). The four phases (Understanding Cultural Diversity, Differentiation, Identifying Various Discriminations, and Social Justice) are applicable for teacher-librarians, since their profession requires them to be both licensed teachers as well as librarians. We contend that a daily application of these four phases will lead to competency in multicultural education. We will now highlight each phase with activities that teacher-librarians may employ with relation to each phase that helps create safe educational spaces.

Understanding Cultural Diversity

Teacher-librarians enter the first phase, Understanding Cultural Diversity, in their path to multicultural competence by studying existing literature on how society perceives "culture" and how this relates to the "diversity" of individuals. Culture refers to the socially transmitted ways of how individuals think, believe, feel, and act within a group from one generation to the next (Gollnick and Chinn 2009). Most individuals choose to associate themselves through gender, ethnicity, religion, socioeconomic status, exceptionality, regional (national origin), and language (Banks 2006). Diversity, in relation to culture, tends to become a more difficult term to define, as the term tends to describe any given number of individuals representing a multitude of cultures inhabiting any given space at any particular time. Koppelman and Goodhart (2005, 12) define diversity as "the presence of human beings with perceived or actual differences based on a variety of human characteristics, and that it may exist both in classrooms having no minorities and in classrooms where all the students represent members of various minority groups." Cushner, McClelland, and Safford (2006, 68–76) define diversity, in relation to culture, as a way that "individuals tend to identify themselves in a broad manner and in terms of many physical and social attributes that include criteria as ethnicity/nationality, race, ability/disability, language, social status, social class, religion, sexuality, geographic region, age, health, and sex/gender."

Teacher-librarians will achieve the first phase by understanding that individuals represent various cultures and in any given time at any given space, a gathering of individuals creates diversity. Rosa Hernandez Sheets (2005, 15) hints at this best as she defines diversity as

> the dissimilarities in traits, qualities, characteristics, beliefs, values, and mannerisms present in self and others . . . displayed through predetermined factors such as race, ethnicity, gender, age, ability, national origin, and sexual orientation and changeable features such as citizenship, worldviews, language, schooling, religious beliefs, marital, parental, socioeconomic status, and work experience.

Her definition hints of a gathering of individuals in a space via her use of key words like dissimilarities and key phrases such as "mannerisms present in self and others." The teacher-librarian who implements this phase through action must view the school library as an inviting educational space for individuals representing different cultures. School librarians should ask themselves if pictorial images celebrating women and men from Earth's six inhabitable continents exist. These images should highlight such events as religious celebrations, and women in occupations involving politics, religion, military, media/entertainment, and education outside of the home.

Moreover, teacher-librarians should use a variety of communication media to highlight these images daily (posters, computer/LCD display, museum displays). Furthermore, teacher-librarians may want to ask their students if they possess any knowledge of where their ancestors originated and then look for flags to display that represent the places mentioned. The researchers have visited and worked in schools where flags from South Africa, Israel, Ireland, Australia, India, China, and other countries have been displayed in school libraries as a celebratory representation of the cultures existing in those schools. Successful implementation of this first phase demonstrates an understanding that individuals represent different cultures, and this ideally will help decrease the opportunity to develop a prejudicial perspective of any student who represents a culture outside of a school's majority culture.

Differentiation

Teacher-librarians reach the second phase, Differentiation, when they choose to reflect upon the prejudices they have come to the realization of possessing from an epistemological nature. De Melendez and Beck (2010, 432) define prejudice as "a social perspective or attitude of a negative nature not supported by facts or evidence [that] is based on ideas and stereotypes about individuals and/or groups." These prejudices stem from preconceived notions of a cultural majority, but librarians (including teacher-librarians) must not make assumptions that students come into a library knowing how to properly conduct research based on the comfort of working with a particular majority (Hall 2003). Teacher-librarians also reach the Differentiation phase if they accept the realization that a failure to not examine the epistemological nature of their prejudicial ideas will most likely lead to discrimination—an action or behavior that serves to reinforce a prejudice towards a particular cultural group (Colbert-Lewis 2011). This behavior leads to the arbitrary denial of privileges for a minority group, while it rewards a societal majority group with privileges (Gollnick and Chinn 2009). Teacher-librarians engaging in the Differentiation phase through their actions will realize that students' cultural backgrounds affect how they individually perform in a library setting. Consequently they will adjust their instruction based on the particular needs of any given group of students (Tomlinson 1995). Teacher-librarians must conduct research on what library skills their individual multicultural patrons possess. The use of an anonymous survey of questions regarding students' current knowledge of how to find books through a cataloging system or how to use tertiary sources as search engines (Google, Ask.com, Yahoo, etc.) may help determine the correct pedagogical approach to engage a student.

Differentiated instruction describes any proactive effort on the part of an educator to instruct each student according to the particular needs of that individual student (Tomlinson 1995). Consequently, differentiated instruction also serves as a proactive means for librarians to identify the most prevalent forms of discrimination that take place in school settings. Identifying the most prevalent forms of discrimination that take place in a school setting represents the third phase of gaining multicultural competency for teacher librarians. Individual and institutional agents have targeted individuals or a distinct cultural group in school settings for discrimination. These agents (perpetrators of the discrimination) have been able to retain the power to maintain their oppressive behavior (Hardiman, Jackson, and Griffin 2007). Hardiman, Jackson, and Griffin (2007) identify governments, businesses, and religious organizations as institutional agents.

Identifying Various Discriminations

In the Identify phase, teacher-librarians possess the knowledge of the various forms of discrimination that take place. Far too many times, both individuals and scholars of multicultural education theory mistakenly focus their knowledge on discrimination based on ethnicity (racism) and gender (sexism). To proactively create an educational setting void of discrimination, teacher-librarians must review current multicultural education literature that identifies the most prevalent forms of discrimination and those affected most by them in a school setting: ableism (individuals' mental abilities), classism (lower socialeconomic standing), creedalism (religions outside of Christianity), heterosexism (gay and lesbian citizens), sexism (women), and racism (non-white individuals) (Colbert-Lewis 2011). Lately discrimination toward individuals who speak a primary language other than English (logocism) has been on the rise, as well as discrimination toward individuals based on their geographic origin (rural residents) and their age (physical and behavioral development) (Gollnick and Chinn 2009).

Teacher-librarians have opportunities to make their students feel more comfortable by convincing their school districts to work with vendors that specialize in presenting databases that provide support for programming and cater to a student's particular cultural background. For example, vendors such as Cengage Learning/Gale and EBSCOhost provide databases for use in public and private K–12 schools. These vendors provide resources and support for teacher-librarians. These databases have the feature of changing the initial language used on the computer screen to a different language. This option serves students who do not speak English as their first language, who wish to learn English, or who wish to learn multiple languages. Spoken languages, like Spanish, have become an increasing identifier of a student's culture. Teacher-librarians have an opportunity to create an inviting place for learning for students who do not speak English as their first language through their application of their knowledge of school media technology by providing those students with these distinctive support features in the databases mentioned.

Moreover, teacher-librarians proactively create safe educational spaces by having the courage to speak up when they see students engaging in a form of discrimination toward other students or adults. They must also speak up if they witness other teachers engaging in discrimination toward students or their fellow teachers. A thorough review of the literature gives teacher-librarians preparation to address discrimination as it happens, and by possessing the knowledge of the different types of discrimination, teacher-librarians have an opportunity to create activities, media, and so on that promote transformative learning for the purpose of social justice in the school library and beyond.

Social Justice

Teacher-librarians enter the fourth and final phase, the Social Justice Phase, when they incorporate social justice through their instruction. Social justice describes an environment void of systemic oppression through the deliberate application of instruction highlighting an understanding of diverse cultures. Moreover, this type of instruction, known as critical pedagogy, encourages students not only to appreciate global diversity but also to take the lead in the peaceful addressing of any form of discrimination they see that takes place beyond the classroom (Freire 1970). The development of lessons through critical pedagogy helps teacher-librarians convert their libraries into educational spaces that promote social justice by creating opportunities for their students to bring their lived experiences into an instructional setting (Kubal et al. 2003).

The creation of lessons that allow students to bring their real-life experiences into the classroom is not a new concept. Kopetz, Lease, and Warren-Kring (2006) found that the majority of teachers (white, female, and possessing middle-class values) have a challenge in working with non-white students due to the negative stereotypes they learned before becoming teachers. Kopetz, Lease, and Warren-King (2006) and Ladson-Billings (2000) found that teachers promote multiculturalism by incorporating their knowledge of their students' personal experiences into their lessons. Teacher-librarians demonstrate critical pedagogy through their engagement of their students, allowing both the students and the teacher-librarians to develop an awareness of how institutional practices (discrimination) have led to inequality for different cultural groups.

CREATING LIBRARY ENVIRONMENTS
THAT SUPPORT SOCIAL JUSTICE

Teacher-librarians help provide an environment that promotes social justice by giving their multicultural patrons opportunities to explore aspects of their respective cultures that they consider significant to them. Teacher-librarians accomplish this feat by changing their respective libraries into inviting educational spaces. They could follow the mode of popular bookstore chains like Barnes and Noble and convert their school library into a "coffeehouse bookstore" type of environment. Jackson and Hahn (2011) find that college librarians have attempted this model by adding a coffee or snack bar along with some "relaxing rules regarding the possession of food or drink." Moreover, teacher-librarians promote social justice by inviting diverse members of the community to their school libraries to promote culturally relevant activities that have meaning to a patron's respective culture. For example, teacher-librarians may have daily or annual cultural fairs or events take place at their respective school libraries.

Cultural fairs should serve as schoolwide programs throughout the school year, when students, their families, and other diverse members of the community receive invitations to give day-long lessons on their respective culture's poignant holidays, favorite foods, music, and so on. School librarians may want to follow the example of academic librarians who have created inviting spaces for their college-level multicultural patrons by scheduling musical performances or having film screenings (Jackson and Hahn 2011). For instance, one of the authors for four consecutive years gave presentations to the entire sixth-grade class of two middle schools that serve an affluent, mostly white populated school district outside of Pittsburgh, Pennsylvania, as part of their Cultural Exploratory Day Celebrations. He helped promote and develop these celebrations as the official diversity consultant for the school district. His forty-five-minute presentations centered on one of his family's favorite holidays, Kwanza, and its relevance to the African American community as a means to promote unity while dealing with racism. In addition, direct one-on-one tutoring of multicultural students in need of more assistance helps encourage students to feel comfortable enough to want to come back to the school library.

Moreover, the popularity of bookstore/coffeehouse chains like Barnes and Noble serves as a model to create a comfortable learning space for multicultural patrons. In this model, the teacher-librarian places highlighting signs over specific bookshelves, media materials, and so on that emphasize topics to research or read such as African American history, Asian geography and history, Latino/a America history, Native American history, world religions, U.S. women's history, world women's history, and so on. Multicultural patrons visiting their respective school libraries will feel, as the authors of this chapter have felt, that their respective cultures have significance due to the teacher-librarians' effort at placing these visible signs.

CONCLUSION

Teacher-librarians have an opportunity and an obligation to create school libraries that foster learning for multicultural patrons. The four-phase process highlighted in this chapter will serve teacher-librarians as a model to address any forms of discrimination that they encounter or possess within themselves that potentially impedes the learning of their multicultural patrons. When teacher-librarians create environments that promote social justice through their critical pedagogy, they allow both themselves and their students to address any individual or institutionalized form of discrimination that impedes their mutual learning. Their work at converting school libraries into educational spaces that invite learning serves as an integral conduit of education promoting reading, writing, and research in the same fashion as the libraries of the ancient Mediterranean civilizations.

WORKS CITED

Banks, James. 2006. *Cultural Diversity and Education: Foundations, Curriculum, and Teaching.* 5th ed. Boston: Allyn & Bacon.

Colbert-Lewis, Sean C. D. 2011. "The Role of the University Supervisor in Developing Multicultural Competency for Pre-Service Teachers during Their Field/Student Teaching Experience." *Field Experience Journal* 8 (Fall): 1–26. http://www.student-teacher-supervision.org/yahoo_site_admin/assets/docs/fall_2011.348100729.pdf.

Cushner, Kenneth, Averil McClelland, and Philip Safford. 2006. *Human Diversity in Education: An Integrative Approach.* 5th ed. New York: McGraw-Hill.

de Melendez, Wilma R., and Vesna Beck. 2010. *Teaching Young Children in Multicultural Classrooms: Issues, Concepts, and Strategies.* 3rd ed. Belmont, CA: Wadsworth/Cengage Learning.

Eyles, John D. 1989. "The Geography of Everyday Life." In *Horizons in Human Geography.* Edited by Derek Gregory and Rex Walford. London: Macmillan.

Freire, Paolo. 1970. *Pedagogy of the Oppressed.* New York: Continuum.

Gollnick, Donna, and Philip Chinn. 2009. *Multicultural Education in a Pluralistic Society.* 8th ed. Upper Saddle River, NJ: Pearson/Merrill.

Hall, Patrick. 2003. "Perspectives on Developing Research Skills in African American Students: A Case Note." *Journal of Academic Librarianship* 29(3): 182–88.

Hardiman, Rita, Bailey W. Jackson, and Pat Griffin. 2007. "Conceptual Foundations for Social Justice Courses." In *Teaching for Diversity and Social Justice: A Sourcebook.* 2nd ed. Edited by Maurianne Adams, Lee Anne Bell, and Pat Griffin. New York: Routledge.

Hernandez Sheets, Rosa. 2005. *Diversity Pedagogy: Examining the Role of Culture in the Teaching-Learning Process.* Boston: Pearson/Allyn & Bacon.

Jackson, Heather Lea, and Trudi Bellardo Hahn. 2011. "Serving Higher Education's Highest Goals: Assessment of the Academic Library as Place." *College and Research Libraries* 72, no. 5 (September): 428–42.

Johnston, Melissa P., and Bradley W. Bishop. 2011. "The Potential and Possibilities for Utilizing Geographic Information Systems to Inform School Library as Place." *School Libraries Worldwide* 17, no. 1 (January): 1–10.

Kopetz, Patricia, Anthony J. Lease, and Bonnie Z. Warren-Kring. 2006. *Comprehensive Urban Education.* Boston: Pearson/Allyn & Bacon.

Koppelman, Kent L., and R. Lee Goodhart. 2005. *Understanding Human Differences: Multicultural Education for a Diverse America.* Boston: Pearson/Allyn & Bacon.

Kubal, Timothy, Deanna Meyler, Rosalie Torres Stone, and Teelyn T. Mauney. 2003. "Teaching Diversity and Learning Outcomes: Bringing Lived Experience into the Classroom." *Teaching Sociology* 31, no. 4 (October): 441–55.

Ladson-Billings, Gloria. 2000. "Fighting for Our Lives: Preparing Teachers to Teach African American Students." *Journal of Teacher Education* 51, no. 4 (May–June): 206–14.

Mestre, Lori. 2009. "Culturally Responsive Instruction for Teacher Librarians." *Teacher Librarian* 36(3): 8–12. San Jose State University School of Information and Library Science, "Teacher Librarianship Program." http://slisweb.sjsu.edu/classes/careerpathways/teacherlibrarian.htm.

San Jose State University School of Information and Library Science. 2012. "Teacher Librarianship Program." http://slisweb.sjsu.edu/classes/careerpathways/teacherlibrarian.htm.

Segall, Avner. 2002. *Disturbing Practice: Reading Teacher Education as Text.* New York: Peter Lang.

Tomlinson, Carol A. 1995. *How to Differentiate Instruction in Mixed-Ability Classrooms.* Alexandria, VA: Association for Supervision and Curriculum Development.

Tuan, Y. F. 2001. *Space and Place: The Perspective of Experience.* Minneapolis: University of Minnesota Press.

University of North Carolina at Chapel Hill School of Information and Library Science. 2012. "Courses" homepage. http://sils.unc.edu.

Chapter Ten

Expanding Services to International Students and Scholars at Midsize and Small Universities and Colleges

Amauri Serrano and Elizabeth Cramer

International education is increasingly becoming a key focus in many institutions of higher education in the United States. Recruitment of international students and scholars is on the rise, with colleges and universities recognizing the value of increased global awareness and cultural diversity. According to the Institute of International Education's Open Doors data (Chow and Bhandari 2011), the number of international scholars at U.S. institutions of higher education has grown by almost 30 percent in the last decade, while the number of international students has increased by 19 percent. The greatest numbers of international students and scholars are at the large research universities, but with the growth of comprehensive internationalization in higher education, international recruitment at small and midsize colleges and universities is on the rise. From 2009 to 2011 alone, international enrollment at master's colleges and universities increased by 3.2 percent, and 2.7 percent in baccalaureate colleges (Chow and Bhandari 2011, 66).

This chapter addresses how libraries at small to midsize universities and colleges can help meet the needs of growing numbers of international students and scholars while also contributing to a culturally diverse campus atmosphere. With smaller campuses increasing their international recruitment, libraries have new opportunities to provide specialized services and resources to meet the needs of a growing international community. Library initiatives and projects at Appalachian State University Library are presented as a possible model for libraries in small to midsize campuses with growing numbers of international students and scholars, while also contributing to campus internationalization and cultural diversity awareness.

LEARNING FROM THE LIBRARY LITERATURE

The literature on U.S. library services for international students is extensive and covers an array of issues that are important for any library regardless of size, number of international students enrolled, or campus diversity. Although there is less written about library services for international scholars, many of the issues and initiatives discussed in the literature and reviewed in this chapter are beneficial to both groups. For an extensive list of publications covering academic libraries and international students and scholars, see the ACRL Instructions Section's *Library Instruction for Diverse Populations, Bibliography: International Students* (Association of College and Research Libraries 2008) and Diane Peters's (2010) *International Students and Academic Libraries: A Survey of Issues and Annotated Bibliography.*

LANGUAGE BARRIERS AND COMPREHENSION OF ACADEMIC AND LIBRARY JARGON

Some of the literature on language barriers focuses on drawing upon campus diversity to offer multilingual services, such as library handouts in translation (Chau May 2002), multilingual library tours (Hensley and Love 2011), and bilingual library instruction (Bosch and Molteni 2011). Multilingual library services are not always practical at smaller schools; they may not have sufficient numbers of international students and scholars from one particular country or language group to warrant such an approach or multilingual librarians to offer such services. However, libraries may find the following useful: using second language acquisition techniques in the classroom (Amsberry 2008), the use of a simplified vocabulary and sentence structure at the reference desk (Brown 2000), and listening techniques and staff training (Amsberry 2009).

Research has also shown that international students have difficulty understanding library and academic jargon (Howzc and Moore 2003). As a result of the research, the ACRL Instruction Section's Committee on Instruction for Diverse Populations created a multilingual glossary of terms. The committee also proposed that library research and terminology be integrated into intensive English courses when possible and that early exposure to the library and its resources may help to mitigate international student misconceptions of the library and promote comfort and security in academic research.

LIBRARY STAFF AND CULTURAL SENSITIVITY

Although the literature about academic library services to international populations covers aspects of staff competency, the most useful recommendations in this area are found in publications about services for minority and underserved populations. A central component of any training program involves developing cultural competence (Overall 2009). Some larger academic libraries have hired librarians with the specific task of overseeing diversity efforts and outreach. Although a diversity librarian or multicultural librarian position at smaller universities may not be viable, a committee of librarians that is interested or experienced with multicultural populations can provide diversity programming and workshops while drawing upon the knowledge and expertise of university faculty and staff on campus.

INTRODUCTION TO ACADEMIC LIBRARIES AND RESEARCH SERVICES

Orientation to the library and its various services is an integral part of an international student's or scholar's success at an institution. International student orientation need not be restricted to on-campus events but can also be delivered virtually with the creation of web resources (Ruswick 2011). Such an approach requires building strong relationships with the office of international student services, who in turn can act as a referral service for students and scholars (Switzer 2008). International instructors will benefit from individual consultations with subject specialists in order to familiarize themselves with subject-specific resources and collections. Moreover, many international scholars have families whose needs the library should address as part of its community engagement program. The library literature covering outreach efforts by public libraries to immigrant populations is especially useful in this area.

CONSIDERATIONS FOR INTERNATIONAL STUDENTS AT SMALL AND MIDSIZE INSTITUTIONS

Although the literature does a good job of proposing new and innovative strategies for libraries to better support the success and enrichment of international students and scholars on American college campuses, it unfortunately (yet understandably) tends to focus on campuses with large international populations and does not adequately cover smaller campuses that possibly have fewer resources and a much different international student and scholar population. Librarians at smaller institutions often serve predominantly international undergraduate students of whom a significant portion is non-degree-seeking exchange students. Like their American undergraduate peers, they face the challenges of navigating the world of American libraries and scholarly research but have the additional barriers of language and cultural differences. Unlike their domestic peers, who often get information literacy and an introduction to library services as part of the institution's general education curriculum, international exchange students often take upper-level courses in the major and do not receive information literacy instruction. Moreover, as librarians in a midsize public institution with few, although increasing, numbers of international students, we face the challenge of an international student population that changes biannually and represents many countries of origin.

In order to address the lack of opportunities for library instruction and limited staff and financial resources, it is instrumental that the library be creative and

- collaborate with the campus office of international student and scholar services to determine who is on campus, for how long, and from where;
- be a part of the campus's international student orientation programming;
- provide international students with specialized library information that addresses their specific needs, and preferably make it available online;
- provide international student library tours to showcase library facilities and services;
- assess services offered continuously with focus groups, exit interviews, or surveys and be prepared to modify services as needed;
- become involved in campus internationalization efforts that are not necessarily library related.

CONSIDERATIONS FOR INTERNATIONAL SCHOLARS AT SMALL AND MIDSIZE INSTITUTIONS

In order to develop an outreach program and services for international scholars, it is important that the library understand the international scholar population on campus and the length of their stay. For those scholars who teach, your institution's new faculty orientation program may be an excellent opportunity to highlight library services and, most importantly, individual consultations. Other initiatives that may be feasible for smaller campuses include the following:

- Library tours for international scholars and their families.
- A librarian and international scholar partnership program, in which librarians can provide subject specific assistance.
- Creation of an information packet about the academic library and local public library resources for the families of international scholars to be provided by the office of international student and scholar services or a appropriate unit.
- Subject-specific workshops for international scholars; this is especially useful if your institution hosts significant numbers of scholars in certain disciplines such as STEM or business.

APPALACHIAN STATE UNIVERSITY LIBRARY:
A POSSIBLE MODEL

Appalachian State University is a midsize master's degree–granting university located in a remote Appalachian Mountain region of North Carolina with a homogenous student population. In the autumn 2011 semester, 87.7 percent of enrollees self-identified as white and 90.5 percent were in-state residents (Appalachian State University 2011). In response to the remote locale and the uniform student population, Appalachian is focusing on recruitment of international students and scholars to increase diversity on campus. In addition to diversity needs, the growing number of international students and scholars increases global awareness on campus, a recognized goal as stated in the university's strategic plan (Appalachian State University 2008).

International Student and Scholar Services (ISSS) reported an enrollment of 151 international students from sixty-two different countries enrolled at Appalachian during the 2010/2011 academic year (ISSS 2011). This number represents a 32 percent increase in the number of international students from the previous year. In addition to the increase in the international student population, the ISSS also reported 12 international visiting professors and scholars at Appalachian during this time period, as well as 62 additional international scholars and visitors who came to the campus for periods ranging from two days to four weeks (ISSS 2011).

In response to this growing community, Appalachian State University Library recognizes the importance of meeting the needs of these campus constituencies. The increase of foreign students and scholars on campuses with little diversity has created new challenges and opportunities in the areas of outreach, services, resources, and programs. The Appalachian State University Library provides a possible model of creative outreach efforts and services to a small but growing international campus community.

OUTREACH

To best meet the needs of incoming international students and scholars at Appalachian State University, librarians work closely with the University's Office of International Education and Development (OIED) to stay informed about international recruitment, international partnerships, and campus events related to global awareness and cultural awareness. Twice a year, at the beginning of the autumn and spring semesters, the library participates in the university-wide international student orientation, a two-day event facilitated by the OIED. In preparation for the orientation, OIED sends the library a list of new international students and their home countries. Knowledge of home countries of the incoming international students helps the library prepare in many ways:

- keeping current on geographic origins of our international student population
- gauging current needs for specialized services and resources based on cultural and linguistic backgrounds
- organizing future focus groups for feedback and suggestions

As part of the university-wide orientation, the library hosts a one-and-a-half hour session that includes a brief discussion of library services and resources, a presentation from the University Writing Center, a walking tour of the library building, and an informal reception for librarians, library staff, and international students. The brief discussion about library resources and services is accompanied by an online guide, a resource that international students consult throughout their stay at Appalachian. In recognition of the potential differences between Appalachian's library and the student's home institution's library, we discuss open stacks, the accessibility of our librarians, and the library's social environment. Librarians explain library jargon that arises during the program—terms such as *stacks*, *periodicals*, or *checkout*. A short glossary of academic research terms is included within the online library guide for further consultation. There is also a list of print and online travel guides for popular destinations within the United States, public transportation information, and a description of the library's film collection, which is the most extensive within the community.

Appalachian librarians also participate in the university's orientation for new or visiting international scholars at the beginning of every fall semester. During the session, librarians provide a summary of services available and emphasize the availability of one-on-one librarian consultations, providing contact information for library departmental liaisons. Being a nonresearch institution, we also emphasize interlibrary loan and the comment box on the library's homepage, encouraging them to make requests or suggestions for future acquisitions. The relationship that develops between librarians and visiting international scholars is beneficial to the library's goal of internationalizing collections. For example, visiting scholars in the Foreign Languages Department have suggested various regional authors, critiqued existing collections, and reviewed books donated to the library in non-Romanized text.

In order to promote cultural sensitivity among librarians and staff, the library has a Library Diversity Committee that is active in outreach activities within the library and throughout the campus and community. Internally, the Library Diversity Committee coordinates and presents cultural awareness workshops for librarians and staff, educating them on relevant topics such as communication with nonnative English speakers, special needs of nontraditional students, and current university recruitment efforts of underrepresented and international students. The committee also coordinates the International Student Orientation twice a year and represents the library at a variety of campus international activities, including the Diversity Celebration, International Education Week, and International Coffee Break.

RESOURCES AND SERVICES

In support of the university's internationalization efforts, the Appalachian State University Library has acquired relevant resources in a wide variety of formats and languages. One popular resource is international satellite television from Asia, Arabic-speaking countries, Western Europe, and Latin America. Professors from a variety of disciplines, including political science, foreign languages, religion, and philosophy, create assignments based on comparative studies of media coverage and popular entertainment from around the world. In addition, international (and domestic) students may reserve television viewing rooms to watch sports, news, or popular serials from their home country.

For both international students and scholars, individual research assistance is available. Through the various outreach efforts mentioned above, international students and scholars are connected with Appalachian librarians who specialize in specific disciplines or languages. One outstanding example of a librarian working with a targeted international group is the library's ASU Faculty Fellow Librarian. Seven years ago, Appalachian State University recruited a Chinese national to serve as an ASU Faculty Fellow, an initiative to attract a more diverse student population through recruitment of a more diverse faculty. The Library's Faculty Fellow has been wonderfully successful in connecting with Chinese students and scholars and serves in several related capacities on campus.

PROGRAMMING

The library also sponsors a campus-wide program called Doorways, which focuses on international issues and encourages new and/or visiting international faculty to present their research to an audience of students, faculty, and local community members. The library views each Doorways program as an opportunity to evaluate and strengthen library resources relevant to the program topic. At each program, the library promotes relevant library resources through the creation of a subject bibliography and presentation of selected items.

Recently the library has also partnered with student groups, the Diversity Office, and the Office of International Education and Development to present a Global Film Series. International student groups have proven invaluable in suggesting films from their home country that would appeal to domestic students as well. In this way, the Global Film Series includes popular feature films that appeal to a younger group, in addition to the documentary films that may be more appealing to university faculty. By having students promote films, the Global Film Series has become part of the student social scene, bolstering attendance at a previously poorly attended event. Faculty members are invited to introduce the films, and student organizations participate by offering cultural activities before the screening.

ASSESSMENT

Assessment is key not only for evaluating and improving current programming and services but also for acquiring input from cultural and ethnic groups in order to determine gaps in the library's current offerings and to strengthen relationships. For the past two years librarians at Appalachian State University have received feedback from students through focus groups and online surveys sent out to international students at the end of every semester. Focus groups have proven the most effective, since librarians were able to ask follow-up questions in an informal and relaxed setting. Through student feedback, Appalachian librarians realized that international students lacked awareness about many library services, even after attending short orientation sessions. Based on this information, the library expanded the International Student Orientation to include a formal sit-down introduction to library services with a question-and-answer session, a speaker from the Writing Center, and the creation of an online research and services.

CONCLUSION

Libraries that serve small to midsize campuses with little diversity have a unique opportunity to use their creativity and size to better serve an increasing number of international students and scholars, and in so doing, contribute to the success of university internationalization efforts. The library literature provides a host of case studies and projects that can help determine which services, resources, and outreach and programming initiatives may be appropriate for your campus. However, the literature does not adequately address some of the issues that smaller schools may face such as limited staff and fiscal resources, campus diversity, and relatively transitory international population. Building strong partnerships with campus units concerned with internationalization is critical to the library's success. Appalachian State University Library has taken the campus's commitment to internationalization as a central goal and can provide similar libraries a model of possible services and outreach and programming efforts.

WORKS CITED

Amsberry, Dawn. 2008. "Talking the Talk: Library Classroom Communication and International Students." *Journal of Academic Librarianship* 34(4): 354–57.

———. 2009. "Using Effective Listening Skills with International Patrons." *Reference Services Review* 37(1): 10–19.

Appalachian State University. 2008. "Strategic Plan 2008–2012: Reach Greater Heights." http://www.appstate.edu/about/strategic_plan.pdf (accessed December 16, 2012).

———. Fall 2011. "IPEDS Enrollment Statistics by Race and Gender." http://www1.appstate.edu/dept/irp/FB/1112/SI/s60_enroll_race_gender.pdf (accessed January 18, 2012).

Association of College and Research Libraries (ACRL). 2008. Instructions Section. "Library Instructions for Diverse Populations Bibliography: International Students." http://www.ala.org/acrl/sites/ala.org.acrl/files/content/aboutacrl/directoryofleadership/sections/is/iswebsite/projpubs/internatlstudents.pdf (accessed January 12, 2012).

———. "Multilingual Glossary of Terms." 2011. http://www.ala.org/acrl/aboutacrl/directoryofleadership/sections/is/iswebsite/projpubs/multilingual (accessed January 12, 2012).

Bosch, Eileen K., and Valeria E. Molteni. 2011. "Connecting to International Students in Their Languages: Innovative Bilingual Library Instruction in Academic Libraries." In *International Students and Academic Libraries: Initiatives for Success*, edited by Pamela A. Jackson and Patrick Sullivan, 135–50. Chicago: Association of College and Research Libraries.

Brown, Christopher C. 2000. "Reference Services to the International Adult Learner: Understanding the Barriers." *Reference Librarian* 69/70: 337–47.

Chau May, Ying. 2002. "Helping Hands: Serving and Engaging International Students." *Reference Librarian* 79/80: 383–393.

Chow, Patricia, and Rajika Bhandari. 2011. *Open Doors 2011: Report on International Educational Exchange*. New York: Institute of International Education.

Gilton, Donna Louise. 2005. "Culture Shock in the Library: Implications for Information Literacy Instruction." *Research Strategies* 20(4): 424–32.

Hensley, Merinda Kaye, and Emily Love. 2011. "A Multifaceted Model of Outreach and Instruction for International Students." In *International Students and Academic Libraries: Initiatives for Success*, edited by Pamela A. Jackson and Patrick Sullivan, 115–34. Chicago: Association of College and Research Libraries.

Howze, Phillip, and Dorothy Moore. 2003. "Measuring International Students' Understanding of Concepts Related to the Use of Library-Based Technology." *Research Strategies* 19(1): 57–74.

International Student and Scholar Services (ISSS), Appalachian State University. 2011. "Annual Report." Unpublished university document, December 16.

Overall, Patricia Montiel. 2009. "Cultural Competence: A Conceptual Framework for Library Information Science Professionals." *Library Quarterly* 79(2): 175–204.

Peters, Diane E. 2010. *International Students and Academic Libraries: A Survey of Issues and Annotated Bibliography*. Lanham, MD: Scarecrow Press.

Ruswick, Janelle. 2011. "Engaging International Students before Welcome Week." In *International Students and Academic Libraries: Initiatives for Success*, edited by Pamela A. Jackson and Patrick Sullivan, 19–46. Chicago: Association of College and Research Libraries.

Switzer, Anne T. 2008. "Redefining Diversity: Creating an Inclusive Academic Library through Diversity Initiatives." *College and Undergraduate Libraries* 15(3): 280–300.

Chapter Eleven

Reaching Out to International Students at the University of Lethbridge Library

Nicole Eva

The University of Lethbridge is a medium-sized research institution with an undergraduate and graduate population of approximately 8,500 students (University of Lethbridge Institutional Analysis 2011). The main campus is located in Lethbridge, a small city of nearly 88,000 people (Neufeld 2011) in southern Alberta, Canada. There is one library on the main campus, which serves the Lethbridge campus as well as two satellite campuses located in Calgary, Alberta, and Edmonton, Alberta, located approximately 250 and 500 kilometers, respectively, from Lethbridge.

The Student Engagement Team (SET) at the University of Lethbridge (U of L) Library has a mandate to "provide leadership within the University Library on all services, activities and innovations, both in person and virtual, that support the University Strategic Plan and Strategic Direction of *enhancing the student experience*," as stated in the 2010 SET Charter. We try to keep this purpose in mind with all of the activities we engage in as a group, getting involved in recruitment and retention activities, university fairs and orientations, and projects and initiatives designed to engage students both academically and socially. We are constantly planning and seeking out new ways to provide new or enhanced services and activities that support the overall experience of students as well as partnering with other service providers across campus and within the Lethbridge community. We want to engage not only the students at the University of Lethbridge with the library, but also those on the remote campuses, as well as staff, faculty, and members of the larger Lethbridge community. In today's times, it is important for us to reach out to as many potential users as we can and make our valuable resources and services known to as wide a group as possible.

With this purpose in mind, the SET members sought out student groups to target that we felt would benefit the most from exposure to the library and the help we can provide. These groups included transfer students (transferring from other programs, usually at colleges, and continuing their degrees at the university level), students studying at the satellite campuses, and international students. These international students come to the U of L on exchange, to gain English as a Second Language for Academic Purposes (EAP) accreditation, or to complete undergraduate or graduate degrees. They come to us in southern Alberta from all over the world and nearly every continent—Asia, Africa, the Americas, Australia, and Europe. In fact, in fall 2011 the U of L admitted over 700 undergraduate and graduate students from over ninety different countries, not including Canada and the United States, according to Nicole Bach, University of Lethbridge Institutional Analysis, in an e-mail communication on December 14, 2011. At the reference desk, staff have noticed a high percentage of international students seeking help. Not only do they require research assistance, but their English language skills are often very poor, setting them even further back in their attempt to find suitable resources for their assignments. They seem to be struggling a great deal with using the library and finding suitable library materials, and with understanding the requirements of research and their assignment. The SET felt that perhaps by tailoring messaging and services towards this group, we could reach more of them and give them personalized attention that could help them reach their academic goals.

We know from both experience and the literature that international students are often less likely to seek help for a wide variety of reasons (see Walker and Click 2011; Liu and Winn 2009; Gilton 2007; Morrissey and Given 2006; Wang and Frank 2002). Some have a cultural belief that it is rude to ask questions and that one should not question authority; some are shy or insecure with their language skills, which inhibits them from asking questions; and some don't think of people who work in libraries as being people who are capable of helping them with their research because libraries (and librarians) may function very differently in the countries from which they came. So not only do they likely need our help more than many students, but they are less likely to ask for it. International students face many overwhelming challenges when studying abroad—not only with language, but also with cultural and traditional differences.

The author, chair of the SET, arranged a meeting with the Liaison Officer from the International Centre for Students on campus. This woman arranges events for all international students to participate in and tries to make their transition to Canadian culture as smooth as possible. Her work includes helping students find appropriate housing, helping them fit socially into their new environment, and dealing with any academic issues that may arise. She runs a monthly International Café for all international students to come together and socialize and sometimes invites guests to speak to them. We arranged for a librarian, designated as the International Librarian, to attend the Café, introducing herself and some of the library's services. The librarian chosen for this role enjoys working with international students and had already met some of them while delivering a bibliographic instruction class on APA style for EAP students. She has also traveled extensively worldwide, giving her a greater knowledge and respect for various cultures.

At the Café, the librarian emphasized the research help available and the wide variety of resources the library contains, and she made it clear that she was available for individual appointments. We felt that students might be more comfortable contacting someone they had met rather than approaching a stranger at the reference desk, due to the aforementioned studies which suggested that international students are less likely to seek help from a librarian. She also handed out a survey (see textbox 11.1) created for this event to ascertain the international students' wants and needs with respect to the library. The results of this survey can be seen in table 11.1.

Textbox 11.1: International Café—Library Questionnaire

Please take a moment to complete this questionnaire about the university library. We value your feedback, and it will help us develop future sessions for you. Thank you!

1. Have you had any contact with the U of L Library? Please check all that apply:

- Someone from the library has visited my class.
- I have had a tour of the library.
- I have used space in the library to study or meet with classmates.
- I have used library services—e.g., checked out a book, asked a question.
- I have visited the library website.

2. What did you think about the U of L Library when you first saw it?
3. How is the library at the U of L different from libraries in your home country?
4. Please RANK these items in order of importance (1 being the most important) in terms of what you would you like to learn about the U of L Library, its services, or its resources.

- ____ How to look for books, DVDs, etc.
- ____ How to use the library databases

- _____ How to write citations and create bibliographies
- _____ How to avoid plagiarism
- _____ How to evaluate websites
- _____ How to request items from other libraries
- _____ Other: _____

Comments received from the students included that they felt the library was a good place to study; that they appreciated the quiet and variety of study spaces; that it is bright and well-lit; that the library staff were helpful; that they would appreciate longer opening hours for the library; and that the U of L Library was larger in physical size and size of collection than the libraries in many of the students' home countries.

One outcome of the librarian's attendance at the International Café was the idea to offer a workshop geared exclusively to international students, focused on how to use the library's catalogue and databases. A desire for this type of instruction was expressed in the Café surveys; it was advertised

Table 11.1.   Results of International Café Survey

Total Surveys Completed	40

Have you had any contact with the U of L Library? Please check all that apply.

A librarian has visited my class.	14
I have had a tour of the library.	11
I have used space in the library.	31
I have used library services.	33
I have visited the library website.	30

Please RANK these items in order of importance (1 being the most important) in terms of what you would you like to learn about the U of L Library, its services, or its resources.

RANKING	1	2	3	4	5	6
How to look for books, DVDs, etc.	8	9	5	3	4	4
How to use the library databases	14	7	8	4	0	1
How to write citations and create bibliographies	5	7	8	8	6	0
How to avoid plagiarism	1	2	6	8	6	9
How to evaluate websites	1	2	2	6	10	12
How to request items from other libraries	7	9	4	4	7	7

exclusively to international students through the International Centre via targeted e-mails and posters in the Centre. As noted by Conteh-Morgan (2001), nonnative English speakers may feel more comfortable in a familiar environment with other English as a Second Language (ESL) students. Badke (2002) notes that the cultural reluctance to participate in classroom activities may make international students more comfortable practicing library skills outside of their regular classroom if their regular classes are integrated with native English speakers. Morrisey and Given (2006) found that providing international students with their own library sessions at a time when they may have had more time to adapt to Canadian culture and the English language was more effective than holding them earlier in the term. Wang and Frank (2002) suggest that sessions held exclusively for international students can be better tailored to their unique learning styles and needs. We also felt that these students may feel less hesitant about attending a workshop where all other attendees were at a similar level in terms of language and skills development. Unfortunately, the workshop was not well attended.

The SET tried to communicate to our international student cohort in a variety of ways. The author designed a brochure that highlighted the unique services and resources available to international students. These included the aforementioned dedicated international librarian and workshops, as well as such features as the ability to change the interface language on some databases and our subscriptions to international newspapers. We tried to touch on the basics of library use and heavily emphasized the help available to them through the library. We mentioned the availability of online materials and open stacks, which may not be what they were used to from their home libraries. We also highlighted some of the recent resources acquired on the topics of studying in a nonnative language and Canadian culture, as well as the pathfinder created to showcase these items. This brochure was distributed through the International Centre for Students to all incoming international students.

The library's collection of resources geared to international students was also increased. Recent monographs dealing with Canadian culture, studying abroad, and English language skills were purchased. These new acquisitions were also highlighted in a research help guide, along with other library resources that might be of interest to international students. In addition, the research help guide highlighted several free, authoritative websites geared to those learning English as a second language. Furthermore, we created a table display of these newly acquired titles during the university's International Week, a yearly event promoted by the International Centre for Students. The author also investigated the acquisition of a language learning database, Mango Languages, which could help international students improve their English language skills. We have subsequently obtained this database through one of our consortia.

Another way the U of L Library tried to get involved in International Week activities was to host an international-themed PechaKucha event. PechaKucha is a presentation style that was originated by architects in Japan to keep presentations short and succinct (Klein Dytham Architecture n.d.). Typically, twenty slides of images only are shown for twenty seconds each. For the library's event, we asked students, staff, and faculty to present on their international experiences, be it travel, work, or study. The result was an entertaining and enlightening evening of presentations, ranging from immigration experiences, travels with family members, and class trips abroad, among many others.

Both from the literature and from our own experiences, it is evident that international students require additional guidance to navigate the university library system. Language issues alone put them at a huge disadvantage; imagine having mastered the basics of subject-specific and conversational English, only to be faced with such terms as *catalogue, database, index, thesaurus,* and many more terms that even students who are native English speakers are often unfamiliar with. Added to this confusion are cultural values that include not asking questions of those in authority, inherent shyness and embarrassment at what may be perceived as inadequacies, and unfamiliarity with libraries that are open to user navigation, and it is not difficult to see how the entire scenario of using the library might be terrifyingly overwhelming.

Many librarians may be frustrated when faced with students who can barely utter their question in an understandable way, let alone have any idea about how to go about their research; however, when one realizes the obstacles these students overcome every day just navigating through an unfamiliar city, culture, and educational system, it does not take long to gain some sympathy for them. The author's meeting with the Liaison Officer from the International Centre for Students at the U of L included discussion of holding cultural sensitivity training for all library staff, which would be of great benefit to any library that deals with large numbers of international students and has been suggested by some in the literature (see Gale 2006; Gray 2010; Mestre 2010). Unfortunately, we have not yet held this training at the University of Lethbridge Library, but we hope to soon. Just knowing about some of the cultural differences between Canada/the United States and the wide range of countries from which our international students come can go a long way toward increasing understanding on the part of staff members.

Many basic tips for dealing with international students may seem obvious, but bear repeating and are outlined nicely in Curry and Copeman's "Reference Service to International Students: A Field Stimulation Research Study" (2005). These include speaking slowly, using simple language without library jargon or big words, repeating the asker's question to ensure understanding on the part of the librarian or staff member, and maintaining eye contact and a pleasant demeanor. As so much of these students' reluctance to ask questions may arise from shyness over their inability to confidently express themselves in English, just smiling and nodding at them reassuringly can go a long way toward encouraging them to approach the reference desk and voice their query. It is easy to forget these simple actions when we are used to answering a multitude of questions, but such small courtesies can make a huge difference in the comfort and understanding of a nonnative English speaker. Many other articles in the literature also provide tips on intercultural communication; these include Wang and Frank (2002); Gilton (2007); and Walker and Click (2011).

The ideas implemented at the University of Lethbridge Library are just a few of the possibilities that can be utilized to reach out to and engage international students. Many more ideas are found in the literature, including the articles cited here, and a nice succinct list of easy-to-implement suggestions is provided in Gale (2006). Another valuable resource is the bibliography created by Yusuke Ishimura (2010) which was compiled for the Association of College and Research Libraries (ACRL) Academic Library Services to International Students Interest Group.

The University of Lethbridge will continue our outreach efforts to international students on an ongoing basis through our partnership with the International Centre for Students on campus. Every year brings a new batch of beleaguered and intimidated international students who all need to be told the same message: the library is a helpful, friendly place that can help you with your academic endeavors, so please do not hesitate to come and ask us for assistance. Just providing this information to incoming international students will go a long way in having more of them utilize our services, and, as a result, improve their academic performance while studying in our country.

WORKS CITED

Badke, William. 2002. "International Students: Information Literacy or Academic Literacy?" *Academic Exchange* 6(Winter): 60–65.

Conteh-Morgan, Miriam. 2001. "Empowering ESL Students: A New Model for Information Literacy Instruction." *Research Strategies* 18: 29–38.

Curry, Ann, and Deborah Copeman. 2005. "Reference Service to International Students: A Field Stimulation Research Study." *Journal of Academic Librarianship* 31(5): 409–20.

Gale, Caroline. 2006. "Serving Them Right? How Libraries Can Enhance the Learning Experience of International Students: A Case Study from the University of Exeter." *SCONUL Focus* 39: 36–39.

Gilton, Donna L. 2007. "Culture Shock in the Library: Implications for Information Literacy Instruction." *Research Strategies* 20: 424–32.

Gray, Jody. 2010. "A Different Approach to Diversity Outreach." *College and Research Libraries News* 71(2): 76–78.

Ishimura, Yusuke. 2010. "LIS Literature." Last modified June 10. http://www.acrl.ala.org/international.

Klein Dytham Architecture. n.d. "Twenty Frequently Asked Questions about PechaKucha 20x20." http://www.pecha-kucha.org/what (accessed December 2, 2011).

Liu, Guoying, and Danielle Winn. 2009. "Chinese Graduate Students and the Canadian Academic Library: A User Study at the University of Windsor." *Journal of Academic Librarianship* 35(6): 565–73.

Mestre, Lori S. 2010. "Librarians Working with Diverse Populations: What Impact Does Cultural Competency Training Have on Their Efforts?" *Journal of Academic Librarianship* 36(6): 479–88.

Morrisey, Renée, and Lisa M. Given. 2006. "International Students and the Academic Library: A Case Study." *Canadian Journal of Information and Library Science* 30(3/4): 221–39.

Neufeld, Aleta. 2011. "2011 Census Results: City of Lethbridge Is Home to 1,223 New Residents." Last modified June 22. http://www.lethbridge.ca/NewsCentre/Pages/official-census-results-2011.aspx.

University of Lethbridge Institutional Analysis. 2011. "2010–2011 Facts Book." http://www.uleth.ca/analysis/sites/analysis/files/Facts%20Book%202010_11WEB_0.pdf (accessed December 2, 2011).

Walker, Claire, and Amanda Click. 2011. "Meeting the Reference Expectations of ESL Students." *College and Research Libraries News* 72(1): 20–23.

Wang, Jian, and Donald G. Frank. 2002. "Cross-Cultural Communication: Implications for Effective Information Services in Academic Libraries." *portal: Libraries and the Academy* 2(2): 207–16.

Chapter Twelve

The Solo Career College Librarian

Reaching Out to Nontraditional Students

Alice Graves

Career colleges and their libraries are too often overlooked in the academic literature. Recent research revealed five articles; three were published after 2009, the other two in 2005 and 2006. But as for-profit and career colleges proliferate and their attendance grows, these institutions should be recognized by researchers and treated as seriously as their traditional counterparts.

Unlike other academic libraries, career college libraries are small, limited in the scope of their resources, underused, and often staffed by a solo librarian. Unlike librarians at traditional academic institutions, career college librarians need to lure students into the library to show them what the library has to offer besides access to the Internet and printers.

At my career college library, the computers and printers are in the front area of the library; beyond them are the stacks consisting of four rows of shelves. Like the forbidden attic in *Jane Eyre*, hardly anyone ventures into that area—students or faculty. Thus, uniting students and faculty with the collection is a major priority in a career college library.

I work in a proprietary career college that is in the process of transitioning from a for-profit to a not-for-profit. It is accredited by the Accrediting Commission of Career Schools and Colleges, but this will change as the process of transitioning is complete. The medical assisting program is the school's largest. The other programs include cosmetology, dental assisting, personal fitness training, computer and network administration (CNA), and criminal justice (CJ). Most of these are diploma programs; CNA offers an associate's degree, while CJ offers associate's and bachelor's degrees. My campus, one in a network of seventeen nationwide, currently enrolls 195 students. This serves to create a small-community atmosphere at the campus, where almost all faces are familiar.

The college's demographics are mostly young (twenties to early thirties, with some older students). African Americans account for more than half the students on campus, followed by Hispanics. The students are nontraditional in many senses of the word. They are single parents, veterans, and have been on both sides of the law. They live on the economic edge. Their support systems are precarious; sometimes their role models are their own children. A change in job schedule or a sick child can throw a student's life into chaos. The students use their streetwise social skills when they are not on the street. The Career Development class teaches them soft skills, such as teamwork, problem solving, effective communication, and dependability. These students did not have teachers or librarians in their past who inspired them or made them feel that they matter. At best, they have avoided both. The careers that they have chosen to pursue will transform their lives dramatically. Many of the students have been out of school for several years, recognize their past mistakes, and are finally ready to take their education seriously.

If there is a career college stigma, these students are not aware of it. Some have attended community college and found it "too much like high school." They have no time for academics that will not prepare them for jobs. They need to move into a career quickly and start being adults.

The campus library consists of about four thousand volumes, mostly old textbooks no longer in use. (The college provides all necessary textbooks to each student when classes begin. This ensures that each student will *have* the textbook.) The small fiction and literature collection consists of mostly old, donated books—an ample array of Nora Roberts, Danielle Steele, and John Grisham, but no Hemingway or Woolf. None of the books in the 800s arrived here new. Did I say the 800s? Yes, we use Dewey here. At first I considered converting everything to LCC, simply because this is a college, but DDC may be the best choice for this population. The only other library they use is the public library, so they are familiar with DDC and this gives them a degree of confidence when using the library. And, finally, my campus does not keep circulation statistics because borrowing occurs seldom enough to be a memorable event.

I am the only librarian at my campus, reporting to the director of education, who, fortunately, acknowledges my professional expertise. But many of our students, despite being Gen Yers, have limited computer experience, so I must help them log in for the first time and encourage them to write down their passwords. It is surprising how many neglect to do so and then become frustrated. A large part of my day consists of troubleshooting printer problems; teaching students how to perform tasks on the computers, such as cutting and pasting, choosing fonts and formats, and other Microsoft Word basics; and contacting IT to have forgotten passwords reset. Many students need help using the photocopier as well. Their limited computer experience is a major source of frustration for them, and I have come to think their forgotten passwords are an avoidance technique.

There was no one to train me when I started working here, leaving me to learn how to use the cataloging software on my own. We use bar codes, but the scanner cannot read them, so accession numbers are used for circulation, adding an extra step to the process. Cataloging systems vary by campus, and some campuses use LCC. Sometimes I feel as if this library missed the bus to the twenty-first century.

Library visitors are required to sign in, but some head straight for the computers without signing in, so we lack accurate usage numbers.

The library has no budget. A large part of our collection is made up of textbooks that are no longer in use and donated books. If I need something, I ask. I usually get it, but I never ask for more than I think I will get. Most of my collection development is conducted at used book sales.

When I first came to the library, it was a mess and no one used it. The former librarian, who left several weeks before I started, was a tyrant. Students feared her, faculty ignored her, and both avoided the library. I have heard the lurid details from many different people. It was obvious I needed to quickly create a welcoming, open, dynamic library and to attract students and include faculty.

Thinking specifically about the needs of the students and faculty, I developed the following objectives:

- The students needed a library where they could feel welcome and comfortable.
- The students needed relevant and interesting books.
- The faculty needed to be involved in library initiatives.
- The students needed a librarian who was responsive to their need for information literacy skills and who would provide the tools and skills to help them feel comfortable and confident finding the information they needed from credible Internet sources.
- The students needed to feel respected and trusted by the librarian.
- The students needed a librarian committed to their success by providing tutoring, setting up study centers in the library where groups could work together, and being generally available and welcoming to students.

Then I began putting my plan into effect.

CANDY IS DANDY

Food attracts people. So, there is always candy in the library. At first students were surprised and asked timidly if they could take one. "Of course, help yourself!" I effused, recognizing the need to de-condition their fear. They still ask if they may use "my" stapler, located beside the student printer. Now, students come by every morning, take a piece of candy, say hello, tell me about their classes, ask questions, and browse the 800s. One student brings in a pile of index cards and I help her study for weekly quizzes. Another is writing a book about her life—she is twenty-five and her younger brother is in prison. She gives me pages to read, not to edit or correct, she says, but just to get to know her. We talk about her relationships and family. She is one of our few night students, so we have privacy. It's like therapy. A new student needs help finding scholarships, explaining she is a single mom, a battered woman, and an ex-convict. A male student, in a conversation about holding grudges, tells me that he will never forgive his sister for stabbing him. A student I tutored for the GED exam comes in before class to chat as we both await his results. A few weeks later, he brings his certificate to the library first. Congratulations and hugs are in order. If my knees were in better shape, I'd jump up and down. This is the first time I've seen him smile, and it is an endless one.

BOOK DISPLAYS

This may sound like a no-brainer, but after I realized that no one had any idea what books were in the library, I began setting up displays on the front table. The books may be similar thematically (like during the week of Dr. Martin Luther King's birthday) or they may be purely recreational reading—a mixture of Nora Roberts, a Michael Jordan biography, and Ray Bradbury. I change the display weekly. Students and faculty are surprised at some of the books we have. "I didn't know we had this book. What else do we have?" We have begun to see some circulation and have had some requests for new books. Fines for late returns have been discontinued. These students barely have bus fare. Getting them to read is more important than penalizing them for not being able to return a book on time. My predecessor charged 25 cents per day, which may help explain the lack of circulation.

WEEDING AND NEEDING

The library's collection development policy, as written, is to support the school's curricula. That explains the old textbooks. But the general reading books had no rhyme or reason. I found books on pre-Elizabethan drama and Jewish humor, and essays on the works of Sinclair Lewis. These were removed. There was also a healthy collection of thrillers, mysteries, and popular fiction, which were retained. I added books that are absolutely necessary to any college library. I purchased *To Kill a Mockingbird*, *Push*, *The House on Mango Street*, and the *Hunger Games* series. I regularly troll used book sales at local public libraries, and I have been able to add books by Toni Morrison, Ishmael Beah, Isabel Allende, and a biography of Michael Jordan. Neighbors who were getting ready to sell their house invited me to pick through their books. I found a copy of *The Color Purple* and Alex Haley's *Roots*, both conspicuously absent from our library.

LIBRARY SURVEY

Even the briefest library surveys can determine users' needs. As students enter the library, I hand them a brief survey, consisting of four questions:

1. What is the title of your favorite book?
2. What kinds of books do you like to read (science fiction, mystery, vampire, etc.)?
3. What books would you like to see in the library?
4. If the library had new, interesting books, would you read more?

I discovered that the students had varying tastes and interests, they do read, and everyone answered "yes" to question number four. One student told me his favorite book was Machiavelli's *The Prince*—proof that one cannot stereotype career college students.

GETTING FACULTY INVOLVED

Faculty buy-in is essential in a career college library because their daily contact with the students can be a great influence. I sent an e-mail to faculty asking what course-related books they wanted to have in the library and received several suggestions. Ironically, some of the books suggested were already in the library—that's how well-kept a secret the library is. Those that the library did not have were added, including multiple copies of a pharmacology handbook for nurses.

I also asked faculty and staff to donate their gently used books to the library, specifically asking for fiction, general nonfiction, and biography. One instructor thrilled me the morning she lugged in a shopping bag loaded with mysteries and thrillers.

LIBGUIDES

Students come into the library and ask for books on very specific topics, such as pancreatitis. Most of our books are textbooks with chapters on these topics containing general, limited information. Because I want them to become information literate and to understand that the most current information is found online, I send students to Medline Plus, the CDC, and the Merck Manual online. While all of the college's programs require a term paper using at least minimal research, there is no instruction offered on how to do that research. Students are expected to find the school's three online databases on their own. They simply do not.

One morning a student in the medical assisting program came in asking for books on diabetes for a report. Instead, I showed her MedlinePlus. She was extremely impressed. "Do they have high blood pressure too? What about HIV?" It was all there. She ran back to class to tell her classmates and instructor.

That led me to compile library guides for each program. The one for medical assisting, for example, lists the CDC, MedlinePlus, and the Merck Manual online. Our college subscribes to three databases: Infotrac, Ebrary, and Google Scholar, and the guide explains how to access all of them. Also included are the Florida Electronic Library and the Internet Public Library. The criminal justice guide contains the U.S. Supreme Court online, Florida State Courts, and the Legal Times blog, among others. It is imperative that students become comfortable finding information electronically. It isn't their fault that they are still asking for books—they are just discovering the world of the library and all it has to offer, and they are learning that there is more to the Internet than Google and Wikipedia. I am their information Sherpa.

I distribute the LibGuides to the instructors and invite them to comment and make additional suggestions. The instructors then distribute the guides to their students. This makes the guides a collaboration between the librarian and the instructor, and encourages faculty buy-in.

LIBRARY NEWSLETTER

The library newsletter comes out every month and is my way to communicate with the students. The newsletter reports on new books in the library with short summaries and background history about the authors, news about upcoming events, and library trivia. One newsletter included a guide to the Dewey Decimal System, along with an article about Melvil Dewey and his thriftiness with letters. The newsletter is e-mailed to the faculty, but because the students do not have school e-mail addresses, fifty copies are printed and placed in the student lounge and the library. I requested and received a color printer to add to the attraction of the newsletters.

LIBRARIAN WEBSITE

Students are unaware of electronic sources of information (besides Google), so in addition to the LibGuides, I built a simple website using a free website-building template. The website mimics a lot of what is in the LibGuides, but I included pages on plagiarism, using online citation builders and the limited utility of Wikipedia. Each page has links to outside websites or, in the case of the page on Wikipedia, a link to YouTube and two minutes of a "30 Rock" episode in which the writers edit a Wikipedia entry with wrong information to play a joke on the narcissistic actress. The website is not sanctioned by the corporation, so the name of the school does not appear on it.

BOOK CLUB

In an effort to encourage reading, I started the First Thursday Breakfast Book Club. The group meets before classes on the first Thursday of each month, and I bring doughnuts (food!). The first selection was *Fahrenheit 451.* I chose it because it is in our library, it is relatively short, science fiction is usually gender-neutral, and it is about book burning and censorship. Ray Bradbury, in his genius, predicted reality TV shows, large-screen TVs, and ATMs in this 1953 book. Several students were enthusiastic and read the book. I assured them ahead of time that the discussion would be very informal, not at all like an English class. And we could talk about the irony of firemen starting fires and about book censorship. Still, only two students attended the first meeting. As our second meeting approaches, I am confident that attendance will increase.

OTHER LIBRARY INITIATIVES

Almost every month of the year comes equipped with a celebration. For Black History Month I distributed a black history quiz from the Florida Electronic Library website. Students were told that all the answers are available on the Internet. This intrigued them. I suggested they type key words from the questions onto Google—like "Medgar Evers" or "13th Amendment," and they would find the answers to the questions. At the end of the month, the correctly answered quizzes were put into a brightly decorated box and the winner received a prize. This was followed by a Women's History Month quiz, and a contest to identify faculty members from their childhood photos. Since the campus is small and all faculty photos are posted in the hallway, images can easily be compared. As long as the campus president continues to approve the purchase of inexpensive prizes, these quizzes will gain momentum and become a regular part of the library's programs.

JOIN THE REGIONAL LIBRARY CONSORTIUM

During my first week in the library I began going through the disorganized files, and I noticed that in the past, the library had been a member of the regional library consortium. In 2007, for some reason the membership was not renewed. I made the case to the director of education and campus president, explaining the benefits of membership, the fact that the consortium has over two hundred member libraries and library systems, and that other proprietary career colleges were among them. This request was enthusiastically approved, and the college is reaping the benefits of training opportunities and greater access to information.

CONCLUSION

Career college students take their education seriously and make full use of services if they are easily accessible. While some students never come to the library, others use it every day. The library has become a comfortable place for students to study alone or in small groups, and they ask for help confident that they will not be judged or ridiculed. They finally feel respected, and they reciprocate. Best of all, these students from tough neighborhoods who have seen the worst life has to offer are no longer afraid to enter the library.

We cannot predict what our first job will be. In library school I wrote my final paper for Library Management on solo librarians in special libraries, never dreaming that this would be my fate. Although I sometimes miss the company of other librarians—who else would appreciate an article in a medical journal about Jane Austen's symptoms and differential diagnoses (it may not have been Addison's) or about the fact that the Poe graveside visitor has not returned for the last three years, or about the latest news in the war between e-book publishers and libraries. And I may stand out as the only person in the building wearing striped socks. But the librarian is now an integral member of the community. I love my work, and in the spirit and memory of my high school librarian, who listened without judgment when I couldn't talk to my own parents, I am in turn helping people who need someone to make a difference in their lives.

Chapter Thirteen

Serving Diverse Populations

Outreach to Chinese and African American Users

Kelly Rhodes McBride and Xiaorong Shao

Chinese and African American students enter higher education in the United States with a variety of experiences, a range of expectations, levels of information-gathering skills, and degrees of comfort with writing in English (Ardis 2002). Such potential disadvantages underline the need for supportive services to help those students better cope with the education experience.

THE AFRICAN AMERICAN STUDENT EXPERIENCE

African American students attending predominantly white institutions face challenges particularly in the areas of social and academic integration and institutional environment. These factors can have an impact on their overall academic success (Strayhorn and Terrell 2010).

African American students can find the transition to college difficult. Colleges and universities routinely recruit for diverse populations by offering potential students visits to campus to gain insight into the college experience of their institution. These brief experiences do not always accurately reflect the campus climate they will experience as a full-time student; as a result they may struggle to adjust socially and academically and may experience difficulty finding a community.

THE CHINESE STUDENT EXPERIENCE

Universities and colleges in the United States have seen a steady growth in the number of diverse and international students and scholars during recent years, especially students from China. According to the Open Doors report in 2011, Chinese student enrollment in the United States rose to a total of nearly 158,000 students, or nearly 22 percent of the total international student population, making China the leading country of origin for the second year in a row (Institute of International Education 2011).

Unlike African American students, Chinese students encounter more difficulties studying in an American university due to the differences between the U.S. and Chinese educational systems. In addition, the students may experience cultural and language barriers. In China, teaching is more lecture based and textbook centered and heavily directed by teachers. Communication tends to be more one-way. Chinese college students seldom engage in discussion or cooperative learning activities. Learning consists of memorization of factual information from lectures and textbooks and is driven by exams. The American educational system generally requires students to be self-reliant and independent in their quest for knowledge, thus making it difficult for students from China to adapt to the educational process in the United States (Johnson, Shi, and Shao 2010, 188).

According to Wang (2006), contemporary Chinese students are not only different from students from other countries, but also different from Chinese students in the 1980s and 1990s. Their education today has changed in the level of education sought, areas of studies majored in, degree of English language preparation, and exposure to Western culture prior to arriving in an English-speaking country. Liu and Winn (2009) noted that the difficulties facing Chinese students are mostly attributed to personality traits and language as well as cultural barriers. Chinese students are more modest and quieter than their American counterparts. They tend to solve problems by themselves rather than asking for help. Cultural differences are still barriers to Chinese students, and those differences have prevented them from taking full advantage of library resources and services, whether they are aware of them or not. In addition, Chinese students have different experiences with libraries in China. For example, some libraries in China still use card catalogs. In other Chinese libraries, students may have to pay to use computers, or they have limited access to databases and e-resources. In addition, the physical environment of Chinese libraries is often overcrowded and thus less conducive to learning.

THE ROLE OF DIVERSE LIBRARIANS

A review of the library literature reveals numerous articles addressing how academic libraries provide services to diverse populations. Examples include the establishment of professional positions, such as multicultural or diversity librarians, specialized programs for particular ethnic populations, and the creation and maintenance of collections and services specifically geared to diverse patrons. The consensus found in the literature is that diverse librarians have advantages when assisting diverse populations of similar backgrounds.

Keith Lance (2005) noted that if libraries are to be welcoming institutions to all regardless of race and ethnicity, librarians and other library workers should be more diverse. Adkins and Espinal (2004) indicated that when people do not see themselves represented in libraries, they may not approach the librarians. They may not even approach the libraries. In the best situations, students benefit from being able to "see themselves" reflected throughout the campus.

According to Adkins and Espinal (2004), diverse librarians have more advantages to offer better services to those who have similar backgrounds, as their services can reflect a deeper cultural, linguistic, and racial understanding. It is time for libraries to address the information needs of growing diverse populations on campus and help this group integrate into the academic community.

How are libraries and librarians providing service to diverse populations? The following outlines the experiences of two diverse academic librarians in addressing the information needs of Chinese and African American students on the campus of Appalachian State University.

APPALACHIAN STATE UNIVERSITY LIBRARY

Appalachian State University, one of sixteen universities in the University of North Carolina system, is located in the Blue Ridge Mountains of western North Carolina and offers degree programs at the baccalaureate, master's, specialists, and doctoral levels (Appalachian State University 2012). Appalachian's fall 2011 enrollment data indicates a total student enrollment of 17,344 and a total minority enrollment of 1,750 (Appalachian State University Institutional Research, Assessment, and Planning 2011–2012).

Like many public institutions, Appalachian demonstrates its commitment to diversity education and outreach through the establishment of educational programming, community outreach, faculty fellowships, and scholarship programs (Appalachian State University 2012). However, retention of minority students at the same rate as white students is often a challenge for predominantly white institutions like Appalachian. According to Love (2009), recent studies have shown that libraries can positively impact minority student retention because they play a key role in shaping students' academic success and achievement.

The Appalachian State University Library holds a long-standing commitment to diversity and international education, and to assisting the university in developing globally aware and competent students. The library's dedication to diversity and internationalization efforts has been solidified in *The Appalachian State University Library 2008–2013 Strategic Plan*. The plan includes the objective to "provide students, faculty, and staff with opportunities to learn other cultures, peoples, and systems." This commitment is demonstrated in the development of the collections, creation of services to diverse and international students and faculty, and in the ubiquitous access to the library's electronic resources.

The following are examples of the library's internalization and diversification efforts:

- The library's collections reflect the international interests of faculty and students. Over 4 percent of books acquired since 2000 are in languages other than English or have been translated from other languages. Over two thousand electronic serials contain the words "international" or "global" in the title, while more than eight hundred serials include one of these words in the title: African, Asian, Australian, Brazilian, Chinese, European, Japanese, Russian, or Scandinavian. Electronic resources, such as indexes and news databases, cover an international range of journals and subjects.
- The library's Diversity Committee, since its inception in 1998, has worked hard to promote diversity awareness to faculty and staff in the library through various activities. The committee has been a major player in organizing library orientations for new international students and faculty, and in creating the library information display during the University Diversity Education Week held on campus each spring. The committee is identifying campus programs that serve underrepresented, low-income and first-generation students, and is working with these programs to provide library outreach and services.
- In the summer of 2007, three librarians created an international program series called Doorways International Program Series. The library sponsors a series of programs on international issues and offers five to six programs per year. The goal of the program is to provide a platform for people to share their research and knowledge on international issues and to build productive relationships based in their interest in international affairs. An additional goal is to help the library build its collection of international and diversity materials.

EXPERIENCES OF DIVERSE LIBRARIANS AT APPALACHIAN STATE UNIVERSITY LIBRARY

Xiaorong Shao

I have studied in one university in England and two universities in the United States. As an international student from China I can relate to and have experienced some of the difficulties and challenges Chinese students have encountered in the American educational system. These experiences in different educational systems have put me in a better position to understand and help those students, especially during transitions of their academic career to the United States. I came to Appalachian in 2006 as a faculty fellow for diversity and international education. Serving international and diverse users has become one of my passions as well as research interests since I started my career as a librarian.

I serve on the university's international student enrollment and management committee and the library diversity committee. I have been also involved in many diversity and international education initiatives and outreach programs at the campus, at national and international levels. All of these engagements have provided me with the resources and support from administration and colleagues needed for my services to diverse and international library users.

Kelly Rhodes McBride

I have attended three predominantly white institutions and one historically black institution of higher learning in the United States. As a minority student I have experienced many of the same issues and challenges that African American students face in finding a place, developing a sense of comfort, and connecting with others on campus.

I came to Appalachian in 1997 as a minority librarian and was hired to assist the library in meeting the goal of increasing diversity among the library faculty. As the minority librarian my job responsibilities included working to provide outreach to the African American campus. Through my work as a librarian I had interaction with both faculty and staff but chose to focus my attention on working primarily with African American students. I have served as president of the Black Faculty and Staff Association, participated in formal and informal mentoring programs, worked as a faculty adviser to diverse student and campus organizations, and served as chair of the university's diversity scholarship committee.

Because I am a visible face in the library, African American students feel very comfortable approaching me and often stop by my office for research assistance or just to chat. All of these interactions allow me to connect with students, and through these connections I am able to provide outreach and educate students about the library's programs and services.

EFFORTS THAT TARGET CHINESE AND AFRICAN AMERICAN STUDENTS

A number of strategies have been undertaken to introduce library services to Chinese and African American students.

1. *Make an effort to be visible and available.* Pursuing a degree in higher education is a major investment and an important decision for students and their parents. Students often face a period of transition in which they must learn to navigate a new set of academic expectations as well as adapt to a new campus culture. If you have made a concerted effort to be available to diverse students and have demonstrated that you are willing to listen and offer assistance and advice, students will often seek you out. In our experiences these interactions often begins in the context of the library, but it is not uncommon for interactions to blend into other areas as well. We have both found ourselves assisting students in finding housing, providing meals during holidays, and just being available when students need to talk.

2. *Provide assistance with planning and goal setting.* As experienced public service librarians we both understand the role that planning and goal setting plays in college. The Chinese educational system and parenting styles tend to foster more dependence in adolescents. Those students are used to doing what their teachers and parents tell them to do. All of a sudden, they encounter a system where they have to make decisions and live independently. They can become overwhelmed, to say the least. A librarian can help them make plans and set goals about what they want to accomplish so that they can have some direction to follow.

3. *Acknowledge differences.* It is important for both students and librarians to acknowledge that Chinese and African American students are different from other students, including international students from other countries. They differ in their academic preparation, experiences with group projects, class discussions, and in their library research and writing skills. Students and librarians can work together to bridge the gaps to help these students adapt to a university system. We find it is

important to discuss these differences with the students and talk about how and what they may have to do to overcome challenges during their transition.

4. *Promote and encourage library services.* It is important to assure that students are both aware of library services and programs and encouraged to make use of the services. As public service librarians we provide library classroom instruction, work public service desks, and participate in research consultations. Students should know these services are available to help them. We want students to overcome their reluctance to ask for help and not to fear that doing so is admitting to a deficiency. Toward that goal we provide outreach and promotion of library services to assure these students that it is normal for them to encounter situations in which the assistance of a librarian is necessary. Chinese students are of special concern because they may not be aware of reference services and library instruction programs in academic libraries in the United States, since their libraries in China usually did not have prominent reference desks, nor did they provide library user education programs.

5. *Focus on the research process.* When students from these populations acquire some idea of how the U.S. higher education system works and what to do to succeed in this environment, it becomes easier to introduce them to the library services and resources. For Chinese students, I have tried to help them with their assignments, especially their first essay assignments. For example, during the first week of fall semester 2011, two graduate students from China needed help with their library research and with writing up a five-page essay. I assisted them with searching for materials, putting together their ideas, and citing references. I was also there to help edit the draft.

6. *Language choice.* Language is still a barrier for Chinese students. On occasions, I adjust my pace of speaking to improve the students' comprehension. In other cases, based on their preference and comfort level with English, I speak English, Chinese, or both. As we get more new Chinese students (five to eight each semester), we are able to offer a combination library tour and introduction to library resources to these students in Chinese. In the future, we have plans to translate key information about library resources and services into a bilingual format to improve the understanding of these students.

7. *Network across campus.* Identifying faculty, staff, and students across campus who can assist diverse students is an important step in sustaining the effort. As our university continues to pursue diversity there will be an increased need for more resources. Knowing what university offices, support services, activities, and programs on campus will

benefit these students and being able to connect them with these critical resources around the campus is important, since libraries and librarians simply cannot do all the work by themselves.

8. *Maintain balance with other job responsibilities.* Our work and commitment to diverse students must be balanced with other job duties. We are not exclusively diversity librarians and it can be difficult to find both the time and motivation to meet all of our work demands. As faculty librarians we have responsibilities in the areas of teaching, scholarship, and service. It is often the case that we feel that work with diverse students is in addition to our other duties. How do we manage this? We are fortunate that our work with diverse students is known and supported by the library administration. Ultimately, however, we do have a responsibility to make sure that we maintain a good balance in all of our work and commitments.

9. *Collections.* Library collections need to reflect and support the institution's commitment to diversity. Libraries can achieve this by purchasing materials that assist minority and international students in learning languages and cultures and by providing ethnic leisure reading materials that enhance the comprehensive nature of the collection for all users. We work to ensure that the collections address the needs of Chinese and African American students, staff, and faculty.

CONCLUSION

Providing services to diverse populations should not be the sole responsibility of diversity librarians, but rather it should be a broader commitment taken by all librarians to provide the best quality service to all of members of the campus community. Gulati (2010, 289) states that the strength of libraries has always been the diversity of their collections and their commitment to serving all people. As librarians endeavor to meet the challenges of providing services to increasingly diverse users, it is important that we recognize the needs of each and every patron and make them all feel welcomed and included.

Serving international and diverse patrons requires dedication, commitment, and passion, and it is not always an easy task. However, it can be extremely rewarding to see these students make a successful transition to the academic campus culture.

WORKS CITED

Adkins, Dennis, and Isabel Espinal. 2004. "The Diversity Mandate." *Library Journal* 129(7): 52–54.

Appalachian State University. 2012. "About Appalachian." http://www.appstate.edu/about/ (accessed December 15, 2011).

Appalachian State University. Institutional Research, Assessment, and Planning. 2011–2012. *Fact Book.* http://irap.appstate.edu/fact-book/2011-2012-fact-book (accessed January 23, 2012).

Ardis, Susan. 2002. "An Idea from the Field—21st Century Service to all Users. *IATUL Proceedings*, 12. http://veweb.hwwilsonweb.com/hww/results/results_single_fulltext.jhtml (accessed January 26, 2012).

Gulati, Anjali. 2010. "Diversity in Librarianship: The United States Perspectives." *IFLA* 36 (June): 288–93. doi: 10.1177/0340032510388244 (accessed January 19, 2012.)

Institute of International Education (IIE). 2011. "International Student Enrollment Increased by 5 Percent in 2010/11, Led by Strong Increase in Students from China." *Open Doors Report 2011.* http://www.iie.org/en/Who-We-Are/News-and-Events/Press-Center/Press-Releases/2011/2011-11-14-Open-Doors-International-Students (accessed January 4, 2012).

Johnson, Megan, Weihua Shi, and Xiaorong Shao. 2010. "Exploring Library Service Models at Fudan University and Appalachian State University: Experiences from an International Librarian Exchange Program." *International Information and Library Review* 42(3): 186–94.

Lance, Keith Curry. 2005. "Racial and Ethnic Diversity of U.S. Library Workers." *American Libraries* 36(5): 41–43.

Liu, Guoying, and Danielle Winn. 2009. "Chinese Graduate Students and the Canadian Academic Library: A User Study at the University of Windsor." *Journal of Academic Librarianship* 35(6): 565–73.

Love, Emily. 2009. "A Simple Step: Integrating Library Reference and Instruction into Previously Established Academic Programs for Minority Students." *The Reference Librarian* 50, 4–13.

Strayhorn, Terrell L., and Melvin C. Terrell, eds. 2010. *The Evolving Challenges of Black College Students: New Insights for Practice and Research.* Sterling, VA: Stylus.

U.S. Census Bureau. "Overview of Race and Hispanic Origin: 2010." http://www.census.gov/prod/cen2010/briefs/c2010br-02.pdf (accessed January 22, 2012).

Wang, Belle Xinfeng. 2006. "Academic Library Services to Chinese International Students in New Zealand." Master's thesis, Victoria University of Wellington, New Zealand.

Part III

Community Connections

Chapter Fourteen

The Community Speaks for Itself

Indigenous Speakers in the Labriola
National American Indian Data Center

Joyce Martin

The Labriola National American Indian Data Center is one of seven special collections within the Department of Archives and Special Collections at Arizona State University (ASU) and is one of the only repositories within a public university library devoted to American Indian collections. Students and faculty researching American Indian issues across many disciplines at ASU frequently use the Labriola Center's unique primary and secondary resources. However, the Labriola Center always seeks an even wider base of patrons.

The Labriola Center has strong partnerships with American Indian organizations both on campus and in the community. With the help of these key partners, the Labriola Center reaches out to the American Indian community at ASU and in the greater Phoenix metropolitan area by hosting regularly scheduled outreach events in the Labriola Center, including an Indigenous speaker series, poetry reading, and national book award presentation. The Labriola Center's outreach efforts have brought in noted American Indian authors, academics, artists, and lawyers to speak in the library.

The Labriola National American Indian Data Center, dedicated on April 1, 1993, is endowed by Frank and Mary Labriola. In 1973 the Labriolas opened an aluminum company called Pimalco, or Pima Aluminum Company, located on the Gila River reservation. Frank and Mary had such a positive experience working with the Gila River Indian Community and with members of various tribes that they founded the Labriola National American Indian Data Center as an "expression of our friendship and respect" for the individuals they had come to know over the years. As Frank and Mary said on the dedication plaque, "It is our wish that the Labriola Center be a source of education and pride for all Native Americans" (Labriola 1993).

In addition to having a top-notch research collection focused on American Indian issues, the Labriola Center also strives to be a place for interactive shared learning. To borrow the words of Devon Abbott Mihesuah and Angela Cavender Wilson in *Indigenizing the Academy*, the Labriola Center aspires to be "a space where Indigenous values and knowledge are respected" (Mihesuah and Wilson 2004, 2). The Labriola Center works to accomplish this goal and to fulfill the mission set out by Frank and Mary Labriola by hosting regularly scheduled outreach events throughout the year featuring Indigenous speakers from various professions and areas of expertise. All of the events in the Labriola Center are free and open to the public, and the Labriola Center is an inviting space that promotes interaction between guests and speakers.

While the Labriola National American Indian Data Center is one of seven repositories within the Department of Archives and Special Collections at ASU Libraries, the Labriola Center has its own unique reading room on the second floor of Hayden Library, the social sciences library at Arizona State University. The Labriola Center reading room is a beautiful, intimate space that, when set up classroom style, holds around forty-five to fifty guests. In comparison with events held in lecture halls or auditorium-type rooms, the Labriola Center reading room space holds a small enough crowd to encourage a real exchange of ideas between speaker and audience.

Adjacent to the Labriola Center reading room is a smaller room that is typically set up as a mediated classroom for the curator of the Labriola Center to provide bibliographic instruction for students in American Indian Studies classes as well as the many other disciplines at ASU that examine Indigenous knowledge as part of their classes. During outreach events, the Labriola Center staff converts the classroom into an area for refreshments, providing an additional space for people to mingle and talk. The physical spaces, both the size and the layout, contribute to the creation of an environment conducive for speakers and audience to come together and share ideas and speak about their professions, experiences, research, and writing.

The Labriola Center participates in three types of regularly scheduled outreach events, which bring in speakers from the Indigenous community to engage the Labriola National American Indian Data Center patrons in discussion and intellectual exchange. The first is an annual poetry or short story reading held in conjunction with the American Indian Studies Association (AISA) Conference at ASU hosted by the American Indian Studies Department. In this outreach effort, the speakers are Indigenous authors of note from the ASU campus. The second outreach event is the Simon Ortiz and Labriola Center Lecture on Indigenous Land, Culture, and Community. And

the third outreach event is an interview with a member of the judging committee of the Labriola Center American Indian National Book Award and the
book award–winning author.

POETRY READING—PARTNERING WITH AN
ACADEMIC DEPARTMENT

Each February the Labriola Center curator organizes a poetry reading and
reception held in the Labriola Center in conjunction with the annual AISA
Conference on the Arizona State University Campus. The ASU American
Indian Studies Department sponsors the AISA Conference and has invited
the Labriola Center to host a reception and poetry or short story reading since
2006.

Holding the poetry reading in the Labriola Center is a great way to bring
in new patrons, as American Indian Studies faculty and graduate students
from across the country attend this conference at ASU, and the reception and
poetry reading brings them into the library. While the conference is typically
held in the Memorial Union (the campus student union), the reception and
poetry reading is held in Hayden Library in the Labriola Center. Conference
participants who attend the poetry reading often become future customers of
the Labriola Center, taking time to explore the library's resources following
conference sessions.

Faculty and graduate students in the ASU Department of English and/or
the American Indian Studies Department, as they read to a packed house in
the Labriola Center reading room, create an emotionally charged as well as
intellectually thought-provoking outreach event. The ASU American Indian
Studies Department does a great job advertising the AISA Conference both
to American Indian Studies scholars around the world and to interested community members. The link between this national conference, the ASU
American Indian Studies Department, and the Labriola Center benefits the
Center by expanding our audience beyond Arizona State University to
American Indian Studies scholars and community members in Arizona and
beyond.

SPEAKER SERIES—PARTNERING WITH BOTH ACADEMIC
DEPARTMENTS AND COMMUNITY PARTNERS

In 2008, the Labriola Center partnered with the American Indian Studies
Department, the Department of English, the American Indian Policy Institute, the Faculty of History in the School of Historical, Philosophical, and

Religious Studies, the Indian Legal Program in the Sandra Day O'Connor College of Law, Women and Gender Studies in the School of Social Transformation, and the Heard Museum to cosponsor the Simon Ortiz and Labriola Center Lecture on Indigenous Land, Culture, and Community. This lecture at Arizona State University "addresses topics and issues across disciplines in the arts, humanities, sciences, and politics. Underscoring Indigenous American experiences and perspectives, this series seeks to create and celebrate knowledge that evolves from an inclusive Indigenous worldview and that is applicable to all walks of life" (Arizona State University 2008).

The Simon Ortiz and Labriola Center Lecture on Indigenous Land, Culture, and Community is held twice a year in March and in October. This lecture series invites prominent Indigenous intellectuals working in a variety of fields to speak both at Arizona State University and at the Heard Museum. The Heard Museum is a world-renowned museum of American Indian art and culture located in the heart of Phoenix, Arizona. The connections the Heard Museum has to the American Indian tribes in Arizona help the Labriola Center reach a broader range of patrons.

The Heard Museum has connections with American Indian media outlets, which promote their events. The Heard also has a strong volunteer and donor program, and their members help spread the word about upcoming outreach events to an interested audience. The Heard Museum hosts the formal Speaker Series lecture in their auditorium, and the Labriola Center hosts a more intimate gathering with the speaker earlier in the day.

In fact, each speaker who is invited to give the Simon Ortiz and Labriola Center Lecture on Indigenous Land, Culture, and Community is in for a full day of activities. The visit of Arlinda Locklear will serve to illustrate: On October 6, 2011, invited speaker attorney Arlinda Locklear (Lumbee) came to the Phoenix metropolitan area to speak about the history of the Oneida land claims case. In the morning Locklear spoke in the Labriola National American Indian Data Center about her career as an attorney. In the afternoon she spoke in the ASU Sandra Day O'Connor College of Law building, addressing specific questions about federal Indian law from an audience composed mostly of law students, American Indian Studies students, and ASU faculty and staff. The formal lecture took place that evening at the Heard Museum, where Locklear spoke about how attorneys for tribes have used the doctrine of discovery or federal common law to assert claims in tribal land claims cases. Locklear laid out the history of the Oneida land claims case against the state of New York, beginning in 1784 when the state began an aggressive campaign to acquire Oneida territory to the present (Locklear 2011). The audience at the Heard Museum lecture is usually quite large and varied, including students and faculty from ASU as well as both

Native and non-Native community members. An outreach event such as this one is a great way for interested people living in the Phoenix area to learn about the Labriola Center and become future patrons.

Another way the Simon Ortiz and Labriola Center Lecture on Indigenous Land, Culture, and Community helps increase the number of Labriola Center patrons is through the strong web presence for the speaker series. The ASU English Department hosts a web page advertising the lecture series. ASU Libraries records the Simon Ortiz and Labriola Center Lecture on Indigenous Land, Culture, and Community at the Heard Museum and places the streaming video of all past lectures on the ASU Library Channel website and on YouTube. A DVD of the lecture is also created and placed in the Labriola National American Indian Data Center collection, as well as in the Hayden Library.

Since the start of the lecture series in 2008, the Labriola Center has hosted such amazing intellectuals as Professor Leroy Little Bear (Blackfoot) and Wilma Mankiller (Cherokee), just to name two. In 2011, Professor Little Bear, head of the SEED Graduate Institute, former director of the American Indian Program at Harvard University, and Professor Emeritus of Native Studies at the University of Lethbridge, spoke about the potential for collaboration between what he called "Native science" and "Western science." Professor Little Bear discussed the tenets of Indigenous thought and compared them to the Western paradigm. Professor Little Bear spoke about how Indigenous language explains nature without depending on the language of math. He spoke about how the collaboration of Indigenous thought and string theory could potentially complete the Grand Unified Theory of physics (Little Bear 2011). The Labriola Center also hosted former principal chief of the Cherokee Nation and internationally known Native rights activist Wilma Mankiller in October 2008. Mankiller's talk was titled "Challenges Facing Twenty-First-Century Indigenous People," and she spoke of the wide diversity among Indigenous people today and about their sense of responsibility to protect the natural world (Mankiller 2008).

Hosting a variety of Indigenous speakers through the Labriola Center's involvement in the Simon Ortiz and Labriola Center Lecture on Indigenous Land, Culture, and Community has helped increase awareness of the Labriola Center's resources among community members.

BOOK AWARD—PARTNERING WITH INDIVIDUALS

Another way to bring in speakers from your community is to sponsor a book award for authors from your target community. Four years ago an ASU professor in the School of Historical, Philosophical, and Religious Studies,

Native American history scholar Dr. Donald Fixico, approached the curator of the Labriola Center with the idea of creating a book award that would recognize authors writing about contemporary American Indian issues. The Labriola National American Indian Data Center happily agreed to work with Dr. Fixico to organize and sponsor such a book award.

The resulting Labriola Center American Indian National Book Award encourages scholarship that crosses multiple disciplines or fields of study, is relevant to contemporary North American Indian communities, and focuses on modern tribal studies, modern biographies, tribal governments, or federal Indian policy. The Labriola Center solicits nominations from about a dozen publishers who are especially strong in American Indian Studies. The judging panel is comprised of Dr. Donald Fixico and Dr. Katherine Osburn from the School of Historical, Philosophical and Religious Studies and Dr. David Martinez from American Indian Studies.

The winner of the book award is invited to the Labriola Center for an award presentation and to speak about his or her book. A member of the judging committee conducts an informal interview with the award winner. The book award ceremony attracts students and faculty from ASU, as well as community members. The award ceremony is widely advertised on ASU public event calendars and in ASU media. In fact, the *ASU News* has written two feature articles on the Labriola Center American Indian National Book Award.

ASU News author Judith Smith wrote about both the 2010 winner, Dr. Malinda Lowery, assistant professor of history at the University of North Carolina at Chapel Hill, and her book *Lumbee Indians in the Jim Crow South: Race, Identity, and the Making of a Nation* and the 2011 winner, Dr. Cathleen Cahill, assistant professor of history at the University of New Mexico, and her book *Federal Fathers and Mothers: A Social History of the United States Indian Service, 1869–1933*.

Additional past winners of the Labriola Center American Indian National Book Award include the inaugural winner, Dr. Daniel Cobb, for his book *Native Activism in Cold War America: The Struggle for Sovereignty* and Dr. Paul Rosier, associate professor of history at Villanova, for *Serving Their Country: American Indian Politics and Patriotism in the Twentieth Century*.

Publishing companies for the winning books have been quick to promote their books as having won the Labriola Center American Indian National Book Award on their websites and in their print catalogs. Having the Labriola Center mentioned on publishers' websites and in their print catalogs has been a great way to raise awareness for our repository.

CONCLUSION—HOW TO MAKE THESE OUTREACH TECHNIQUES WORK FOR YOUR LIBRARY

While it may seem like hosting a poetry reading, starting a speaker series, or creating a book award might be an expensive or difficult undertaking, this is not necessarily the case. It is possible for all libraries and special collections to get involved in similar events on a scale that fits your library. The Labriola Center, while located within a large library, only has one full-time staff member. The rest of the staff consists of very hard working and dedicated interns, volunteers, and student workers. So you really do not need a large staff to successfully pull off outreach events of this type.

What you really do need are good partners. Those partners could be academic departments if you are a special collection or library in a university system, or they could be a local historical society or museum if you are a public library. Finding a partner to cosponsor an outreach event in your local community, such as a local museum or historical society, is a great way to expand your patron base.

Sometimes, as in the example of the Simon Ortiz and Labriola Center Lecture on Indigenous Land, Culture, and Community, your partners are both academic department partners and community partners. Or, as in the case of the Labriola Center American Indian National Book Award, your initial key partner could be one individual.

Money is always a concern in these times of tight budgets; however, the budget for each of the Labriola Center outreach events is manageable, with refreshments often being the largest expense. The expenses can be managed through scaling events to meet the capacity of your library. And keep in mind, the more partners you have when organizing an outreach event, the more affordable the event becomes. For a larger-scale event such as the Simon Ortiz and Labriola Center Lecture on Indigenous Land, Culture, and Community, the Labriola Center has eight partners, widely distributing both the workload and the cost.

Frequently it is necessary to actively seek out partners when planning an outreach event in your library. However, I have also found that collaborations can happen unexpectedly, and it is very important to be open to new ideas when in conversation with your colleagues from the museum, library, and archives fields and beyond. When you are positive and open to talking through an idea, great cooperative projects will often find you.

Do not be deterred by the cautious voice in the back of your head whispering that your resources are already stretched too thin. Talking about a potential collaboration is not the same as agreeing to participate. It is okay to have a conversation or an initial meeting to determine if the proposed project is feasible for your library. Even if the initially proposed project does not come to fruition, you have made a connection that may lead to a successful future event which is just right for your library. Such library outreach events can help your library build bridges to new patrons.

Every library wants to serve the needs of its entire community. It is important that members of the community have a chance to make the library their own by having an opportunity to speak and participate in knowledge creation. The Labriola National American Indian Data Center believes an important step toward reaching patrons is for the library to be a place where the Indigenous community speaks for itself. The Labriola Center hopes to continue to reach new patrons and foster a sense of community by hosting regularly scheduled outreach events featuring Indigenous speakers from a wide variety of professions.

WORKS CITED

Arizona State University. 2008. "The Simon Ortiz and Labriola Center Lecture on Indigenous Land, Culture, and Community." Last modified April 2012. http://english.clas.asu.edu/indigenous/.

Labriola, Frank. 1993. "Dedication Plaque and Reading Room, Labriola National American Indian Data Center." (LAB FILM S21:1–3). Labriola National American Indian Data Center. Department of Archives and Special Collections. University Libraries. Arizona State University, Tempe, Arizona.

Little Bear, Leroy. 2011. "Native Science and Western Science: Possibilities for a Powerful Collaboration." Lecture, Heard Museum, March 24.

Locklear, Arlinda. 2011. "Tribal Land Claims: A Generation of Federal Indian Law on the Edge." Lecture, Heard Museum, October 6.

Mihesuah, Devon A., and Angela Cavender Wilson. 2004. *Indigenizing the Academy: Transforming Scholarship and Empowering Communities*. Lincoln: University of Nebraska Press.

Chapter Fifteen

Connecting with Multicultural Teens (and Their Families by Extension)

Ashley Ansah

One of the most effective manners for encouraging public library usage among immigrant families in our community has been to reach out to area middle school (sixth to eighth grade) English Language Learner (ELL) classrooms. As the teen specialist serving two culturally diverse neighborhoods through the Des Moines Public Library system in Des Moines, Iowa, it is my responsibility to develop programming that is responsive to the needs of students ages twelve to eighteen.

With a background in anthropology and international studies and as a fluent speaker of both English and Spanish, I have also become involved in efforts to create a welcoming environment for multicultural patrons in the library.

When I began working at the library, a majority of our multicultural outreach was in-house only, but it was a necessary first step. We created signage for the collections in prominent community languages; translated the policies brochure into the two most common languages spoken in the neighborhood, Spanish and Vietnamese; and developed relationships with patrons who assisted in the selection of materials purchased for the foreign language collections. Through a partnership with a local community college, an ELL class for adults had been offered at the library for several years prior to our in-house efforts, and yet the library was not attracting a substantial number of new patrons from the immigrant community.

I regularly received questions from our existing immigrant patrons regarding basic library usage, such as "How much do your books cost? Why do you let us take the books home? Why do you want my address?" A particular challenge when serving multicultural patrons is our tendency to judge other cultures through the perspective of our own culture, a phenomenon referred to in the anthropological world as "ethnocentrism."

In order to serve patrons who hail from a background different from your own, you must first be aware that you do this. Have you ever watched as a group of teens (or adults) who are immigrants have a rowdy conversation right in the library entrance? Were you outraged? Did you feel as though the library, or your profession, was being disrespected by the actions of this group? If so, you judged the behavior of this group (or another like it) by the standards of *your* culture: ethnocentrism in action. The challenge is to mentally take a step back and view the situation through a new or different lens. Yes, this is a skill that must be practiced. How can anyone cease behaving as they were taught to behave from a time before they can remember the lesson? First, acknowledge that you do it. I, Ashley Ansah (insert your name), judge others as though they were raised as I was raised. Now you're in good company—I admit that I do this too.

Now that we've confessed, let's begin recovery. Using the example from above, do not take this loud conversation in the entrance of the library personally. Ask yourself, "Have I ever informed this group that the library prefers a certain noise level? Have I approached this group and asked them not to block passage to the library previously?" If you have not done these things prior, do them now. Did the group disrespect you and maintain their rowdy behavior or did they apologize and move on, or redirect their behavior? If the latter is true, you can assume that the members of the group innocently did not understand the environment of a public library in the United States. You provided an excellent learning opportunity for the group by informing them of the proper manner in which to utilize a public library. If the former happens, you are entitled to feel disrespected and should inform your supervisor of the situation. However, in my experience, this is not usually the case.

We often assume, as avid library lovers and users, that others must feel the same about libraries as we do. But often, other cultures do not have access to public libraries, and if they do have access, the policies and regulating rules are certainly different from those of public libraries in the United States. Take the time to explain these differences to others without making assumptions based on your own personal biases. The ability to do so is a work in progress, and reflecting on your patron interactions will be very beneficial as you begin to check your own worldview.

In the case of my library, successful interactions with multicultural patrons really took off when I combined my services to the teen population with efforts to create a welcoming space for adult users from a variety of backgrounds. It was then that I discovered a consistent manner for bringing in new adult users who were born outside of the United States to the public library.

I must give credit where it is due and admit that it was the ELL teacher who appeared in the public library, asking if her classes could take a tour of the building. I was new to this particular neighborhood at the time and was excited by the opportunity to introduce teens to the public library and all of its offerings. We decided a brief discussion of what a library was, how to use the library card, and where to find materials would be the agenda for our tour. In addition, each student was issued a student library card, allowing them to take home five items. I created a small scavenger hunt so that the students could hunt for materials from a variety of library collections, allowing for a discussion on the Dewey Decimal Classification (DDC) system and alphabetizing of author names.

The students completed the scavenger hunt with a partner and received a small treat when they found each item on their list. I informed the classes that the library offered programming for teens, sent them home a flyer for our upcoming programs, and felt quite accomplished. The students were engaged and asked many excellent questions about the library; they were polite and excited to take home books. I was confident that at least some of the students would become fixtures of the library.

It was the influx in adult users from a multitude of cultural backgrounds signing up for library cards over the next several weeks that surprised me. It seemed as though a stream of adults was entering the library for the first time, requesting books for learning English, movies to educate and entertain, and Internet stations. When I noticed a few of the students from the ELL class with the adults, I realized who had brought them in. I asked the teens if they were with their parents. Some said yes they were, while others had come in with family friends or other adult community members who needed their help translating my words.

I realized something after witnessing this change. Multicultural teens are the perfect library marketing tool for reaching members of the community who may not have previous experience with a public library. Why? The teens who had taken a tour of the library with their ELL class asked many questions common among immigrants. Why did the library request photo identification and proof of residence in Des Moines? How much did using the library books and computers cost? Did they need to bring anything to attend the programs? Adults typically have the same questions, but for a variety of reasons, may never ask them. Cultural differences may deter them, or fear or a lack of confidence in speaking English may make the task of initiating dialogue with library staff daunting. Moreover, misconceptions of the public library as a government entity are also a factor to consider for immigrant communities.

Most teens are typically independent enough to walk to the neighborhood library, gaining confidence in their personal usage of materials. It did come to pass that several of the students who toured as an ELL class (now entering our third year of collaboration) began regularly attending the weekly programs at both of the library branches where I host them. The programs provide the teens with a safe and welcoming place to meet other students in the community. As their confidence in their library experience increases, they begin asking more questions, using new services, and voicing concerns when they arise. The teens unknowingly initiate a dialogue about the library with their parents or caregivers each time they ask permission to attend a program or bring home a new book or a craft created during a do-it-yourself class.

A comfort with using the library generates an interest in learning and doing more with the services provided by a public library. So, how can you establish a relationship with teens from a multitude of backgrounds? Below I outline four tips for beginning your experience in working with ELL teens.

Learn about their home country or culture. Make sure that you know the generalities of the culture to avoid missteps in communication, both verbal and nonverbal. If you have questions regarding their culture, try to approach them when you have a reasonable amount of privacy, as they may not feel comfortable discussing the differences between their native culture and American culture while in a group setting.

Never assume that everyday library usage is an innate behavior. While most of us in the library profession grew up using books and libraries, this may not be true of multicultural teens using the library today. Take the time to explain, using clear everyday language, the library's policies. For noisy teens, calmly explain that a library is a quiet place because many people are here to study and work. Try to use verbiage that they may be familiar with—"more time" as opposed to "renewal" or "return" rather than "due date." This simple language will be more easily understood by teens and adults who may not have encountered library lingo prior to their experience in your library.

Take all questions from teens seriously. I know this can be challenging. I know because I have answered some questions from teens that I was not sure I should have answered. When a teen asks "why" to anything you might have told them (one person to a computer, no play fighting in the library, etc.) give him or her an honest answer. Do this for two reasons: they may truly want to know and/or it takes the fun out of trying to flip an answer at the librarian.

The library makes policies for a reason, and teens (whether or not they appear disrespectful or mocking of our rules) deserve to know the why behind the what. For example, I approach a group of multicultural teens who are playfully hitting or kicking their friends. I say to the group in a calm and level voice, "How are you guys doing today? Did you have a good day at school?" Then I wait for their answer(s) before continuing. "I wanted to let you all know that here at the library we do not allow physical hitting or kicking, even if it is playful." I only continue this dialogue when all the students have stopped to look at me; this way I am sure they have heard my message. Generally, you will get one of two responses: "Okay, we won't do it again" (mission accomplished) or "Why? She's my friend, she doesn't care." And here's your opening! There is a reason that the library enforces this policy—calmly explain to your teens that "the library does not allow playful fighting because it is unclear to the staff and others using the library what is fun and what is dangerous. It makes people uncomfortable, and my job at the library is to make sure everyone has a comfortable space to do their work. If you, playfully or not, hit or kick again, I will ask you to leave the library for the day. You are welcome to come back tomorrow and try again." This last part, the invitation to return, is crucial. This clarifies for the teens that it is the behavior, and not the person, that is unwelcome in the library. Using a calm tone of voice and making eye contact with the teens during this conversation will diffuse the "fun" that comes from seeing an adult librarian get flustered by teens presumably sassing back.

Learn as many names as you can. It is much more effective to say to a teen patron, "Luka, you may not sit next to José on the computer" or "Shaw, how was school today?" The teens feel as though someone cares for them on a personal level and respects them as an individual, rather than lumps them into a category (teen, Latino, African, etc.). For those who have naughtier tendencies, your knowing their name takes the anonymity out of the action. It is difficult to correct misbehaviors when you do not know who is responsible. The ability to identify the teens using your library will empower you to more accurately moderate behavior. For instance, you witness three girls in your library who are speaking and laughing loudly; other patrons are glancing between the girls and the reference desk, so you know this behavior is disruptive to others. Address the girls by name if possible, "Cubaniqua, Llanet, and Mamie—I know you are all enjoying your time here, but when I can hear you from across the library, others can hear you as well, and many people here are working on important things. If I have to speak to you again about the noise you are making, I will ask you to leave for the day. You will be welcome to come back tomorrow, of course." Always clearly explain the consequence for not following policy, as well as the invitation to return when they are capable of adhering to your library's policy. By using the teens' names and clarifying the problem(s) and consequence(s), you have empowered the teens to make a choice about their library usage.

Learning names, particularly if the names are not common among your own personal culture, can be a challenge. Do not be afraid to ask the teens for their names. Admit that you have trouble remembering if that is the case. When I help a teen find a book, or when a new teen joins our programming, the first question I ask is for his or her name. If I predict the name will be a challenging one for me to remember, I often say to the teen, "I may have to ask you to remind me of your name later, but I'm Miss Ashley and if you have any questions, please ask me." This way, if I do forget a name, the teen was given notice and my asking him or her to repeat it will not be a surprise. During programming, perhaps you could have the teens wear name tags or make name plates to get you started. When I began our teen book club, each student displayed a personalized name plate for the group to see. This helped all of us learn names, and because the program was centered around our conversations about the book, I wanted each student to feel as though he or she could easily address the others in the group.

By remembering the four tips outlined above, you will be able to bridge the gaps in culture, age, and experience between multicultural teens and the library in which you work. Of course, these tips are guidelines and you will need to customize them to fit your particular situation. The best teachers for interacting with multicultural teens will be the students themselves. Begin with the steps I have discussed, and be sure to give yourself the opportunity to reflect on your interactions with multicultural teens. Their reactions, both verbal and nonverbal, will provide you with the necessary feedback for re-structuring your approaches to reaching this demographic. Do not forget to reflect on your own cultural experiences when observing your teen base.

The benefits of reaching multicultural teens in the library are many. Aside from the aforementioned influx of adult immigrant patrons applying for li-brary cards to begin their personal journeys through the library's resources, another positive outcome has stemmed from my collaboration with the mid-dle school ELL teacher. I have a new marketing tool for my teen program-ming.

Each year that the ELL teacher brings in her students, I have a brand new group of teens who are eager to take advantage of the library's programming. In addition to our in-house programming, I have also brought the library's message to the schools. There is nothing like the positive feedback of a teacher who was well received by the library to encourage classroom visits. When I am invited into a classroom by a teacher, I am usually rewarded with a classroom of teens who have been prepped for my visit. Because their teacher reached out to the library, I am guaranteed to meet with a profession-al who values the services provided by the library. I mention this aspect of the classroom visit because I have visited several classrooms after having contacted the school and scheduled a visit in a more general sense. While this method has proven successful at times, there is less of a guarantee that the students or teacher are interested in my message. However, when a teacher approaches me to speak to the class, he or she will often take the necessary steps to ensure that I will have a captive and receptive audience.

In the past I sent out e-mail blasts to area teachers informing them of the happenings for teens at the public library. I eagerly waited for the replies and phone calls inquiring about tours and programming opportunities for students. Those replies never came. Teachers are so inundated with students, standards, and testing that e-mail blasts tend to get lost in the mix. However, teachers often talk to one another. One good experience is all they need to hear about to personalize what the library can do for their classroom. In my case, luck brought an attentive and caring ELL teacher right to my library's doorstep. You may need to canvas your neighborhood for the right teacher to initiate a working partnership between English Language Learners and your library. Maybe it isn't an ELL teacher, but a neighborhood organization that serves immigrant teens. You will know the right teacher when you find one. You will see in him or her the willingness to reach out to partners within their community.

The right educator will value what the library offers and transfer that enthusiasm for the library to his or her students. This partner will understand your library's limitations and feel comfortable asking for resources that are needed by the students. And when you find that teacher, hold onto him or her for dear life. That teacher will be a walking advertisement for why multicultural teens and their families depend on public libraries. He or she will bring new faces in to your library, and those new faces will bring in more new faces. By reaching out to multicultural teens, you will be reaching out to entire immigrant communities by extension.

Chapter Sixteen

"¡Soy Culto!"

Connecting with the Hispanic Population

Joyce Nutta and Julie Ventura

The Orange County Library System (OCLS) serves the metropolitan area of Orlando, Florida. Over 1.1 million people call this part of Central Florida home. Of that population, 26.9 percent are of Hispanic origin. OCLS was awarded a congressionally directed grant administered through the Institute of Museum and Library Services in 2010. This grant was used over three years to help better serve the Hispanic community in the metro Orlando area, more specifically at two of the branches that have a Hispanic population of approximately 44 percent.

OCLS identified five specific areas on which to focus:

- material acquisition, including books and media (67% of the budget)
- educating patrons about library resources
- new computer class offerings in Spanish
- identifying barriers to service via focus groups
- a new ESL program in conjunction with the University of Central Florida

This chapter will explore the changes made possible by this project, including measurable results and adjustments made in the process between June 2010 and December 2012. The final segment will cover lessons learned during the course of this grant.

BRIEF BACKGROUND

OCLS received word that funding would be provided and immediately began planning and developing a campaign in the spring and summer of 2010, which included allocation of funds, a patron education campaign, purchasing of books and media, and other facets of the grant. By the fall of 2010, the first in a series of computer class booklets had been ordered, a patron education campaign was mapped out, and discussions were under way with the University of Central Florida to finalize an ESL program.

On January 11, 2011, the South Creek Branch hosted a press conference to announce the grant and the associated projects. Nearly eighty people were in attendance. A large number of Spanish language media outlets attended, along with a local authors' group and the active Spanish book club based at the South Creek Branch. Richard Maledecki, president of the library board of trustees and president of the Central Florida Hotel and Lodging Association, gave the welcome speech. The president of the Hispanic Chamber of Commerce of Metro Orlando, Ramon Ojeda, gave a short speech. OCLS has been a member of the Hispanic Chamber of Commerce of Metro Orlando since 2005.

MATERIAL ACQUISITION

In addition to major purchases of books and media of interest to the Hispanic community, OCLS purchased new databases, software, and other material for Spanish speakers. Among these purchases were Spanish-language Playaways. Playaways are smaller than a deck of cards and contain the audio for an entire book. They are powered by one AAA battery. Just plug in a headset and enjoy the book! In addition, OCLS added over six hundred titles to our digital, downloadable book collection. A Spanish-language lease program was developed to keep materials fresh and current. Freegal Musica Gratis was developed with a vendor and purchased with grant funds. Freegal is a free music database that allows patrons to download up to three songs a week using their library card. The music is then the patron's to keep. Freegal Musica Gratis was the development of a full Spanish language interface for Freegal. Use of the Spanish language interface was surprisingly low, despite our best efforts, and the decision was made at the end of the grant cycle to migrate users to the English interface and discontinue the Spanish one.

The Southeast and South Creek branches of the Orange County Library System were the two branches targeted to receive funding, but all materials are available to all members of the OCLS. Our free, home delivery service, Mail Access to Your Library (MAYL), allows materials to be couriered to patrons' doors to provide easy access to most materials.

Working with local Spanish-language book clubs and authors' groups, OCLS added works by local authors and increased collections based on requests and suggestions by the local groups. Additional media purchases include *Ingles sin Barreras*, a popular English-language learning program on DVD, and *Words for Work*, a software program that helps English language learners in a variety of work-related scenarios. *Career Cruising*, a vocational guidance database that helps students and unemployed or job-seeking adults find information on careers, was also purchased. Also, a user interest page was developed to gather links to many of our resources in Spanish.

EDUCATING PATRONS ABOUT LIBRARY RESOURCES

During the first funding year of the grant, we developed a community/patron awareness campaign designed to connect our Hispanic community with their library. OCLS worked with a local advertising agency to develop a series of strong patron education pieces for the community. Hernan Tagliani, founder and leader of The Group Advertising, assisted OCLS in developing a series of campaigns. The phrase "Soy culto" was used, which loosely translates to "I'm cultured." A logo was developed as well.

We also used some other key phrases:

> *Yo soy Músico.¡Y la biblioteca es mi DJ!* ("I am a musician, and the library is my DJ!")
>
> *Yo soy Bilingüe.¡Y mi biblioteca también!* ("I am bilingual, and my library is, too!")

This branding was used on all materials associated with the grant. OCLS staff members were featured in these pieces, so patrons would connect with them on a personal level.

During the second year of the grant, OCLS developed a texting strategy to inform our Spanish-speaking population about our system and services. This strategy was based directly on the results of our nonuser focus groups, of which more will follow. Using the backs of local buses and other sites, our education campaign was developed to encourage people to sign up for a text service that would inform interested parties about upcoming events. OCLS also included our campaign in the Spanish-language newspapers *Las Prensa* and *El Sentinel* and placed banners and audio on local Spanish radio stations, including KQ103 and Jose98.1. A series of text messages in Spanish was created, offering specific programs and general information. We have not seen great results and will not renew the contract once the current one is finished.

NEW COMPUTER CLASS OFFERINGS IN SPANISH

Funds were set aside to provide translations of additional computer classes into Spanish. By using a simple patron survey, staff at the two branches provided a list of classes that were recommended for translation. This was done over the course of a year. Current class offerings include the Office suite of products, 2007 and 2010 versions, in addition to QuickBooks, Photoshop, and other, home-grown classes. Since the inception of the grant, 871 classes with 4,313 people in attendance have been taught at the two branches. The average attendance is 6 people per class, which is higher than the English-language classes at the two locations. The maximum per class is 8 or 12 people, based upon the size of the lab. We found that a majority of students were interested in improving job skills, so we focused on the Office suite of products. Many attendees used the certificate of completion to prove to employers or prospective employers that they were willing to improve and/or enhance their performance. All locations of OCLS that teach classes in Spanish now use the translated booklets created for these classes.

IDENTIFYING BARRIERS TO SERVICE VIA FOCUS GROUPS

Another aspect of this grant was to identify barriers to service. We looked to the Hispanic community, specifically to those without library cards, to see why they didn't use the library. With the assistance of a local business development consultant, Sami Haiman-Marrero of Urbander, OCLS surveyed 228 individuals living within the service area of the two library branches. Of the 228 surveyed, 13 were invited to attend a focus group to further discuss library use or lack thereof. Five conclusions were reached using the information provided in the focus groups:

1. Spanish preference is prevalent and serves as a conduit for a positive experience. While many Spanish speakers speak English, there is a sense of connection and community when using Spanish.
2. Aside from the Internet, outdoor activities are the library's main competitor in terms of viable entertainment options for Hispanic families. In addition, "free time" is considered "family time." By creating fami-

ly-based programming, rather than "adult" or "children's" activities, we were able to attract larger groups to our events. For example, a Superhero Saturday, promoted as a family event, attracted 159 attendees. A local comic-book store provided costumed characters and information about comic books, as well as face painting and other events. Many of the adults were as eager as the children to meet the characters. A Motorcycle Madness program provided patrons with a chance to see some spectacular motorcycles, talk to the riders, and create leather crafts, including wrist bands, hair ornaments, and other ornaments. This event was enjoyed by 82 people, children and parents.

3. Hispanics are interested in group activities where people can interact with each other and also with experts in different disciplines. An example would be OCLS's Spanish Book Clubs, which provide a regular time for social activities and often host local musicians, as well as experts such as publishers, foreign dignitaries, and doctors. The South Creek Spanish Book Club enjoys an average weekly attendance of more than 25 people.

4. Grassroots marketing and digital platforms are key channels to communicate and engage with the Hispanic community. Word of mouth plays a major role in attracting people to the library. As mentioned above, the connectedness of the Hispanic community suggests that texting should play a major role. At this juncture, however, our text messaging efforts have not provided the return we expected.

5. Primary targets are young Hispanic adults who are forming lifestyle patterns and children who can serve as ambassadors for the library in Hispanic households. Many young families look to the library to provide educational information and entertainment through DVDs, books, and programming. By providing programming and computer classes, we can instill in this group a pattern of using the library to meet their needs.

NEW ESL PROGRAM

As part of the Hispanic community outreach, the Orange County Library System partnered with the University of Central Florida to develop English as a Second Language (ESL) classes. Seeking to avoid duplication of existing adult ESL classes offered at local schools, the program designers determined that there were needs not being met in these sectors nor within current class offerings at the libraries. In particular, many adults who had participated in library English conversation sessions or computer-based ESL programs had developed spoken English skills that were adequate for daily interactions on the job and in the neighborhood, but they lacked the level of English proficiency required for promotion at work, admission to postsecondary study, or handling more delicate situations. For example, the patrons knew how to order a meal at a restaurant, but they didn't know how to write a letter of complaint about bad food or service. They could perform the routine tasks of their jobs, but they couldn't take advantage of job openings that required supervisory communication skills. It was clear that the ESL classes should focus on building participants' knowledge of and competence in using more formal and academic English than the survival-level English they had developed through incidental or self-directed learning or conversation-based classes.

Because the ESL classes were designed and taught by university faculty and graduate students, many academic resources were available to shape the content of the curriculum. The University of Central Florida offers an intensive English program for international students striving to develop the requisite academic English proficiency for university study in the United States. This type of program is structured to build upon previous formal study of English or to launch absolute beginners into expedited development of communicative ability, always with an emphasis on English for academic purposes. As designed, this program would not be suitable for library patrons who had picked up basic communication skills in English from immersion in an English-speaking environment but had not studied English as adults. In addition, the program's narrow emphasis on academic language development for university study was not flexible enough to meet the diverse needs of the adults interested in the library ESL classes. However, many features of this type of program could be beneficial to the library ESL program.

The program designers decided to offer the formal, academic emphasis of a university-based ESL program but to also strategically build upon the existing conversational abilities of the adult immigrant students in order to further participants' diverse English development goals. The program was designed to develop students' communicative competence and linguistic accuracy for a variety of language functions, including professional and academic language use, through focusing on the four skill areas of listening, speaking, reading, and writing. Writing, including attention to grammar, style, and spelling errors commonly made by ESL students, was emphasized. Using reading as a means to expand vocabulary and foster command of grammar patterns was a logical strategy for a library-based course. Listening and speaking skills were developed for specific communication purposes, such as interviewing for a job or bringing a problem to the attention of the teacher of one's child. Differences between formal and informal expressions were highlighted and practiced. Because university-based curriculum developers designed and taught the course, it focused on developing accuracy and excellence in English comprehension and expression.

Those interested in joining the class were assessed prior to the first session, and only those whose English proficiency was adequate to fully participate in the curriculum were selected. Those who were not selected were referred to the conversation and computer-based courses offered at the same library branches and were invited to reapply. Instruction was pitched at a level of challenge slightly beyond each student's competence in English, with the goal being the ability to use English in formal ways and settings. Additionally, because adults have so many competing demands on their time, the course was designed and promoted as a free course that is worth paying for. Everyone loves getting something valuable for nothing. Some people will wait hours to get a free gift from a store or restaurant. The designers wanted to offer a greater challenge and better potential outcome than what was available elsewhere and wanted students to feel that their time was well spent on engaging, useful activities with outcomes focused on accuracy and excellence.

The university team found that one way of accomplishing this was incorporating an amount of rigor into the classes proportional to the reduced instruction time as compared to university academic English programs. Technology was incorporated into the curriculum through a wiki that the instructor developed and maintained, including all class materials as well as related files and websites for further study. The instructor and students experimented with Skype as a way to improve phone communication, but use of the branches' computer labs was limited and that aspect was abandoned. Students were consistently given approximately two or more hours' worth of homework per week. Each week, students received a homework assignment related to the week's grammar instruction; a reading on the theme, which included target vocabulary; and a writing component as a capstone activity. Instructors always collected the capstone assignment and gave both positive and corrective feedback. When the instructors approached the class with high expectations of student involvement, the students rose to the occasion.

Because adults often drop out of community-based classes, attrition is always a concern. Three main benefits of the course were publicized to recruit and retain students: (1) a university-quality ESL program offered at no cost; (2) a well-defined set of skills that program completers master through faithful attendance over a six-week period; (3) a flexible curriculum based on students' needs. Rather than ask students to sign up for continuous, open-ended sessions of English, the program established a six-week curricular cycle. Participants were required to commit to attending without absences. At the end of the six-week session, the students received a certificate indicating the level of mastery achieved and were referred into English-speaking educational opportunities at the library, including book clubs and computer literacy courses. It is important to note that these referrals mainly directed students into mainstream library classes, programs, and group activ-

ities because encouraging language learners to interact with native speakers is a key goal of our program. Some students were also able to transition to community college courses and even university study.

Word of mouth and OCLS promotion has kept the classes at full enrollment with constant waiting lists. The classes have developed a strong sense of community. They are often composed of several generations of one family, neighbors, and coworkers attending as a group. Students continue to provide testimonials about the gains they see in their personal and professional lives. Since its inception in January 2011, this program has had over fourteen hundred attendees at the two locations, with a total of eighty-six classes taught to the date of this writing. The biggest success of this class can be illustrated through one student's experience. This student had lived and worked in the United States for years but had never studied English in a classroom setting before. The student was uncomfortable about speaking English. At the end of the Soy Culto English program, the student felt confident enough with English to sign up as a full-time English language student at the local community college. Because of the student's experiences in Soy Culto, the goal of being bilingual felt within reach for the first time.

LESSONS LEARNED

Several lessons were learned that helped OCLS best connect to the Hispanic community.

First, it is not enough to translate material. Information must be trans-created. A catchphrase in English might not translate directly into Spanish. By shaping the campaigns around the culture and language, we were able to be more effective in attracting people.

Second, developing relationships with local media staff and community leaders was successful. By inviting media to the press conference, then working to develop a relationship with them, OCLS was able to garner much more support from these groups.

Third, using staff members in promotional pieces was extremely popular. A number of staff members were invited to a photo shoot, and their photos were used on educational pieces and brochures. First, staff members could see themselves in educational pieces, radio website banners, and even on the backs of buses. Second, members of the community could come in and actually see the people from the pieces. Finally, patrons of the specific branches could enjoy the knowledge that the people portrayed were "their" library workers.

Fourth, by creating relationships with other organizations, OCLS has woven itself more firmly into the Hispanic community. Being a member of the Hispanic Chamber of Commerce of Metro Orlando has helped demonstrate our commitment to serving the population, just as attending the Hispanic Business Expo at the Orange County Convention Center proved that we are reaching out to that community.

Fifth, the connectedness of the Hispanic community suggests that texting should play a major role. At this juncture, this has not proven to be true in our experience. Similarly, using Skype to enhance ESL classes was proven ineffective. Person-to-person contact, especially with a teacher leading a group, has proven a much more popular approach.

Last, by seeking out experts in other fields, we were able to best use the grant funds. Trying to develop an ESL program, a promotional campaign, or surveys would have been possible, but by partnering with Joyce Nutta and Allison Youngblood at UCF, Hernan Tagliani of the Group, and Sami Haiman-Marrero of Urbander, we were most able to be effective and productive in our efforts.

CONCLUSION

OCLS was fortunate to receive this grant, especially during this difficult financial time. The monies provided have helped us shape and expand our collections as well as create new services and opportunities for a large part of our community. The programs and services instituted by this grant will continue to help us serve our community for many years to come.

Chapter Seventeen

Fotonovelas and Historietas

Adult Comic Books from Mexico in American Libraries

Cynthia Houston

LA LITERATURA POPULAR: THE POPULAR READING TRADITION IN MEXICO

In my southern California childhood, no trip to the local supermarket would have been complete without furtive glances along the row of Spanish-language adult comic books on display by the check-out counter. To me, these small-sized illustrated booklets, with covers showing muscular men and buxom women, represented a strange and mysterious world of melodrama in print. These items did not exist in lower shelves of the comic-book section where I was allowed to browse for my weekly *Archie* or *Wonder Woman* title.

I did not fully understand my fascination with these adult graphic novels until many years later, when a librarian at a local Reforma meeting mentioned that these *fotonovelas* are great items to include in collections for Hispanic patrons because they are an important part of the Mexican and Latin American popular reading tradition. Suddenly the light went on—these are the little books that fascinated me as a child! In later adulthood, during my many travels in Mexico, I encountered hundreds of fotonovelas displayed in street-side newsstands at less than a dollar per title, in flea markets for a fraction of that price, and in the hands of commuters and workers on their lunch breaks. I saw everyone—young, old, rich, and poor—reading these little *libros de bosillo* (pocket books) in Mexico. So if fotonovelas are this popular, they belong in our libraries in the United States!

In a recent article published in the *Mexican Review of Communication*, fotonovelas focusing on romantic or western themes such as *El Libro Vaquero* (The Cowboy Book) or *El Libro Semanal* (The Weekly Book) have been described as "lo major de lo peor" or "the best of the worst" due to the fact that they are printed on cheap paper, use flimsy bindings, and are typically the least expensive item on the newsstand (López Parra 2005). However, their circulation of over seven million copies per month gives testimony to the fact they are wildly popular with the Mexican and Latin American reading public (Campbell 2009). According to Campbell (2009), fotonovelas represent a significant portion of periodical print literature in circulation in Mexico and approximately 12 percent of the materials read by Mexican adults. Consequently, to satisfy the public demand for their regular dose of melodrama, each week publishers in Mexico and Latin American countries distribute new issues to newsstands based on either a romantic, Wild West, detective, or gritty urban theme, depending on the series. Typically, after they leave the newsstand, every fotonovela purchased is read by at least five other people, either by resale or by "renting" from a local used bookseller (Campbell 2009).

FROM FOTONOVELA TO HISTORIETA AND BACK: A BRIEF INTRODUCTION TO THE ADULT COMIC-BOOK TRADITION

Fotonovelas have been part of the popular reading tradition in Mexico and Latin America for over a hundred years. Based on the millions of fotonovelas in circulation, it cannot be denied that the illustrated stories, which take up one or two panels per page, are captivating and entertaining. The dedicated readers of fotonovelas are well aware of the fact that between the pages of every issue is an entertaining world of richly illustrated and tightly narrated high drama—where men and women are locked in mortal combat between good and evil, love and lust, rich and poor, powerful and weak—all of which are developed and resolved, for better or worse, within 50 to 150 pages.

In Mexico, the first *historieta* or "little story," titled *Historia de una Mujer* (Story of a Woman), began as promotional item for a brand of cigarettes in the 1880s. Then, in the early decades of the twentieth century, historietas became a standard item in weekly papers, ultimately emerging in the 1930s as an independent genre of comic book. In the 1970s, the term *fotonovela* was coined to refer to series that used photo stills from films and soap operas as a way to repackage these programs in printed format. Currently, although the term *fotonovela* is used to refer to this genre, it is illustrations rather than photographs that dominate the pages. Currently there are over fifty fotonovela series published by more than ten different publishers (Ulloa

2008). The most common themes are westerns, digested adaptations of literary classics, historical biographies or accounts of historical events, informational texts published by government agencies, detective stories, superheroes, romance, daily drama, and terror. The story lines are familiar, including good against evil, love triumphs above all, and beware of the seven deadly sins. The short sentences that make up the dialogue often use clichés and familiar phrases so that the reader can easily understand the plot and identify with the characters. According to Campbell (2009), the most popular series incorporate themes that reflect twenty-first-century realities of economic and cultural globalization. For example, in the fotonovela series *El Libro Vaqureo*, the main characters are molded on cowboy stereotypes from the American Wild West, while in *El Libro Semanal,* characters reflect U.S.-style upper-middle-class consumer lifestyles and concomitant personal and professional ambitions.

SI SE PUEDE! LITERATURA BARATA IN LA BIBLIOTECA: CHEAP LITERATURE IN THE LIBRARY? YES WE CAN!

Forty years ago, when I first noticed fotonovelas at my local grocery store, they never would have been considered appropriate items for a library in the United States because they were dismissed as pulp fiction. However, in the twenty-first century, as Spanish-speaking populations have increased dramatically all over the United States, finding ways to attract new immigrants to the resources available in the library makes including these items an essential part of any culturally responsive collection development plan (Cuesta 1990; Flythe 2001; Marquis 2003). Because of their wide appeal, these publications have the potential to bring a new population of Spanish speakers into the library and should be viewed as a gateway to other genres of reading materials in Spanish and English. Many librarians and literacy experts firmly believe that once people get into the habit of reading, they will begin to explore other materials available to them in the library, widen their reading experience, and ultimately seek out reading for both entertainment and education (Krashen 2004). In fact, librarians serving Spanish speakers in the United States and library organizations such as Reforma have promoted the inclusion of fotonovelas in collection development plans serving Spanish-speaking populations (Boulé 2005; Naylor and Frey 2006). For this reason, many public libraries such as the Denver Public Library, the Cleveland Public Library, and the Forth Worth Public Library have been incorporating fotonovelas into their collections for many years. In testimony to this fact, a simple search of the Worldcat library database lists 1,790 titles under the subject heading "fotonovela" in libraries across the United States, with titles such as *Bajo el Fuego de Tu Piel* (Under the Fire of Your Skin) and *¡Justicia Divina!* (Divine Justice!).

Understanding the readership of fotonovelas in Mexico is an important beginning for understanding the needs of patrons accessing these materials in libraries in United States. Given the fact that these types of periodicals are popular artifacts from home for immigrants from Mexico and Latin America, we could assume that although all social classes of Spanish-speaking patrons read fotonovelas, the target population for these items in public libraries in the United States would be recent immigrants from Spanish-speaking countries who are migrant workers, domestic workers, or urban day laborers, from rural or urban backgrounds, possibly with limited literacy skills in Spanish (Cuesta 1990). This assumption is based on the fact that fotonovelas are clearly designed with literacy in mind, using simple sentence structures, a minimum of one to two illustrated panels per page, and illustrations supporting the narrative. The size of the fotonovela, about four inches by four inches, allows workers to keep them in their back pockets and available for reading at any time during the day. One writer suggests that these types of popular publications serve to maintain functional literacy among people who may be able to read and write, but rarely do so because of their type of employment, economic situation, or access to reading materials (López Parra 2005). Recent studies of Mexican reading habits also support the assumption that fotonovelas in general can be considered the "poor man's novel" (Güereña and Pisano 1998). Statistics from these studies indicate that 40 percent of readers of western-themed fotonovelas such as *El Libro Vaquero* are working-class males, with 22 percent earning minimum wage or less, while 52 percent of readers of romance-themed fotonovelas such as *El Libro Semanal* are housewives, 62 percent of whom earn $25 a day or less (Campbell 2009).

Recently, fotonovelas have been used extensively by government agencies in the United States and Mexico to provide information on political, health, and safety issues to the Spanish-speaking population. In 2004, the Mexican government published *Guía del Migrante Mexicano* (Guide for the Mexican Migrant), which used the fotonovela format to educate Mexican citizens on surviving the trek of migration across the Mexican border. In the United States, health agencies and public libraries have used the fotonovela format to educate Spanish-speaking populations on important health and safety practices and provide orientation to the public library. The Fotonovela Company specializes in the development and production of fotonovelas for public health and safety organizations and provides many examples of their publications on their website.

LOVE, VIOLENCE, AND THE OLD WEST: POPULAR SERIES OF FOTONOVELAS AND HISTORIETAS IN LIBRARY COLLECTIONS

The terms *fotonovela* ("photo novel") and *historieta* ("little story") are often used interchangeably, but in technical terms the fotonovela format involves still photo or movie image stills used in the production process, while the historieta format makes use of color or black-and-white line drawings. In the 1960s and 1970s the fotonovela was a widely popular format for the romance market, read by teenage girls and housewives, while the historieta was used for the western-themed series and catered to adolescent and adult males. Although it does not appear that any fotonovelas are actually using photo stills in their production, librarians in the United States generally refer to all of types of Spanish-language melodramatic adult graphic novels from Mexico and Latin America as *fotonovelas*. This is because the term *historieta* is a more general term for comic books in the Spanish-speaking world, while *fotonovela* is a term that can be used to refer to a particular type of melodramatic graphic novel. When patrons are making a request for these materials, they may not use the term *fotonovela* and instead ask for "historietas," "libros de bosillo," "comic tipo libro vaquero," "sentimentales," "novelas," "novelitas," or "tiras cómicas." For this reason, mentioning specific fotonovela series during the interview process might help identify the patron's information need.

As fotonovelas are commonly found on newsstands in Mexico and Latin America, patrons would expect them to be in the periodicals area of the library rather than in the stacks—but because of their small size, they should not be shelved with the other magazines. Many libraries use revolving CD display racks for their current fotonovela collections and place them on top of the periodicals shelves, allowing easy patron access. Although their shelf life may be short because of their cheap paper and bindings, many libraries do include fotonovelas in their library catalogs so that circulation statistics can be compiled. There are over a thousand electronic records for titles in fotonovela series on OCLC, so creating a new collection of titles should not require creating original catalog records. During processing, it is also a good idea to reinforce the covers and bindings so that they can withstand heavy circulation.

Because fotonovelas are published in Mexico, their distribution in the United States is limited. Currently there is one distributor of fotonovelas in the United States: Latin American Periodicals (http://www.lapmagazines.com/home.html), based in Nogales, Arizona is the sole provider of fotonovelas to libraries in the United States. Currently, the company serves over six hundred libraries across the United States and offers subscriptions to many popular series including *El Libro Vaquero, Frontera Violenta, Libro Semanal, Libro Sentimental,* and *Amores y Amantes.* Subscriptions to these series can be purchased as packages or individually.

In most collection development plans serving Spanish speakers, fotonovelas are listed as must-haves, primarily because patrons enjoy reading them (Boulé 2005; Cuesta 1990; Marquis 2003). In a recent study of reading habits of Spanish-speaking library patrons in North Carolina, 17 percent reported they read fotonovelas (Flythe 2001). Unfortunately, the decision about whether or not to include fotonovelas in the library collection is sometimes controversial, because in the past fotonovelas have been subjected to challenges from conservative community organizations. For example, in 2005 the anti-immigration group Colorado Alliance for Immigration Reform reviewed the 6,569-item fotonovela collection in the Denver Public Library system and found that four out of the fourteen series in circulation contained questionable content ("Denver Reconsiders Fotonovela Collection" 2005). In this case, according to *American Libraries,* the library cancelled the popular *El Libro Vaquero* (Cowboy Book) series, along with *Frontera Violenta* (Violent Frontier), *La Novela Policiaca* (The Detective Novel), and *El Libro Policiaco* (The Detective Book) series. These are all titles preferred by male Spanish-speaking patrons, so this decision was an unfortunate one for that segment of the service population. However, it must be noted that not all titles in a series contain questionable content, but because of the sheer volume of new issues of fotonovelas published in Mexico every week, it is hard for the government to monitor the contents of every new issue. Sometimes, when driven by the need to increase sales, writers and illustrators take some license with their creativity and include language or pictures that libraries might consider objectionable (López Parra 2005). For this reason, it is suggested that during the cataloging process, individual issues should be reviewed for objectionable content prior to placing them on the shelves.

Fotonovelas developed for an adult audience must be distinguished from Mexican comic books, called "historietas," "comics," or "tiras cómicas," which are geared for middle- and upper-class children and adolescents and are largely based on popular comics from the United States or manga from Japan. Furthermore, these series are also distinct from classic Mexican comic books such as *La Familia Burrón* or *Kalimán,* which are comic books read by all age groups. In contrast to these and other Spanish-language graphic novel formats, fotonovelas are intended for adult readers of illustrated romances, westerns, or gritty police dramas. In recent years fotonovelas have been criticized for containing sexually explicit or excessively violent language and illustrations that are demeaning to women. For this reason it is important to be aware that there are different categories of fotonovelas. The *fotonovela rosa* or *fotonovela suave* (pink or soft photo novel) is the traditional romance genre with sentimental themes and quasi-fairy-tale endings.

Series such as *El Libro Semanal* and *El Libro Sentimental* are examples of these series, in which female characters have exaggerated features and typically play a passive role in determining the outcome of the story, even when they are the main character. The *fotonovela roja*, which is a more contemporary category and often moderately pornographic, deals with a gritty reality and includes themes such as rape, poverty, and drug addiction. The series *Valle de Lagrimas* (Valley of Tears) is an example of this variety of fotonovela.

The annotated list of fotonovela titles below includes series in the fotonovela roja and fotonovela suave categories, most of which are available by subscription from Latin American Periodicals and are currently in public library collections across the country. Exemplary titles from most of these series are available for review online from *Popular Print: Hermosillo*, a digital archive dedicated to collecting popular print materials from Mexico.

FOTONOVELAS SERIES TITLES

El Libro Vaquero (The Cowboy Book). Published by Nueva Impresora y Editora, each title is illustrated in color and set in the nineteenth-century Old West. The stories generally revolve around strong male characters and beautiful female characters engaged in some kind of violent conflict or struggle. Although the settings are often along the U.S.-Mexico border, the stories typically do not mention Mexican history or take on the national perspectives of that historical period.

Frontera Violenta (Violent Frontier). Similar in look and feel to *El Libro Vaquero*, *Frontera Violenta* is published by Nueva Impresora y Editora, illustrated in color, and set in the nineteenth-century Old West, most often along the border areas. The stories feature strong male and beautiful female characters, who are Mexican, Anglo-American, or American Indian, engaged in some kind of struggle or conflict, and often involve violence.

El Libro Semanal (The Weekly Book). Published by Nueva Impresora y Editora, *El Libro Semanal* is illustrated in black and white—each title featuring middle- and upper-class male and female characters in modern urban settings such as Mexico City. The stories are typically organized around a moral lesson and bear a striking similarity to the plots of popular television *telenovelas* (soap operas).

El Libro Sentimental (The Sentimental Book). Published by Nueva Impresora y Editora and illustrated in black and white, each story in *El Libro Sentimental* is set in middle-class, urban or suburban surroundings in the United States or Mexico. The stories typically feature conflicts in relationships between women and men and contain themes focusing on the sins of greed and vanity, or stories of domestic abuse, love, and passion from a woman's point of view.

Amores y Amantes (Loves and Lovers). Published by Editorial Mango and illustrated in black and white, this romance series features tales of young love, forbidden love, and true love in a middle-class urban setting.

Aventuras de Vaqueros (Cowboy Adventures). Published by Mina Editores and filled with rich color illustrations, this series features tales of adventure, passion, and love between men and women set in the Old West. The stories often take place along the border country between the United States and Mexico and involve violent conflicts among Native Americans, Mexicans, and Anglo Americans.

El Libro Policiaco (The Detective Book). Published by Nueva Impresora y Editora and illustrated in color, each story is set on the urban city streets of the United States, Mexico, or Latin America. These stories feature traditional detective fiction themes, with contemporary characters of all ethnicities and urban villains such as drug dealers—many of whom meet a violent end.

WORKS CITED

Boulé, Michelle. 2005. "Examining a Spanish Nonfiction Collection in a Public Library." *Library Collections Acquisitions and Services* 29: 403–11.

Campbell, Bruce. 2009. *Viva la Historieta: Mexican Comics, NAFTA, and the Politics of Globalization.* Oxford: University Press of Mississippi.

Cuesta, Yolanda J. 1990. "From Survival to Sophistication: Hispanic Needs = Library Needs." *Library Journal* 115(9): 26–28.

"Denver Reconsiders Fotonovela Collection." 2005. *American Libraries* 36(8): 12–13.

Flythe, Frances H. 2001. "Identification of the Information Needs of Newly Arrived Hispanic/ Latino Immigrants in Durham County, North Carolina, and How the Public Library May Address Those Needs." Master's thesis, University of North Carolina, Chapel Hill. http:// ils.unc.edu/MSpapers/2666.pdf.

Güereña, Salvador, and Vivian Pisano, eds. 1998. "Other Periodicals: Fotonovelas." In *Latino Periodicals: A Selection Guide.* Jefferson, NC: McFarland.

Krashen, Stephen. 2004. *The Power of Reading.* 2 nd ed. Englewood Cliffs, NJ: Libraries Unlimited.

López Parra, Raul. 2005. "El Libro Vaquero: Un Clásico de la Cultura Popular." *Revista Mexicana de Comunicación* 99.

Marquis, Solina. 2003. "Collections and Services for the Spanish-Speaking." *Public Libraries* 42(3): 172–77.

Naylor, Shelly, and Susan M. Frey. 2006. "Where Cultural and Information Literacy Meet: Serving Spanish-Speaking Library Users in Indiana." *Indiana Libraries* 25(4) : 2–7.

Ulloa, Sergio. 2008. "Pulp Fiction: Mexico's Historieta." *Mexconnect.* http:// www.mexconnect.com/articles/1759-pulp-fiction-mexico-s-historieta.

Chapter Eighteen

Reaching Out through Graphic Novels

Michael Buono

Graphic novels belong in the library. There is a large body of literature in library journals about why graphic novels and other comics should be included in a library's collection. There are a few factors that make graphic novels especially important to multicultural populations. First, comics are great ESL material. Second, there are significant numbers of devoted fans from minority groups. Third, comics often have themes of empowerment and a focus on the trials of day-to-day life. Fourth, they are an international art form and recognizable to most people.

A BIT ON COMICS AND LITERACY

Comics are often touted as great literacy tools, because of their simple text and visual nature. For adult readers who are also nonnative English speakers, comics are easy to read and understand and don't talk down to them. The story lines are complex, and the characters are detailed. This makes them an excellent tool to teach literacy and an excellent opportunity for much more.

Most of the text in comics is dialogue. This means the majority of the words are conversational style, and the sentences are framed after the way American-born people speak. Accents from different parts of the country are represented consistently in the spelling of words and the cadence of the sentences. Jargon, idioms, and other difficult facets of English are also explained. Many of these comics have found their way overseas, and this means that patrons may have grown up reading the same book in their native language.

DEVELOP A DIVERSE COLLECTION

Diverse collections are immensely important. I have learned five very important lessons while developing my collection.

Lesson one: not all minority heroes should be included in your collection.
Depending on who is writing the comic, these portrayals can range from
laughable to offensive.

Lesson two: there are a lot more minority heroes than I thought. Many of
these relatively unknown heroes have touched minority comic fans deeply,
but they are virtually unknown outside of those groups.

Lesson three: the best multicultural collection development resource is
the minority fans themselves. Graphic novels make up a relatively small
percentage of professional review literature. Minority reviewers make up
relatively small portions of professional staff, so I turn to the Internet.

Lesson four: diverse collections do not mean collections without Spider-
Man, Batman, and the rest. Even if these characters are extremely common,
they are also immensely popular. Spider-Man, Batman, and Superman are
known across the world.

Lesson five: manga breaks all the rules. The depictions of non-Japanese
people in manga is frequently comically bad or offensive, but the fan base is
diverse. Manga frequently focuses on the story of the underdog. Struggle,
faith in oneself, and hard work are recurring themes. These universal themes
keep fans of diverse backgrounds coming back for more, despite the questionable depictions of non-Japanese.

TRUST IN THE INTERNET NERDS

To find materials that entertain and enlighten minority patrons, it is best to
turn to Internet nerds. There are many blogs written by minority fans about
minority characters. The authors of these blogs have a more advanced understanding of their culture than I ever will have, and they are more aware of the
issues their culture faces. Despite their possible issues with the medium, the
fact is they are still fans. They comb new publications for gems, and they
offer heartfelt endorsements when they find them. Not all comics they recommend will feature a minority main character, and some of the most be-
loved examples of minority characters were written by people of another
nationality.

These blogs are also helpful if one wants to stay aware of issues that
confront minority fans. Hollywood is still whitewashing characters. Women
artists and writers are still excluded from big-name titles, despite their talent
and popularity. The most frequent advice comic creators, even minority com-

ic creators, have for fans who want more minority characters is "Create them yourself." Entire websites are dedicated to these issues, but a lot can be gleaned by reading review blogs such as Geekquality, Has Boobs, Reads Comics, Racialicious, and Black Superhero Fan.

MERCHANDISING COMICS

Merchandising is of general importance to booksellers and librarians, and the cover art is key to "selling" the book. Comic companies pay artists specifically for cover artwork, because they know how much the cover can sell the book. The cover art is an important part of selling comics to patrons. When I am working in the Young Adult department, I will often take books and graphic novels that have great covers and leave them on our tables. I love watching the teens tentatively pick them up when their friends aren't looking.

Retail bookstores make heavy use of "face outs." This involves turning books on the shelf so the front cover faces outward. This is a great way of using a quantity of a single title to make a display, but you can also put cheap plastic blocks behind the book to provide support. Many of the traditional merchandizing methods librarians employ work especially well for comics.

Minority heroes are frequently members of a team, or they are technically side characters. Almost all superheroes from Marvel and DC debut in titles in which they are not title characters. Sometimes they are not on the cover of the graphic novel. I have seen many libraries arrange printouts of book cover images for a display, and the same thing can be done with the characters within comics. Marvel, DC, and other companies release promotional images of the characters in books. So you can pull out the characters and their profiles, and make a display that way.

RESPECT COMICS EVEN IF YOU DON'T LIKE THEM

Despite all the research, the size of the industry, the proliferation of superhero movies, and the purchase of Marvel by Disney, people are still dubious about the value of comics. The truth is some people just don't like them, and that is okay. Comics and graphic novels are not for everyone. But all mediums of expression deserve respect, and here are some reasons to respect comics.

The characters from Marvel and DC are featured in materials targeting people of all ages, beginning with preschoolers. No physical skill or special talent is required to participate in a discussion of comics or books. A nurtured enthusiasm for comics can lead to a lifelong fan. A lifelong fan reads, and he or she is likely to read noncomic materials as well. For instance, renowned authors such as Orson Scott Card, Dean Koontz, Stephen King, and Neil Gaiman all write comics. Granted, Gaiman started in comics, but you can still easily hand Sandman fans his book *Neverwhere* and get them reading prose.

Comics are something easy for an adult (parent, family member, mentor, or teacher) and child to enjoy together. They have several generations of fans, and they have a community behind them. This fan community overlaps with other fan communities. The fan base is incredibly active, vocal, and participatory in the industry. It has also been a community that is welcoming of isolated individuals.

KEEP AWARE OF FAN ACTIVITIES IN YOUR LOCAL AREA

Connecting a new or old fan with activities in your area can be a great service to any of your patrons. There are Comic Cons all over the country. Some are big and famous, and others are small. Nearly all of them have some opportunity for fans to volunteer or run events. Whether or not you like comics, connecting fans to these events can help you form a relationship with them. This goes beyond respecting the medium, and it shows that you are interested in connecting them with information they want.

FAN FICTION

A large number of fans engage in fan fiction. They make up their own stories in the world of the comics they love, or they make up new scenarios for the characters to participate in. Fan fiction may not be the best-written material, but it is an opportunity to get a fan reading and writing prose. It is an easy thing to get started doing, and it provides fans with the opportunity to cultivate their imagination.

CONVENTIONS

If your interest is to get your patrons to read prose, noncomic authors frequently show up at conventions as well. Pointing out their titles may be a good way to get someone reading prose. Most of the time, volunteers get to go to conventions for free. If you are looking to learn more about the industry, it may be worth volunteering at your local convention. You would be surprised at how much you can learn by giving up a weekend.

I attended New York Comic Con in October of 2011 with the intention of getting some ideas for my collection and keeping up on the comic news. At the convention, I decided to attend a panel called "Always Bet on Black" by Dyami and Hakeem Pipkin for some ideas. It was marketed as a history of black people in comics, and I figured I would find out about some classic titles I missed. The experience was truly inspirational because I was able to glimpse the interior workings of the black comic-book fan. I was exposed to comic heroes I did not know existed, and I felt like I was able to more critically view my collection.

I returned with a strong desire to make my collection represent the ethnicity and interests of my community. That is a mission harder to accomplish in comics, but here is my final tip: When a fan comes to you upset about a depiction of their ethnicity in comics, do what you always do. But also suggest that means the market is open for a realistic hero of their ethnicity, and that the fastest way to change the industry is from the inside because there are not enough minority characters or minority creators.

Part IV

Applying Technology

Chapter Nineteen

The Multilingual Glossary Project and myLanguage

Two Online Programs to Assist Libraries to Deliver Services to Multicultural Patrons

Oriana Acevedo and Nicky Lo Bianco

The role of public libraries is to be accessible and relevant to all members of the community. It is often difficult for libraries to find ways to achieve this with limited resources and time. To address this challenge, two programs have been created, one through the State Library of New South Wales, Australia and the other through a consortium of state and territory libraries around Australia. These two programs have been specifically designed to provide practical support for library staff wishing to make their libraries more engaging and relevant to the needs of their multicultural communities. Both programs employ the use of online tools to bring together practical resources for library staff, no matter where they are or how small their library might be.

THE MULTILINGUAL GLOSSARY PROJECT

Background

New South Wales (NSW) is one of the most culturally diverse communities in Australia. People come from over two hundred birthplaces, and around 26 percent of the population speaks a language other than English at home (Australian Bureau of Statistics 2006). The State Library of NSW is one of the oldest libraries in Australia, with a history tracing back to the establishment of the Australian Subscription Library in 1826. In 1869, the NSW government took over responsibility for the library, forming the Sydney Free Public Library, the first truly public library service for the people of New South Wales. In 1895, the name was changed to the Public Library of New South Wales. It was renamed the State Library of New South Wales in 1975. The Library Council of New South Wales is the governing body of the State Library of New South Wales (Library Council of New South Wales 2005, 4).

The State Library of NSW is committed to the provision of quality, integrated multicultural library services that are responsive to both changing migration patterns and the changing information needs of a culturally diverse community. It provides access to its own multicultural services and collections in forty-three languages and also provides support to all 274 NSW public libraries to help them offer multicultural library services. There is a multicultural consultant who has a specific responsibility to promote and support multicultural library services in NSW public libraries and the NSW communities and to develop policies on multicultural issues for the State Library of NSW.

Under NSW legislation, the public library service has a social responsibility, incorporating the concepts of access and equity. Library services sustain the principle of citizens' unrestricted access to information and ideas. Information literacy is fundamental for a participative citizenship, social inclusion and the creation of knowledge, and learning for life.

The Multilingual Glossary: A Communication and Signage Tool

This tool is an example of one of the ways in which the State Library has hosted a product to meet the needs of library staff, not only in NSW, but globally via the Internet. The multilingual glossary is a professionally translated, and culturally appropriate, signage tool for libraries. It is a free and innovative contribution to international library-based multicultural services.

The need for a Multilingual Glossary became clear for the following reasons:

- In a library environment the level of provision of translation services is low in relation to community need.
- Library best practice internationally has highlighted the need for active engagement with the community and a stronger mediation role for libraries between the languages other than English (LOTE) collections and clients.
- Delivery of future services through the Internet was seen as a priority by library staff.

While some libraries have staff who possess language skills, they are not generally qualified interpreters/translators, nor are they necessarily representative of the major language groups in that community. Also, library staff with the language skills needed to assist the public are not available at all times.

The purpose of the project is to enable culturally and linguistically diverse (CALD) communities to have greater opportunities for participation in community life and to also assist them with equitable access to the information and entertainment resources that are held in public libraries. Specifically, this project aims to assist CALD clients in overcoming language barriers that prevent them from accessing library services and make the library environment more user-friendly. For example, library staff may find the glossary very useful when informing clients that there is health information in their community language or that the library items they requested are now available. They can tell clients that the library has books in their language. Some libraries may want to promote a book sale to draw attention to the fact that they have books in languages other than English to sell.

How the Glossary Was Created

The Working Group on Multicultural Library Services in NSW identified the need to develop a tool that would be easy to access from any library and would not be restricted by available technology or a lack of staff with language skills. Web-accessible alternatives, such as translation software, were also researched but were found to be unreliable, providing grammatically inaccurate or culturally inappropriate translations.

The glossary was developed by a committee of multicultural librarians from public libraries in NSW. Most of them were based in libraries in the Sydney metropolitan area, and English was their second language. Over a period of two years the group trialed different approaches to cooperative translations and developed a glossary of library terms. The group then decided to obtain advice from the State Library of NSW. The outcome was the specifications for a database able to manage images and resizable fonts. In the research stage a feasible model and pilot was built by the information technology (IT) unit at the State Library that proved to be efficient and able to deliver what was needed to assist public libraries to improve communication and outreach with the culturally and diverse communities of New South Wales.

An information technology multilingual specialist company, eTranslate, was awarded the contract to develop the database. Over a period of two months, eTranslate created 6,958 files, the equivalent of 142 words and sentences translated into forty-nine languages. The Working Group identified, across the public library network, people with appropriate language skills to check and discuss the translations, making sure that the words and phrases were appropriate to be used in a library environment.

Project Sustainability

A project management group comprising the Fairfield City library manager, a committee of multicultural librarians, and the multicultural consultant from the State Library of NSW continue to manage the project. The database continues to be hosted by the State Library of NSW on its website. The Working Group reviews the database every two years, making appropriate revisions. Recently, for example, words such as *cassettes* and *videos* that are no longer relevant for public libraries in NSW were removed and the phrase *health information* was added to support a project focusing on multicultural health awareness.

Using the Glossary

The glossary searches specific library service–related English phrases, retrieving a non-English equivalent in one of forty-nine languages, including Arabic, Chinese, Russia, Thai, and many more.

The Multilingual Glossary can be:

- Searched using an English phrase, retrieving a non-English equivalent
- Used to allow libraries that may have differing levels of technology to access the information

The Glossary resides in a SQL 2000 database and is available via Internet using a Cold Fusion front-end.

Outcomes

The Glossary delivered the following benefits:

- A cost-effective means of offering information in multiple languages
- The ability for public libraries to respond promptly to the changing profiles of the community
- An improved ability to serve diverse members of the community
- The ability to promote library services to CALD communities in regional and rural locations (where access to translating services is poor)
- Better use of technology, particularly for non-Roman script
- A degree of independent access to information for culturally and linguistically diverse library clients

- A standardization of signage and information for NSW libraries (this assists CALD clients in overcoming language barriers that prevent them from accessing library services and makes the library environment more user-friendly)
- The opportunity to address a service gap by assisting the delivery of information to the target groups
- Support for both new settlers and established migrant communities with members still facing language barriers

The database concept of gathering commonly used terms in a specific environment has other applications beyond those related to library services. For example, Gold Coast City wanted to explore the possibility of developing a similar database that will allow them to store translated information in several languages for services such as pet licensing, rubbish collection, recycling, and so forth.

Global Users

Via the Internet, the Glossary database is also available to global users. It is a free and innovative contribution to international library-based multicultural services. Positive feedback through "Request a phrase" has been received from the Vancouver Public Library, the Brooklyn Public Library, and Wellington City.

MYLANGUAGE

Background

myLanguage is a website developed in 2005 through a partnership between the state and territory libraries of the Australian Capital Territory, New South Wales, Northern Territory, Queensland, South Australia, Victoria, and Western Australia. Given the impossibility of libraries being able to offer sufficient physical resources in the many languages spoken in Australia, this service has provided online access to information via websites, search engines, web directories, and news in over sixty-five community languages. The website has also provided resources to assist library staff to develop multicultural services and to promote their programs to culturally and linguistically diverse (CALD) communities across Australia.

In 2010 an updated vision and new objectives marked a significant shift for the project, with an emphasis on digital inclusion for CALD communities using new technologies and Web 2.0 opportunities. As a result, in November 2011, stage one of an updated, more interactive website was launched to enable libraries to support Australia's multicultural communities to access information, language, and culture. The site now provides free access to an increased variety of tools and resources for library staff to develop services and encourage library use.

The following statements guide the work of the myLanguage partnership:

Vision 2010–2015:
   myLanguage will use information technologies to enable libraries to empower CALD communities to

• Achieve greater social inclusion
• Maintain and enrich cultural and linguistic identity

Objectives:
   myLanguage will:

• Build collaborative partnerships across all sectors to develop multilingual resources
• Further develop myLanguage, implementing innovative solutions
• Enhance access to diverse information resources in community languages
• Understand and respond to the information needs of CALD communities
• Value the role played by public libraries by supporting their delivery of multicultural services
• Advocate for (the value of) digital and social inclusion for CALD communities

Practical Ways to Encourage Library Use

The new myLanguage website provides an online hub where libraries, service providers, multicultural communities, and individuals can find and share information as well as discover tools for developing effective services and programs. Its major features from a library perspective are described below, with different aspects all based on suggestions from library staff around Australia.

Search Engines, Web Directories, and News in over Sixty-Five Community Languages

This feature is particularly helpful in assisting new Internet users to explore the possibilities of the Internet in their language. It allows direct access to a language without having to navigate too much English first. The site also provides access to online multilingual Internet training manuals that are available via Creative Commons, for any library to adapt to their needs.

Resources for Planning, Implementing, and Promoting Multicultural Programs and Services

This part of the site aims to provide the background information libraries need to develop the most appropriate services for their multicultural communities. It pulls together a wide number of websites and documents covering aspects such as community profiles and statistics, cross-cultural communication, government and library policies, support organizations, collection development and cataloging, program ideas, and training manuals.

Case Studies Highlighting Great Programs Involving Multicultural Communities, Libraries, and Other Support Organizations

This section further assists library staff in providing relevant and attractive services to their communities. Examples are given of different kinds of programs from around the country, with details on how they were developed. Examples include English conversation groups, digital oral history programs, multilingual story times, health information programs, book fairs, and literacy programs.

News and Ideas, Blog for Sharing Resources, and New Developments

This section provides library staff with access to information about the latest developments in libraries as well as in the wider community and supports their work with different groups. It also enables them to comment and share ideas.

Translations of Government and Community Information

Research has shown that while many online translations of important information exist in areas such as health, settlement, the law, and education, multicultural communities find it difficult to access. Given that access to information is a key role for libraries, the myLanguage website brings together translated information to one access point to enable library staff and service providers to support their communities more effectively. This information may be in text format but increasingly includes digital videos or podcasts.

Traditionally, public libraries in Australia have worked with health organizations to provide information in community languages at a local level. This information is normally limited to language and content offered by the information provider. The challenge for CALD communities seeking information about chronic illnesses is to overcome cultural and linguistic barriers, limited access to technology, and a lack of awareness of available resources.

In 2010 the State Library of NSW hosted the first myLanguage national conference. One of the priorities to emerge from the conference was the need to provide effective access to government information and services. In response, in 2011, a collaborative project between myLanguage, the NSW Multicultural Health Communication Service, and the State Library of NSW commenced. A number of interested regional and local libraries partnered with the project.

The aim of the project was to improve awareness and access to health information for CALD communities in NSW and to develop a sustainable model benefiting communities across the nation. The myLanguage website was updated, making access to multilingual health resources easier, with the State Library of NSW acting as a clearinghouse for the distribution of health-related materials in community languages to the public library network.

myLanguage is providing a unique nationwide repository. The site encourages outside organizations to contribute their translations so that it will continue to grow. It also has the following functionalities:

- A guide to language collections across Australia. This tool enables both members of multicultural communities and library staff to identify where language collections of interest to them are held around the country.
- An events calendar for libraries and multicultural organizations. In this section visitors can upload their own events, which are then promoted nationwide. For library staff it is a unique opportunity to highlight their work.
- Information about the national myLanguage conference. This biennial event has become an important event to enable library staff, other service providers, and multicultural communities to come together to discuss issues of importance, as well as to highlight new ways to support and deliver programs.

Developments in new media and greater interactivity on the web mean that libraries can move beyond traditional roles to support all members of the community and to promote access to information, heritage, and culture. This can mean facilitating the creation of resources, not just providing access. For example, small, new, and emerging communities with few resources can be assisted by libraries in recording oral histories using digital video or create e-books using free online software.

Outcomes

myLanguage is the only site that provides national coverage of multilingual services. The website is becoming an online hub bringing together libraries, community organizations, multicultural communities, and individuals sharing ideas, content news, events, and information. It is helping draw attention to the role libraries play in enabling access to information, heritage, and culture, and it is resulting in other service providers contributing their translated information and events to the site. Partnerships are constantly being developed to support the flow of information and ideas throughout multicultural communities, including, for example, the Federation of Ethnic Communities Councils of Australia, SBS (the national multicultural broadcaster), and key government and community health providers.

The Future

As resources on the Internet grow, migrant communities will have increasing access to resources in their own language that many will be able to access independently; however, for many new and emerging communities this is not always possible. Library staff are encountering new language groups as a result of changing humanitarian migration policies, particularly from Africa, the Middle East, and Southeast Asia. In the second stage of its development, the new myLanguage is concentrating on supporting such groups. This involves providing assistance in creating online resources and the development of solutions to enable languages to be displayed correctly and effectively online. Increasingly, new migrants to Australia are being settled in country areas such as Swan Hill, Shepparton, and Wagga. For all library staff, but particularly those in remote regions working on their own, a tool such as myLanguage connects them to the wider world, where they can tap into resources and ideas for working with new residents, developing services that will support them to settle effectively, and also enrich the life of their towns. The myLanguage resources are freely available globally.

CONCLUSION

Both of the projects described recognize and seek to address the issues that public libraries have in meeting the needs of their multicultural communities. The use of online technology and new, more interactive solutions means that ideas, resources, and programs can be shared freely to benefit not only metropolitan libraries but also those in remote regions or indeed anywhere in the world where the online technology is accessible. Library staff working alone have access to ready-made resources that are free and adaptable. The projects also open the way to new solutions, such as the possibility of libraries helping communities create their own resources and information tools where they don't currently exist.

WORKS CITED

Australian Bureau of Statistics. 2006. New South Wales. Census Expanded Community Profile. Latest issue, February 29, 2008. http://www.censusdata.abs.gov.au.

Library Council of New South Wales. 2005. Annual Report 2004/05. Sydney: State Library of New South Wales.

Chapter Twenty

Developing a Job Help and Computer Skills Program for Recent Immigrants

Nyssa Densley and Heather Ross

PROGRAM CONTEXT

Pima County Public Library, located in Tucson, Arizona, has always served an incredibly diverse population, but within the last few years, we began to notice a significant increase in the number of refugees and immigrants coming into the library. Their arrival created new opportunities—as well as significant challenges—for library staff members wondering how best to serve these individuals. Many refugees spoke languages we didn't know and seemed to have trouble making sense of how the library works, which made it very difficult to help them. At the same time, we knew that they were struggling too, not only to communicate with us but also to find new jobs, learn new skills, and acclimate to a new way of life.

In response, a group of librarians applied for a grant and designed a program to provide assistance to refugees. Free English language classes were already available in the library as the result of a partnership with a local literacy organization. However, we found community polls and other local surveys that showed that refugees considered themselves disadvantaged when it came to searching for jobs and using technology.

With this in mind, we decided to focus on offering computer classes. Possessing computer skills can create self-sufficiency and job opportunities, but we didn't see many places in the community where refugees could go for computer instruction. Consequently, we decided to fill in that service gap by providing individualized computer assistance, classes, and curriculum in several target languages spoken by refugees and immigrants within the community. Our primary goal was to reach out to refugees themselves, and our secondary goal was to create documents that staff could use when working with refugees to make those interactions more productive and positive.

In this chapter, we will describe the program that we offered at the Pima County Public Library and make suggestions about how you might adapt it to suit the needs of refugee customers who visit your library.

PROGRAM IMPLEMENTATION

To begin, we hired part-time multilingual computer assistants who were in high school or college. We specifically recruited people who were able to speak some of the languages spoken by refugees and immigrants in the community (Arabic, French, Kirundi, Somali, Nepali, and Maay Maay) and assigned them to the branches with the highest number of refugees. These computer assistants helped customers with basic computer questions, such as how to sign up to use a computer, how to access the Internet, and how to print documents. They served other key roles as well, such as helping people fill out library card applications and explaining how to borrow library materials. People began coming into the library and requesting these computer assistants by name.

Seeing that the youth computer assistants were so well received, we then applied for a Library Services and Technology Act (LSTA) grant to help us further address some of the needs of refugees and immigrants in our community. We hired multilingual instructors who could translate computer curriculum and library documents and provide in-depth computer instruction in a variety of languages.

As you consider how you can offer services to refugees in your community, think broadly about what your goals are and how you can accomplish them. You might recruit employees who speak particular languages and can run programs and classes for your library, or you might recruit volunteers from a local high school. While high school students may not be able to create or translate curriculum, they can provide other valuable services, including working one-on-one with customers and forming positive relationships with them so that they see the library as a welcoming place.

PROGRAM STRUCTURE

We had two primary goals for our computer instructors: to teach classes and to translate computer curriculum and key library documents, such as library card applications and library orientation pamphlets, so they would be available to both current and future library customers and staff. We asked the instructors to teach classes focused on résumé writing and online job applications, since many new arrivals did not have résumés and had not used a computer to fill out an online application. But shortly after the instructors created curriculum around these topics, we discovered that it needed to be revamped. It didn't take us long to realize that the students' goals for themselves were different from our goals for them.

We had been incorrectly assuming that students wanted to learn about résumés and job applications because those skills were directly linked to employment. However, although a few of the more advanced students were interested in those topics, we hadn't realized that the majority of students first needed to master computer and Internet basics before being ready to work on the more complex tasks. Those students needed plenty of individualized attention. So the instructors changed their approach and made themselves available for drop-in help, understanding that it was best to structure computer classes loosely and in a way that could adapt to a wide variety of student needs. This way, students could come in and get assistance with whatever they wanted, whether it was writing a résumé or learning how to operate a mouse. Making the classes more flexible greatly increased both class turnout and effectiveness.

We also learned to be flexible when it came to allowing young children to be present during these computer classes. For most of our other adult education classes, parents are encouraged to come without their children. However, we found that asking new refugees and immigrants to find a babysitter sometimes meant that they wouldn't be able to come to the program because making alternative child-care plans created such a significant burden for them. Consequently, we decided to make an exception to our usual policy and allow parents to bring their children to the classes.

Be creative about how you accommodate children when you are teaching parents. Since most of our classes were taught in a meeting room on laptop computers, we either allowed the children to use an unoccupied computer, or set up board games or coloring sheets on a nearby table. Other locations with more flexible meeting room space offered a craft time concurrent with the computer classes, or another program designed for children, such as story time.

As you're planning your program, consider the immigrants and refugees you see coming into your library. Ask them questions and make program decisions based on what you learn. What languages do they speak? What, if any, computer skills do they already possess? What kind of assistance would be most helpful to them? What might be the barriers that would prevent them from being able to come to a program that would otherwise appeal to them? Having an understanding of what the need really is, as well as a willingness to adapt your program over time, will ensure that your program is successful.

MATERIALS

We were fortunate to already have mobile laptop labs so that we could hold classes inside a meeting room. This structure allowed for classes that didn't disrupt customers in the computer area and didn't tie up the public computers for extended periods of time. If your library has sufficient funding, a mobile laptop lab will be an investment that pays itself off many times over, though of course you could certainly hold classes without one.

Because we already had the computers, we didn't have to buy much else. We did purchase flash drives so people would be able to save their documents and bring them up on any computer, regardless of whether or not they had access to the Internet. We also purchased bus passes to remove the transportation barrier for people who might find it difficult to come to the library otherwise. We didn't purchase special computer programs, though, instead choosing to rely on free, open-source software. Not only did this plan save us money, but it meant that anyone with Internet access would be able to retrieve the documents they created. It also meant that we didn't run the risk of purchasing software that would quickly become obsolete when something new was developed.

Your program can be as high- or low-budget as you like, as small-scale or grandiose as your personnel allows for. If you have limited resources or only a small community of refugees to serve, you might decide not to teach computer classes but still want to provide some assistance. One possibility is to create handouts that list resources that immigrants and refugees would find useful. These might include lists of websites that have information in the target language or lists of relevant library materials. For instance, people from Nepal often requested "Hindi movies." Because they didn't know how to use the catalog to search for what they wanted, we found that generating a list of the Bollywood titles we carried helped to address their question.

PUBLICITY

When publicizing your programs and services, don't rely exclusively on traditional methods. We used the library's online calendar and posted information in the newspaper, as we would do for any library program. But we understood that many refugees or recent immigrants could not read English. So we made bilingual paper flyers and posted them widely—not just on library bulletin boards but also in places we knew many refugees would visit, such as ethnic grocery stores. We also asked local organizations that work with refugees to disseminate the information to their clients and contacts.

In addition, the instructors we hired spread the word within their communities. Personalized, word-of-mouth invitations were often the best way to encourage people to attend a program because of the sense of welcoming provided by those invitations. Our instructors could also alert us to important cultural information we needed to consider when we planned our programs. They would tell us when the community was celebrating a major holiday or planning a wedding, so we didn't inadvertently schedule a library program for that day. In our Kirundi community, for example, we learned that everybody turns out for a wedding, and if we tried to hold a program that day, no one would attend the program.

FUNDING

We funded our program through an LSTA grant. Depending on the scope of your program, you could solicit funds from your local Friends group or apply for a grant (whether LSTA or otherwise). As one example, Microsoft offers technology and software grants for nonprofits. There are a variety of grant opportunities available, if you're willing to seek them out. Books and databases your library subscribes to may provide you with more information about grants. The Pima County Public Library has a dedicated grants page on their website, which is updated frequently.

Additionally, simply changing your frame of mind when recruiting and hiring new employees can be a beginning. You do not have to create a new position. Our system has a "Computer Instructor" position, but if this position does not exist for you, think about already existing positions. Library associates or even librarians can teach computer classes. When you have current openings, consider recruiting multilingual candidates who could begin teaching classes or translating library handouts.

PARTNERSHIPS

Partnerships can broaden your network, provide more outreach opportunities, create ties with the community, and bring allies to your library. Partnerships can also increase your chances of being awarded grant monies.

Partnerships are critical when developing any programming designed for an immigrant or refugee audience. However, partnerships chosen poorly or in haste can threaten the success of your endeavor. In this section we will discuss strategies for choosing the right partner and offer suggestions for agencies you might want to partner with in your community. Our goal is not to give a comprehensive overview, but rather to share some of the tips and lessons we've learned through our own partnerships.

Your first step is to select an appropriate partner. When trying to decide whether or not a potential partner is a good fit, consider several questions:

• Do our objectives align?

A few years ago, our library system partnered with an organization that provided us with workbooks and curriculum for classes. The curriculum was already created, which was a huge benefit for us. But the organization wanted to collect information contrary to our own privacy and information collection policies. It was a constant tug-of-war to find a compromise that pleased both parties. Before committing to any partnership, make sure that both parties have communicated their expectations clearly.

• Is your contact at the organization authorized to speak and make decisions on behalf of the organization?

This might seem like an obvious question to ask, but we didn't, and it would have saved us some work if we had. One representative of an organization we were working with promised more than the organization could ultimately deliver. This set our project back by several months, although in the end we were able to work together in a reduced fashion.

• How would you rate your interactions with this organization in the past?

Don't let a looming deadline or someone else's opinion talk you into a partnership with an organization with which you don't have a good rapport. How hard was it to contact the community relations coordinator? How quickly did they answer your phone or e-mail inquiries? Clear, consistent communication is vital to an effective partnership, particularly if your project is dependent on the information or assistance that the partner provides.

If you choose carefully, partnerships can be fluid and easy. Depending on your project, there are several national agencies who work with refugees and immigrants who may make good partners. Here are a few we used when developing our computer classes and job help.

• The International Rescue Committee (IRC) is a national organization that plays a large role in refugee resettlement. The IRC has twenty-two regional offices in the United States.

- Tucson has an alliance called the Refugee Integration Service Provider Network (RISP-Net), which brings together disparate organizations who work with refugees, such as the library and the IRC, to create a network serving this population. Check to see if a similar network has been created in your community, or maybe your library could assume a leadership role in developing one.
- Translation agencies can assist with translation projects, particularly if the language is not spoken by anyone within the library system. When it came time to translate library resources into our target languages, we tried to rely on people we had hired, but that left out a lot of languages. At this point we turned to a small, community-oriented translation agency that specialized in serving refugee populations.

IDENTIFYING AND ACKNOWLEDGING YOUR COMMUNITY'S LANGUAGE NEEDS

Take the time to identify who lives in your community and which languages they speak. If you're hiring a translator and creating computer curriculum in another language, be sure you're not translating for a largely oral language, like Maay Maay. Many immigrants from African countries speak several languages, but may be more comfortable using one language or another. We have immigrants from Burundi who speak Kirundi, Swahili, French, and Kinyarwanda, but when it comes to technical language and learning new skills, they are most comfortable with Kirundi. Getting to know your community will help you identify these differences.

We also began purchasing dictionaries to augment our classes. There are a few things to keep in mind when evaluating a dictionary:

- Is the dictionary one-way or two-way? A dictionary that is only English into another language will not be helpful to someone who cannot speak English.
- Is the dictionary directed at an English speaker learning a foreign language? Or is it for a second language speaker learning English? The dynamics of the book and the way it is organized will greatly differ. For an example, see the next point.
- Is the dictionary published in an English alphabet or another script? There are many Nepali dictionaries published for English speakers learning Nepali, in which everything is in the English alphabet. To be truly useful for a Nepali speaker learning English, the dictionary needs to be in the Devanagari script. Similarly, Arabic speakers benefit from dictionaries written in an Arabic script.

- Does the language have a written equivalent? If the language is primarily an oral one, there is little use trying to find a dictionary. Don't frustrate yourself searching for a dictionary that just doesn't exist.

Searching for one of these more specialized dictionaries can be tricky. Here are two methods we used to acquire dictionaries that may prove useful to you, too.

- Start with your distributor. Though it can sometimes be difficult to find a dictionary in your distributor's databases, with some creative searching, it can be done. We discovered that starting a more general search using Google or Amazon allowed us to experiment with different spellings and come up with titles and ISBNs for in-print dictionaries. We were then able to transfer those ISBNs into our distributor's database and purchase the titles. Using this method, we located dictionaries in Amharic, Tigrigna, Turkish, and Marshallese.
- The Marston Memorial Historical Center has free print-on-demand dictionaries for Kirundi-English.

CONCLUSION

Using all the elements discussed above, we created a significant program that, two years after the official grant period ended, is still having a positive impact on refugees and immigrants in our community. We hired multilingual computer assistants to aid customers, and as those computer assistants graduate from school and move on to other jobs, we continue to replace them with computer assistants who have the ability to speak multiple languages. We hired multilingual instructors to teach computer skills and job-hunting skills in three branches, in addition to translating library documents and computer curriculum that were made available to the entire library system. After the grant ended, we were able to hire some of these instructors as permanent staff members because our administration recognized the valuable, unique service they provide to the community. We promoted our program using nontraditional outreach methods and built new community partnerships. We also expanded our foreign language dictionary selection to better reflect our new populations and to better serve this new community using our libraries. As a result of these efforts, staff began to feel more confident about serving these new populations, which in turn led to refugees and immigrants seeing the library as a more welcoming place.

We hope our program has given you groundwork to build a similar program at your library and has offered inspiration for new ways to serve your new communities.

Chapter Twenty-One

Opening the World

Creating a Multilingual DVD to Introduce Library
Services to Refugees and Immigrants

Judy Anghelescu

Individuals who have little or no English-speaking skills and are from less developed countries often have difficulty understanding what a free lending library is, let alone how to use a library and what the terminology means. So how do we get the concept of libraries and their essential services across? That was the question Omaha Public Library attempted to answer by creating a "Welcome to the Library" DVD (subtitles and voiceover in Arabic, Sudanese-Nuer, Karen, Spanish, Swahili, and Somali), which has visual representations of the borrowing concept (for preliterate viewers), introduces common library words, and explains library cards and services in simple terms.

Omaha is home to many immigrants, including a large Spanish-speaking population as well as Sudanese, Somali, and Burmese newcomers. Each year the library staffs a table at World Refugee Day. Over fifteen hundred members of the community attend this annual event, which includes first-person education panels, festive music and dance, naturalization ceremonies, and food. We recognized the need for a basic video about what a library has to offer—in the languages of those new to Omaha—while handing out library brochures in English to those did not speak English.

Libraries are an essential component of the Omaha community and its non-English-speaking members. We have bilingual books and story times, events for teens, ELS resources for all ages, Tutor.com for homework help, Learning Express for citizenship exam prep, free computers and meeting rooms, and a warm, neutral place, open to all. The best way to learn about what a library has to offer is through library tours. Librarians are always willing to give tours. However, with those who do not speak English, such tours are easier said than done because of the need for translators. None of our library staff can speak Somali, Karen, Swahili, or Sudanese, the languages of Omaha's underserved populations. On the new DVD, the library tour comes to them comfortably in their own language.

OUR STEPS

We decided to create a simple video that introduces the library as vital to a new start in America. Our first steps were to seek out partners and identify our target audience. We asked what local organizations had a vested interest and in what way. Lutheran Family Services (LFS), a refugee resettlement agency, was our main source of information and guidance. Dedicated to meeting incoming families at the airport and coordinating the housing, medical, and educational needs of the refugees, this organization was both an obvious choice and an indispensable partner. LFS put us in contact with possible translators, told us which languages are written rather than spoken, located ethnic volunteers to serve as extras in the video, and wrote a letter of support for our grant. Another invaluable partner was Omaha Public Schools (OPS). They organize the annual World Refugee Day and provide the Yates Community Program, whose mission is to teach refugees and immigrants skills to live in Omaha.

Omaha is home to a significant Spanish-speaking population, fifteen hundred Somali, and two thousand Burmese refugees, with significant additional monthly arrivals. The Omaha Refugee Task Force meeting is bimonthly. This includes state and government representatives; members of the housing, health and human services, and employment agencies based in Nebraska who contribute to refugee resettlement efforts; and local leaders of the Somali, Sudanese, and Karen communities. Attendance here increased our awareness of the new cultures coming into Omaha, so identifying our target audience was simple. We knew illiterate and preliterate individuals, along with those with learning disabilities, would benefit from a simple, descriptive video. However, to truly define our focus, we turned to our partners LFS and OPS. They provided crucial information on the learning styles, habits, needs, limitations, and lifestyles of the Somali, Sudanese, and Karen culture.

Next, obtaining the funding was paramount. To estimate how much we would need, we asked LFS and OPS to provide a rough estimate of per-hour translator fees and began searching online for a local production company. We applied for a $20,000 Library Improvement Grant through the Nebraska Library Commission and got it! The Friends of the Omaha Public Library offered a 10 percent cash match also. We chose Videobuzz Productions, which had done some work for the Omaha Convention Center; they quoted us $14,800. They frequently work with Grubb Studios for any audio needs, so that was one less company for which we needed to search. Our costs were four translators for $2,000, a professional narrator for $280, and advertising and food/craft supplies for a related event totaling $1,100. With the remaining money, we purchased *Welcome to the U.S.* guidebooks for refugees in their languages from the Center of Applied Linguistics.

The most fun yet time-consuming steps were developing the storyboard and script. It is very important to share your vision and goals of the DVD with the production company. The best source of knowledge on what your library has to offer is you. The production company you hire may not have been in a library for years. The decisions made on what will be described in this DVD are important; it is the one shot you have to show what you have got. If you are in a multibranch library system, which libraries will you film? Will it be the library that is closest to the underserved population you are trying to target or a library that is most conducive to filming? Which exteriors and interiors will look best? If you shoot on a day the library is closed, will the AC/heat be on?

CONTENT CREATION AND TECHNICAL DETAILS

To create the storyboard, we used one PowerPoint page for every screenshot. Each screenshot depicted what would be happening in that scene, what animations or text were to be shown in the finished product, and the dialogue, props, and people that would be in it. We had to determine what we wanted to highlight in each scene. We placed props such as ESL and citizenship materials, foreign language titles, and flyers advertising other library programs and services wherever possible in scenes. It is important that each shot count. To gain the interest of the population you are trying to reach, place books and music CDs of interest to them on circulation desks during shots and on display as someone walks through a scene. In addition, have plenty of props on hand for those last-minute shots. Also, make sure to budget for lunch and have plenty of water on hand for down time.

The storyboard also depicted what age groups were to be shown in each scene and what library services and areas would be shown: book clubs, teens playing games, story times, people using the book return, signage, shots of damaged materials, staff members, and extras. Keep in mind that the storyboard and subsequent video shoot is a work in progress. What looks good on paper as a scene may need to be changed once the video director gets involved. As an expert, he or she sees things in a different way based on lighting, space, and dynamic elements, so be flexible enough to change things at the last minute. If you want representatives of the underserved population and library staff or family members in the video, provide plenty of notice when putting out your "casting call." For the refugees, we asked Omaha Public Schools for volunteers of various ages willing to come dressed in their ethnic clothing, and we provided transportation when needed. Have volunteers who are willing to be "on call," in case the director needs more people during spontaneous shots.

When writing the script, make sure to use natural language that staff would truly say during library interactions. Again, what looks good on paper may not be smooth verbally to those who have speaking lines. Working with the translators and the script took the longest time and was the most challenging part of the project. After obtaining names of people who spoke Sudanese-Nuer, Swahili, Somali, Karen, and Arabic, we e-mailed the script so they could become familiar with it, since they would be translating it in a studio. We assumed they had looked it over before arriving at the studio, but one translator had not. Studio time booked for two days became four. Once the script has been approved, send it out to the cast, especially the translators, as soon as possible.

To keep the project on schedule, have a person-to-person meeting with each translator to go over the script to ensure it has been translated beforehand. Since so much of the language and concepts (such as time, months, and dates) do not translate into the intended language easily, this caused a lot of extra studio time. I had to explain what the line meant to the translator for her to come up with something similar. For example, in English the script said, "A big part of the Omaha Public Library is the friendly librarians that work here. They all wear name tags and are happy to help you with any questions you may have." However, in Somali, there is no such word or concept as "name tag" so the closest translation used was "If you are worried about anything or happy about anything, they will answer questions for you." To minimize stress and costs to the translators, offer to transport them to the audio studio and film locations.

Number each line of the script. This lets the audio engineer know when to start and stop the tape. It lets the video director know which translated line of text to copy and paste for each shot in the final edits. Since none of us knew these languages, we had to trust that what the translator transposed was the correct line and that it was said smoothly. The audio engineer would hear stutters and what he thought may have sounded funny. Unsure of whether it was just a guttural part of the language, he finally resorted to just asking the translator if that was a good "take" or not. In most cases, it was not, and they were glad to do it repeatedly until they felt they got it right.

Our translators definitely worked the hardest. Not only did they have to work with the audio version of the script, they also had to work with the written one as well. In order for the director to know when the sentences ended in each of the languages for proper subtitle placement on the screen, we had to e-mail the translators constantly for months with requests to make appropriate spaces in the written sentences. The video and audio companies certainly had their challenges too. Arabic text reads right to left instead of left to right. Specific language computer fonts needed to be downloaded, copied, and pasted to place subtitles on the slides. With each language, they had to try to place the translations in the correct place in the video without knowing the language. And because the written text is much longer in some of the languages, each video version is a different length! Ensure that the video and audio director know that this is a possibility.

MARKETING THE PROJECT

The "Welcome to the Library" video is available on YouTube (http://www.youtube.com/watch?v=bCzCbYz6Vd0) and from the link to the Immigrant/Refugee Libguide located on Omaha Public Library's website (http://www.omahapubliclibrary.org)—with the intention that it can be used by libraries everywhere. Although it highlights Omaha Public Library, the concepts are the same and much of it is transferrable to all libraries. Originally, 250 copies of the DVD were made. Twelve were cataloged and placed in our library branches, either on displays or in the foreign language sections on the shelves. The DVD was shown to the forty-odd members of the Omaha Refugee Task Force Meeting in January 2010. One hundred copies of the DVD were taken to this meeting. Twenty copies of the DVD were requested from foreign language professors at UNO for use with their students and in orientations. Library staff had requested additional copies of the DVD to hand out to Sudanese and Somali families when they visit the library branches, resulting in the need to get fifty more copies made. All library branches promoted the DVD in displays and regularly mentioned it when foreign language speakers visit the library. Omaha Public Schools pledged to disseminate information on the DVD in their schools.

We promoted the DVD in a TV spot on Omaha's "Morning Blend" show, placed ads in the local Spanish newspaper, and distributed flyers, posters, and handouts to our twelve branches. We also e-mailed a press release to all Omaha area media and promoted it on the library website, social media, and in the Omaha Library Foundation spring newsletter, using a QR code. In March 2011, the library held a multicultural "Welcome to the Library" movie premiere. The event included a continuous showing of the DVD in all of the languages, Arabic and African food from two local restaurants, and a mariachi performance and a Mexican folkloric dance performance coordinated through the Mexican Cultural Arts Association. We also had bilingual story times, a make-and-take craft table in which participants made a door sign that said "Welcome" in many languages, a teen gaming area, and displays of ESL materials, foreign language books, and ethnic cookbooks. Upon request, two publishers provided sixty bilingual books at no cost to us that were given away free to all who attended the event. Invitations to this event were designed, printed, and sent to the library's Friends, foundation boards, and the mayor's staff. This event, lasting three hours, was opened by the mayor, staffed with six staff members and ten volunteers, and had an attendance of 341.

In a collaborative discussion with Omaha Public Schools in the planning of World Refugee Day, it was decided that it would be beneficial to have something for the refugees to learn, instead of only American attendees learning about refugees as is typical practice. Because of the high concentration of refugees performing/attending, selling their wares, and celebrating their culture, this is the ideal venue to reach this underserved Omaha population. In the past, we have staffed a library outreach booth issuing library cards, promoting ESL materials, Mango Languages, and the Learning Express database. Education panels typically involve refugees sharing their stories to the public. However, at World Refugee Day in 2011, we held an education panel in which we played the "Welcome to the Library" DVD throughout the day in an effort to promote the library.

It was a huge success! Sixty-five DVDs were taken home. Over two hundred refugees either came into the library on their own or were brought inside in groups led by an interpreter. They expressed surprise at hearing their language being spoken on the DVD and sat in rapt attention learning about the library and services. Many teens wandered in and expressed "This is in my language!" and proceeded to collect their families and friends to come in to watch. A Russian-born U.S. citizen approached me with a family of three from Burma who had only been in the United States for two weeks. As their sponsor, she confessed that this was their first event outside of their new apartment and that she could relate to their culture shock. She eagerly took a copy of the DVD and asked for advice on how to get her sponsored family acclimated to the United States to draw them out of their shyness.

Because of the partnerships created through this DVD project, I was able to connect her with someone from Lutheran Family Services and introduce her sponsored family to a young man who was in the DVD. Sitting there in the library with the DVD playing in the background, Thu Soe, one of the extras in the movie, was able to tell the family about a church they could attend and an upcoming Karen celebration. He even translated a question the Russian-born sponsor had: "Has their apartment freezer been fixed yet?" Listening to this conversation, I realized how important such connections are in making daily life bearable for newcomers to the United States.

COMMUNITY IMPACT AND EVALUATION

We evaluated the success of this project mainly through visit counts to You-Tube and the Immigrant/Refugee Libguide available on the footer of our library's website, along with verbal and written feedback. Omaha Public Schools is utilizing the "Welcome to the Library" DVD during their refugee and migrant education class; the International Center for the Heartland (ICH) has one hundred copies of the DVD in their office and has included it as part of their orientation to incoming refugees. The ICH has stated that the DVD project "is significant to our community because it expands upon the existing resources available to resettled refugees, secondary migrants, and immigrants." ICH serves as a "one-stop" service in which the DVD is included as a tool to introduce newcomers to Omaha and the community.

We also measured our success based on feedback from our partners. The Education and Employment Specialist for Lutheran Refugee Services had this to say about the "Welcome to the Library" DVD: "The video was great because it was so elementary and took nothing for granted about the level of knowledge among our clients. I really liked the pauses for key words, too!" Lutheran Family Services sent the following e-mail in June 2011:

> As a result of the distribution of the video in the community, more refugees are getting library cards. Whereas before I never heard of a refugee with a library card, I've heard of three refugees with library cards within the last two months! I don't think they really knew about it before, but now people are accessing the library. Since word-of-mouth really spreads fast, I expect that you'll see many refugees at the library.

By increasing our awareness and outreach to specific groups of immigrants/ refugees moving into our neighborhoods and to the underserved populations already here, we are improving our library service to each segment of the Omaha community. The project has continuously impacted the target population as they arrive at refugee resettlement agencies and are given a "tour" of the library. Personal library tours with refugees can be enhanced by sending the DVD home with each patron to share with his or her community. One concept within Omaha Public Library's new strategic plan is developing our long reach in order to discover organizations and help them resolve underlying issues in Omaha. This project allowed us to form a strong strategic alliance, introducing the library as a catalyst and collaborator toward creating a better Omaha. A person's chances of finding work and learning about a new community and available resources are vastly improved with the help of a public library. Once a comfort level with library staff and concepts has been attained, dialogue can be exchanged about common interests, friendships will be forged, and we will be able to culturally customize our programs, personalize our marketing, and enhance collections to meet the unique needs of this group.

Chapter Twenty-Two

Virtual Services to Latinos and Spanish Speakers

Audrey Barbakoff and Kristina Gomez

Effective virtual services are a crucial component to serving the recreation, education, and information needs of individuals and present an exciting opportunity for libraries to engage Latinos online. Virtual services can be defined as the way libraries connect with the public in an online environment; they can include websites, library catalogs, virtual reference, social media sites, and mobile applications. With Spanish being by far the most supported non-English language in public libraries today and Hispanics representing the largest and fastest-growing demographic in the United States, this is an important time for libraries to develop a comprehensive approach to virtual services for Latinos. Virtual services for Latinos can be seen as part of a larger commitment by libraries to ensure equal access to information for all patrons, regardless of language needs. What are some key differences in the way Latinos access and utilize online information, and what strategies can libraries use to develop virtual services? This chapter will describe the ways libraries can address the information needs of Latinos through three virtual services: web content, mobile library applications, and virtual reference service.

DEMOGRAPHIC OVERVIEW

As with any population, we need a fuller demographic picture of Hispanics and Latinos in the United States in order to understand how to approach their information needs. Who are the Hispanic and Latino populations that we serve?

Because much of our demographic information comes from the U.S. Census, we will use the definition of Hispanic or Latino employed by the Census and developed by the Office of Management and Budget's 1997 "Revisions to the Standards for the Classification of Federal Data on Race and Ethnicity." Respondents are asked to self-identify as Hispanic/Latino based on "the heritage, nationality group, lineage, or country of birth of the person or the person's parents or ancestors before their arrival in the United States. People who identify their origin as Hispanic, Latino, or Spanish may be any race" (Ennis, Ríos-Vargas, and Albert 2011).

In our increasingly diverse country, it is not unexpected to find that a growing portion of our population is now Hispanic. Sixteen percent of the U.S. population (50.5 million people) identify as Hispanic or Latino (Ennis, Ríos-Vargas, and Albert 2011). Nearly 40 percent are second- or third-generation Americans (Fox and Livingston 2007). Increases in the Hispanic population accounted for more than half of the country's population growth between 2000 and 2010.

Because of the geographic, linguistic, and cultural diversity of Latinos, each community may have very different needs. Understanding your local culture is critical to developing relevant and meaningful services. Begin your local research by finding the census statistics for your own region on the U.S. Census Bureau's American FactFinder website. No matter where our libraries are located, we would be deeply negligent not to consider the information needs and information-seeking behaviors of this rapidly growing group.

BEYOND "EN ESPAÑOL": DEVELOPING EFFECTIVE AND ENGAGING LIBRARY WEBSITES FOR LATINOS

Library websites often function as a first point of virtual contact for English- and Spanish-speaking patrons and as such serve as an essential component of effective virtual services to Latinos. By providing access to library hours and events, materials, reference assistance, recommended resources and even community connections, library websites have truly become "virtual branches," replicating the services provided by physical locations in an online environment. The most visible way libraries appeal to Latinos online is through Spanish language or bilingual (Spanish-English) versions of their website. Quality Spanish and bilingual library web content is the first step in any effort to provide access to electronic resources to Latinos. However, there is more to creating an engaging and inviting user experience than providing web pages with direct Spanish translations of library content.

Moving beyond translating content into Spanish, we must consider cultural values and expectations in order to effectively engage current and potential Latino patrons.

Latinos Online

The number of Latinos online is rapidly growing. A Pew Internet study shows that Internet usage by Latino adults rose from 54 to 64 percent from 2006 to 2008 and that this group constitutes the fastest-growing online population (Livingston, Parker, and Fox 2009). Market research shows the current Latino online population is characterized as being between eighteen and thirty-four years old and is "more affluent, more educated and more acculturated than the aggregate Hispanic population" (Captura Group 2008). Using research on expectations, preferences and behaviors of Hispanics online, libraries can design web content to address the information needs of and appeal to the online Latino population.

Language Preference

The first step for libraries committed to addressing the linguistic needs and preferences of Latino patrons is to create and provide access to bilingual and Spanish library information online. This can be accomplished through staff language skills, community connections, or paid translation services. Latinos have a range of language skills. Slightly more than half of all U.S. Hispanics are English-only or bilingual; 47 percent are Spanish dominant (Fox and Livingston 2007). Research by companies such as ComScore and AOL shows that 50 percent of Latinos online "prefer Spanish content or both Spanish and English content" (Singh, Baack, Kundu, and Hurtado 2008, 164).

Because Spanish speakers have diverse cultural backgrounds, language preferences can vary. Libraries should create their bilingual and Spanish language text based on the customs of Latinos in their service area. This can be done by using vernaculars of the predominant Latino group in the library service population. However, we should be mindful of informal or too familiar language. A study on Hispanic online consumer expectations shows the importance of proper forms of greeting and politeness in web content. It is important for the library to address Hispanic patrons with respect in virtual communication. This would include using the formal *usted*, steering clear of overly informal phrases (such as "¿Qué tal?"), and ensuring that Spanish language pages have just as much content as their English counterparts (Singh, Baack, Kundu, and Hurtado 2008).

Celebrating Culture and Connecting Community

Cultural relevancy defines Internet usage for Latinos, and incorporating cultural elements and symbols to which Latinos feel connected makes for an inviting online user experience (Korzenny and Korzenny 2005). It is important that web content not depict Hispanic stereotypes but reflect the diversity of the Latino community by including images of Latinos with various skin tones, ages, and backgrounds. E-commerce marketing research shows that Latinos prefer bright, vibrant colors because they convey a sense of cheerfulness (Singh, Baack, Kundu, and Hurtado 2008). These visual preferences are easy to implement in an online environment.

Latinos value community and tend to engage with institutions that demonstrate their commitment to serving the Latino community. Libraries should highlight their community connections online with Spanish or bilingual events calendars, information on outreach activities, community partnerships, patron testimonials, or profiles from local community leaders who are vocal supporters of the library. Libraries can also serve as a connector of virtual communities by providing space online for Latinos to connect with others. This could take the shape of social media connections, library blogs, or patron book reviews in Spanish.

Family Orientation

Strong family orientation is one of the cultural values libraries can address through adapted web content. It is important to recognize that in this context the term *family* includes grandparents, aunts, uncles, and cousins. Libraries can create family-centered web pages by aggregating library information and services for all age groups on a single Spanish or bilingual page. A focus group participant in a study on Hispanic expectations and attitudes toward online information highlighted the importance of family-focused web content: "Don't just have the web site for kids, teenagers, or parents, make it for the whole family. Have something for every family member" (Singh, Baack, Kundu, and Hurtado 2008, 168). For libraries unable to offer a complete Spanish version of all English content, this aggregation into a single, easy-to-locate page becomes even more important to provide easier access to library information.

In addition to a strong family orientation, we know that children in homes with foreign-born parents may serve as "gatekeepers of the Internet," serving as the primary web searcher in the household and making determinations on what information is relevant or of value for themselves and parents (Singh, Baack, Kundu, and Hurtado 2008, 168). For this reason we need to be mindful of creating Spanish and bilingual web pages that are both family focused and kid friendly. Highlight family and multigenerational programming and create an inviting online environment by including images of extended families and especially images of grandparents, which have been shown to evoke feelings of respect and caring.

Content Is Crucial

Promoting the quality information available through our subscription databases, subject guides, and resource lists has always been a priority for libraries. This digital content should also be available to the Latino community in their language of preference. Products such as EBSCOhost Español, with its Spanish language interface and article translation functionality; Informe from Gale; and standby reference favorites such as Britannica's Spanish Reference Center are a key component of providing equal access to information for all patrons. For libraries with little to no budget to purchase access to these products, developing a comprehensive resource list of free Spanish language websites is essential. A Spanish language resource list should contain links to consumer health information, social service agencies, government information, and news sources. Be sure to provide descriptions of these resources in Spanish and make them easily accessible from the library's homepage.

Developing dynamic and relevant web content is an important part of providing meaningful access to library resources, but its impact will be enhanced when it is complemented by other virtual services. How can mobile technology engage Hispanic and Latino users beyond the standard website?

MOBILE TECHNOLOGY

Mobile technology is key to providing successful virtual services to a particular portion of the Hispanic population. Studies and news reports have been rife with headlines about Hispanics' heavy usage of mobile technology for several years. To engage Latinos, libraries must increase the amount of mobile content we provide and tailor it to the cultural preferences of Hispanics. However, we must also recognize that mobile services reach only a portion of this diverse group. Hispanic users of mobile content are predominantly young, native-born, and English-speaking. We should tailor our mobile services to appeal to this demographic, while also seeking ways to reach the older, immigrant, and Spanish-speaking members of our communities.

Hispanics Are Mobile Users—and Often Mobile Users Only

Latinos, especially young, native-born English speakers, use their cell phones far more heavily than their non-Hispanic white counterparts. Fifty-one percent of Hispanics use their cell phones to access the Internet, as opposed to 33 percent of non-Hispanic whites (Washington 2011). They make more calls, send more text messages, and are twice as likely to engage in text messaging campaigns. They use more features and data functions on their phones than the general population (Chang 2009; Mata 2011). Fifty-nine percent of Hispanics consider cell phones a necessity, as opposed to fewer than half of non-Hispanic whites and blacks (Fox and Livingston 2007).

This heavy usage may exist because a cell phone is the primary or only access point to the Internet for many Latinos (Chang 2009). Less than one-third of Latino adults have access to broadband Internet at home and 6 percent report accessing the Internet from a cell phone in lieu of a home Internet connection (Fox and Livingston 2007; Livingston 2011). Commercial advertising campaigns directed at Latinos that use mobile technology have been highly successful and are proliferating rapidly (Chang 2009). Libraries should draw on the research, experience, and success of advertisers and marketers to create high-interest, culturally relevant mobile platforms for young, English-speaking Latinos.

Building a Latino-Centric Mobile App

Once we have committed to introducing mobile apps for our library, how can we design them to appeal to Latinos? Studies by advertising agencies reveal two major factors: interactive or media features and culturally relevant content that clearly targets Latinos.

Hispanic mobile-data users are three times more likely to download videos than non-Hispanics (Ruiz-Velasco 2007). They are also more engaged in streaming or downloading music, playing online games, searching for books and movies, and sampling video and audio clips (Pew Internet 2001). Advertising agencies have addressed these preferences in a variety of ways that libraries can imitate. Telemundo allows fans to post video comments. The Publias Groupe, a multicultural media agency, has driven urban bilingual traffic to a company's site by offering downloadable ringtones, wallpaper, music, and even cocktail recipes (Ruiz-Velasco 2007). MundoYaris.com allowed users to mix music to create their own ringtones (Wentz 2007). Approaches like these are highly consistent with libraries' efforts to integrate more media and interactivity into our web presences, making the physical and digital library a place for content creation. Building interactive, high-interest, creatively empowered applications will be immensely valuable (and enjoyable!) for our Latino users and for the library.

Our content must also be culturally relevant to Hispanics. Surface changes, like featuring Hispanic people and bilingual content, are a start. "Hispanics are curious and interested about messages directed specifically to them and from a source they recognize," according to Felipe Korzenny, professor and director of the Center for Hispanic Marketing Communication at Florida State University (Chang 2009). However, to be truly impactful, our efforts must also align with the deeper values held by this set of users. The Hispanic Institute writes that Hispanic culture depends deeply on "strong, extensive social relationships" (Mata 2011). It surmises that the popularity of mobile technology itself is a manifestation of this value, that "the use of cell phones builds upon the cultural affinity for close connections" (Mata 2011). Libraries must integrate social components into our Hispanic-targeted apps to be successful. We should also be cognizant of mobile technology limitations. It reaches predominantly younger, native-born English speakers and is not ideal for in-depth tasks. Therefore, we must also consider other forms of virtual outreach, such as Spanish virtual reference service to Hispanics.

VIRTUAL REFERENCE

Virtual reference in Spanish is a small but expanding service. While research on its effectiveness is limited so far, librarians are sharing anecdotal knowledge about their experiences (Shapiro 2003). In the same vein, we will share some of our own experience in helping to plan a Spanish-language chat service for the state of Wisconsin. We hope this will build the confidence of other librarians considering implementing Spanish virtual reference.

Virtual Reference Is Feasible for You

Even if your library is small and lacks resources, you can find ways to offer Spanish-language reference. Finding sufficient bilingual staff with reference training is a challenge, but not an insurmountable one. Only 1.8% of the library workforce is Latino (Montiel-Overall and Littletree 2010). Of course, some non-Hispanic librarians are Spanish-fluent, but it is still very probable that there are few or no qualified candidates at your library. At many smaller libraries in Wisconsin, there were no Spanish-speaking reference staff at all. However, we were able to find one of many possible solutions.

Work Together

At Milwaukee Public Library, we already used QuestionPoint for English-language VR. When we chose to add Spanish, we did so as a state. If the state as a whole put in a certain number of hours, every library in Wisconsin would have access to 24/7 Spanish chat. This allowed libraries that did have Spanish-speaking librarians and available staff time to work together to support service for the entire state. Since small communities serve a large portion of Spanish-speakers in America (Davis 2009), this arrangement is one way a small library can provide a significant Spanish-language service without impossible demands on its resources or staff. Consider approaching your department of public instruction, your state library association, or a coalition of libraries to see if you can pool your financial and human resources.

Build an Audience Offline

Once you have arranged some way to provide virtual reference, building interest in the service is key. Only 32 percent of Spanish-dominant Latinos use the Internet (Fox and Livingston 2007), so libraries must build our audience offline as well as online. A successful campaign will involve reaching out to organizations, media, and people with strong ties to the local Hispanic community. Although Milwaukee's service has not made it into the widespread advertising phase at this time, we have begun to brainstorm contacts in our community. Who are the Spanish-speaking advocacy groups, churches, newspapers, clubs, and community leaders in your service area?

Take a Long-Term View

Finally, set reasonable expectations. Because of the many barriers—age, education, and access, for example—that often prevent Spanish-dominant Latinos from using the Internet at all, your audience may be limited. However, this service can still be of significant benefit to your community. Providing Spanish-language reference is a powerful tool to convey your library's commitment to serving Hispanics, which may draw Latino users to engage with the library in a variety of ways. Furthermore, a major barrier to library use of any kind is the lack of language-appropriate material and staff (Montiel-Overall and Littletree 2010). We need to give our users time to realize that we serve our Spanish speakers and become comfortable with those services.

Also, the popularity of Spanish-language computer classes (Davis 2009) implies that the lack of Spanish-dominant Internet use may be due to lack of knowledge, not lack of interest. As we help our Spanish-speaking population become more educated about technology, and as we increase our Spanish-language resources, Spanish virtual reference is poised to become an essential element of library services.

CONCLUSION

Virtual services present significant opportunities for libraries to connect with patrons in new and exciting ways. Armed with an awareness of the specific needs and expectations of Latinos and Spanish speakers, you will be ready to develop virtual services that speak to this underserved population and show a commitment to not only increasing the number of Latino and Spanish speakers reached, but to providing meaningful and equitable access to library services to Latino patrons.

WORKS CITED

Captura Group. 2008. *Hispanic Online Market.* http://capturagroup.com/hispanic-online-market.html (accessed January 15, 2012).

Chang, Rita. 2009. "Mobile Marketers Target Receptive Hispanic Audience." *Advertising Age*, January 26, 18.

Davis, Denise. 2009. "Outreach to Non-English Speakers in U.S. Public Libraries: Summary of a 2007 Study." *Public Libraries*, January–February, 13–19.

Ennis, Sharon, Merarys Ríos-Vargas, and Nora G. Albert. 2011. "The Hispanic Population: 2010." *2011 Census Briefs*, May 2011. http://www.census.gov/prod/cen2010/briefs/c2010br-04.pdf (accessed January 26, 2012).

Fox, Susannah, and Gretchen Livingston. 2007. *Latinos Online*, March 14. http://www.pewinternet.org/Reports/2007/Latinos-Online.aspx (accessed January 26, 2012).

Korzenny, Felipe, and Betty Ann Korzenny. 2005. *Hispanic Marketing: A Cultural Perspective.* Burlington, MA: Elsevier/Butterworth-Heinemann.

Livingston, Gretchen. 2011. *Latinos and Digital Technology, 2010.* Pew Hispanic Center. http://www.pewhispanic.org/2011/02/09/latinos-and-digital-technology-2010 (accessed January 26, 2012).

Livingston, Gretchen, Kim Parker, and Susannah Fox. 2009. *Latinos Online, 2006–2008: Narrowing the Gap.* Pew Research Center. http://www.pewhispanic.org/2009/12/22/latinos-online-2006-2008-narrowing-the-gap/ (accessed January 26, 2012).

Mata, Arnoldo. 2011. "Connected Hispanics and Civic Engagement." The Hispanic Institute. http://thehispanicinstitute.net/files/u2/Connected_Hispanics_and_Civic_Engagement_3_.pdf (accessed January 26, 2012).

Montiel-Overall, Patricia, and Sandra Littletree. 2010. "Knowledge River: A Case Study of a Library and Information Science Program Focusing on Latino and Native American Perspectives." *Library Trends* 59(1–2): 67–87.

Office of Management and Budget. 1997. "Revisions to the Standards for the Classification of Federal Data on Race and Ethnicity." *Federal Register Notice*, October 30. http://www.whitehouse.gov/omb/fedreg_1997standards (accessed January 26, 2012).

Pew Internet. 2001. "50% of Hispanic Adults Now Are Online." Pew Internet and American Life Project, July 25. http://www.pewinternet.org/Press-Releases/2001/50-of-Hispanic-Adults-Now-are-Online.aspx (accessed January 26, 2012).

Ruiz-Velasco, Laura Martinez. 2007. "Mobile Video Booms among Latinos." *Advertising Age*, April 23, S5. http://elibrary.bigchalk.com (accessed January 26, 2012).

Shapiro, Michael. 2003. "Developing Virtual Spanish-Language Resources: Exploring a Best Practices Model for Public Libraries." *Oregon Library Association Quarterly* 9(2): 15–19.

Singh, Nitish, Daniel Baack, Arun Pereira, and Donald Baack. 2008. "Culturally Customizing Websites for U.S. Hispanic Online Consumers." *Journal of Advertising Research*, June, 224–34.

Singh, Nitish, Daniel Baack, Sumit Kundu, and Christopher Hurtado. 2008. "U.S. Hispanic Consumer e-Commerce Preferences: Expectations and Attitudes toward Web Content." *Journal of Electronic Commerce Research* 9(2): 162–75.

Washington, Jesse. 2011. "For Minorities, New 'Digital Divide' Seen." *USA Today*, January 10. http://www.usatoday.com/tech/news/2011-01-10-minorities-online_N.htm (accessed January 26, 2012).

Wentz, Laurel. 2007. "Conill Connects Cultures via Feelings That Resonate." *Advertising Age*, January 8, S9. http://elibrary.bigchalk.com (accessed January 26, 2012).

Chapter Twenty-Three

Web-Based Language Technologies

Frans Albarillo

What are web-based language technologies, and why are they important to librarians? I hope to answer this question in this chapter. This chapter will help librarians use freely available web-based language tools to personalize content and user experience for nonnative speakers of English. These tools and strategies may be readily applied in academic libraries that serve international student populations. They can also be applied to a public library setting, particularly when the library serves a large multicultural population base.

My intention is not to give an exhaustive overview but to address the gap in the library literature that exists when it comes to multilingual approaches to multicultural librarianship. By multilingual approaches, I mean the application of language tools and staffing to better improve service to people whose first language is not English. Increasingly, there are more patrons of this background. Treating other languages as relevant in today's information environment takes us closer to the notion of deep diversity, defined as a space where "minority values, ideas, and beliefs, are regarded as highly as those of the majority" (Kyrillidou et al. 2009, 7). My own training includes graduate work in linguistics in addition to my library science degree, so my interest in language, culture, and libraries comes from working in the fusion of my own professional and academic experiences in institutions with large international student and immigrant populations.

WEB-BASED LANGUAGE TOOLS

A wide variety of online language tools are available. I use the term "web-based language technologies" to refer to a wide variety of online resources that are meant to help individuals who are interested in language learning, individuals who need to access information in other languages, and language communities. Language learning resources include websites with grammars and dictionaries. These resources can be of varying quality and are often created by university language departments, book publishers, grammar aficionados, and teachers. This chapter focuses mostly on individuals who need to access information in other languages, so the emphasis is on tools that include machine translators (computer programs that translate from one language to another) and virtual keyboards. There are many machine translators and virtual keyboards available, but I believe i2Type and Google Translate outshine them all. Language support software is also important. Other tools come in the form of printer drivers and "language packs" for printers and operating systems.

i2TYPE

i2Type is a free virtual web keyboard that allows users to type in many languages. i2Type is useful in the following ways: it enhances the user's ability to search the Internet using non-English languages; there is full physical keyboard compatibility, including the shift and control keys for touch-typing; and what's most impressive is that it supports seventy-one input languages. i2Type can be installed directly in the browser as an add-on (Firefox) or an extension (Google Chrome). Sciweavers LLC, the creator of i2Type, is an academic science group committed to disseminating scientific papers via their online network and website (Sciweavers 2011). Currently, the tools they offer are freely available. In addition to i2Type, they offer other tools including PDF authoring and image applications.

WHY USE IT?

A major problem of multilingual searching is finding a good keyboard input. Non-English languages often have different characters, consonants, and vowel sounds that need to be indicated by accent marks (diacritics) or other special symbols. In addition to symbols, some languages read from top to bottom, or from left to right, or can have complex characters that don't really work like the Latin-based alphabet we are accustomed to in English. Keyboards need to be specially configured to do this. i2Type provides an immediate and simple solution. While I haven't tested all the features for all seventy-one languages, I have experimented with this tool for typing in French and Spanish. I also consulted with my linguist friends who speak and have studied Russian, Mandarin, Cantonese, Korean, and Japanese, and they said that the keyboard works well for these major languages. If libraries serving multilingual populations configured their computers to work with i2Type, more research and testing could be done on these types of tools. For now, the most important aspect of i2Type is that it empowers users to search the Internet more comfortably in their own language by providing a basic keyboard.

USING i2TYPE AT LIBRARY WORKSTATIONS

The advantage to using a virtual keyboard is that it is instant, with minimal configuration necessary. Firefox, the web browser, offers an add-on that can be installed by a system administrator. There is also an extension available for Google Chrome. The advantage to installing i2Type within the browser is that the patron won't need to go to the website to access the keyboard, but can use it directly in the browser. The staff will need to make the patron aware of the extension and how to use it.

As a productivity tool, i2Type's ability to support both virtual and physical keyboards allows the patron to use an English keyboard to touch-type in their native language while viewing the native language's keyboard layout on-screen for reference. Virtual keyboards (keyboards that exist virtually via a web browser or an application) often require the user to input via a mouse (or more recently, via a touchscreen). i2Type allows virtual input using a mouse but also connects directly to a computer's keyboard so that the physical computer keys directly correspond to the keys on the virtual keyboard. This is a very useful feature, since touch-typing is a much faster method than the point-and-click input method found in other virtual keyboards. Another very useful feature of i2Type is that a user can directly copy and paste the text, so he or she can use i2Type as in input tool for word processing programs, library databases, Google Translate, and e-mail programs that support Unicode font standards.

AT THE REFERENCE DESK

The ability to call up a virtual online keyboard and type in a non-English language, combined with a robust machine translator like Google Translate, facilitates the reference interview in a new way that goes beyond consulting physical dictionaries, grammars, and phrase books. For example, it provides an easy way to input the names of books, movies, or pieces of art in the patron's language. This is very useful if the patron does not know the English name or the official translated name of a work. It is also useful when searching for documents that have been translated into multiple languages; this is true with immigration material, health material, and travel, tax, and business information.

ONLINE CHAT

i2Type is a virtual keyboard, so it's easy to send a patron a link over online chat. Why would you want to do this? We've outlined some reasons above, but more importantly, before these keyboards, the patron's ability to search was limited to queries in English; by providing a way to search in their native language, there is an increase in their ability to access and generate web content. Sending the patron the link online makes patrons aware that they can search using a language other than English, which gives them another means of access to information. For me, this type of access and empowerment through language is a new and powerful form of outreach.

GOOGLE TRANSLATE

Why do librarians need a computer translator? How useful is it really? The biggest point that I want to communicate in this chapter is that at a fundamental level, language can be an enormous barrier to information. If the language a person thinks in isn't English, then it's likely that forming English search terms and retrieving non-English information will be more difficult. Much of the Internet's content is in English, and although the non-English web is still in its infancy, other languages are developing an online presence. Machine translators like Google Translate provide a much-needed way of working between languages online.

Google Translate is a web-based translation tool provided by Google that can translate across sixty-three different languages. According to the Google Translate blog, it was designed with the simple goal of reducing language barriers to information (Gilliland 2011). There is a downloadable extension available for both Google Chrome and Firefox, but the interface works best for Chrome. I've personally used these extensions on Mac, Windows, and Ubuntu (Linux) operating systems. The Firefox extension was not created by Google and lacks the auto language detection features of the Google web-page version. In addition to the web tools, Google has created an application for Android phones that imports this functionality with a voice interface on mobile devices (Chin 2011). As Android phones and tablets get cheaper and the technology more robust, Android devices may be an interesting tool in the library setting.

Google Translate isn't a search engine, and it won't automatically search the words you are translating. You'll notice in the interface that there is no "search" button, but rather a "translate" button. There is a search interface that connects Google Translate to the Google search engine called Google Language Tools. This resource translates a query instantly into another language and uses the translation as a search query. I don't recommend using it, because building search terms one keyword or phrase at a time is a good way to scrutinize the translations and the effectiveness of their results. When I search using Google Translate, I create a document that keeps track of the search (search log), while I also take note of other linguistic elements that affect the results. Using Google Language Tools to translate and search bypasses these intermediate steps, when a human being is far more effective at judging the translations than a machine translator.

USING GOOGLE TRANSLATE

In the library setting Google Translate works best as a search term look-up. In addition to search terms, Google Translate gives you the ability to look at frequently occurring terms, navigation of other important text items, and tags in English and to parse out their basic meanings. Frequently occurring terms can indicate relevant concepts and thematic content. Of course, it might be difficult to sort out articles, conjunctions, and pronouns from relevant concepts. Using Google Translate for translating each individual term that occurs frequently is also helpful in separating terms that perform a grammatical function from terms that indicate a concept or theme. I also suggest separate translations of the sentences that contain these terms in order to get the context at the phrase and sentence level. Machine translation is limited, but we can get a feel for the meaning by applying these types of strategies.

In addition to navigation elements on a web page, it is quite common to find hyperlinks or downloadable files in the text. Google Translate can help identify these important page elements. This could be useful when looking at a government website, blog, Twitter post, or other online social media. As librarians we can keep in mind that we only need a basic idea of the information in order to manipulate and navigate it. Tags used on blog posts, news headlines, and website navigation elements can all quickly be looked up. Is the page loading up in a language you don't understand? That's no problem for Google Translate.

Using these new techniques to navigate multilingual environments will take practice and time. As a librarian, I understand that we don't have a lot of time in our workday, and I suggest that becoming proficient with Google Translate works best when you find yourself regularly working with a particular language group. The goal isn't fluency, but rather to become comfortable working in a second language environment, applying your expertise in information to help your patrons. After all, if your patrons have to move out of their comfort zone to work in your language, this is a way to meet them halfway.

STRATEGIES AT THE REFERENCE DESK OR ONLINE CHAT

Using Google Translate or i2Type in a face-to-face or virtual reference interview can improve communication between the librarian and a patron who may not be able to articulate questions because of limited English ability. There may be additional issues besides simple lack of proficiency (particularly in the academic library setting), and these include: jargon, understanding exactly what they are searching, and the patron's familiarity with discipline-specific conventions in scholarly communication. I mention these other factors because this chapter only attempts to unpack aspects of the language layer.

Technologies like Google Translate and i2Type work particularly well when formulating research questions and search terms. I initially started using these tools with international students working on their graduate degrees. These were motivated students who spoke Arabic, Korean, and Mandarin who were frequently at the library. The students had adequate command of the English language but struggled with academic English, and this was often an obstacle when they searched library databases.

The best strategy during these reference interviews was to have the patron type keywords in their native language into Google Translate while watching the English translation. Sometimes, these will be sentences; at other times they can be fragments of phrases. As you progress with the interview, you can do a round of clarification, focusing on nouns within the phrases. Nouns communicate concepts best, and they are often used as descriptors, keywords, or subject headings. What's important to understand in this interaction is that we are looking for rough translations, and that the communicative meaning is more important than creating well-formed questions. Understanding the nouns that the patron is most enthusiastic about is a good sign that the noun is relevant to the information need. Look up synonyms and retranslate those synonyms back into the patron's native language. If the patron is typing in phrases or sentences, reconstruct the sentence by dividing the subject and verb. Groping through language is not a science, and it can be time-intensive. Over time, like any language learner, you will begin to develop a better linguistic understanding of the populations you serve.

NEWSEUM.ORG

Newseum is a museum about newspaper history. Officially opened in 2008 and located in Washington, DC, Newseum's physical facilities boast fourteen exhibition galleries covering 250,000 square feet (Newseum 2008). Newspapers are a type of language and cultural resource that communicate information that is of regional interest. Patrons who are interested in international current events can browse newspaper front pages around the world (with Africa being a noticeable exception). The default setting is U.S. regional newspapers. There is a world map that allows the user to browse different newspapers by geographic region.

Regional newspapers add a nice touch to any personalized cultural workstation. Being able to see what is of important local interest can also help people stay in touch with current events of their region. As I have seen many times, this type of native language leisure reading leads to additional first-language Internet searching for local blogs and local-language news sites.

LANGUAGE PERSONALIZATION AT COMPUTER WORKSTATIONS

Providing productivity solutions for groups who normally wouldn't have ready access to them will require some investment of staff time. Here are some suggestions on how to personalize workstations for multilingual use:

- Create a multiple user/language log-in with the default start screen in English, but different user settings that could be configured for different languages.
- Identify which languages printers support.
- Install PDF printers that will preserve document font formatting.

In the academic setting students need to print all types of documents and correspondence to support their immigration status, personal correspondence, job search, and academic needs. Although it is easy to configure different language settings, doing so requires administrative passwords and downloading free language fonts and input support. Most operating systems like Windows and Mac come with support for multiple languages. Internet search engines and database interfaces (like EBSCO and Gale) also have a wide range of language support. Increasingly, printers are now able to support Unicode font standards that allow printing in languages that don't have Roman fonts. It is essential that the librarians identify and activate these features and be aware which computers and printers are able to support certain languages. My recommendation is to provide a space in the library that handles these information needs.

BASIC LANGUAGE RESEARCH

If you find that you have frequent patrons from a particular language group, it is important to do some basic language research to find out more about the language. Knowing the word order of the language and how the language is written (the orthography) can help you better understand the best way to approach the tools explained above, as well as their limits. English follows a regular pattern of word order. Other languages follow different patterns. This means keywords might fall in different positions in sentences. Below are simple examples of French adjective phrases:

- *Marketing vert* is translated to "green marketing"
- *Consommation durable* is translated to "sustainable consumption"
- *Développement durable* is translated to "sustainable development"

These examples of French subject headings show that adjectival word order tends to be the reverse of English. Doing basic language research can help clarify basic grammatical forms.

In addition to finding a basic language grammar on the particular language you are working with, the following resources are good places to start to get general information on languages, their distribution, and how they function in society.

Laurie Bauer and Peter Trudgill. 1998. *Language Myths*. New York: Penguin.
Bernard Comrie. 1996. *The Atlas of Languages: The Origin and Development of Languages throughout the World*. New York: Facts on File.

Matthew S. Dryer and Martin Haspelmath, eds. 2011. *The World Atlas of Language Structures Online*. Munich: Max Planck Digital Library. Available at http://wals.info.

M. Paul Lewis. 2009. *Languages of the World*. 16th ed. Dallas, TX: SIL International. Available at http://www.ethnologue.com/web.asp.

Online language communities are often good places to find tools and strategies, including culturally relevant information particular to a language group. It's important to note, however, that although people speak the same language, they are not necessarily the same culturally. This is particularly true for many of the major languages like French, English, Spanish, Arabic, and Mandarin. Cultural research is important in addition to language research, before you make any assumptions about the information needs of the communities in your library.

CONCLUSION

Supporting the multilingual information needs of our patrons is the first step to creating a climate for deep diversity. Creating this climate in the library is completely new territory. Technologies improve and create new possibilities; they will entail some experimentation with the types of services that are being offered. In addition to technology, overcoming language barriers means that librarians make an effort to stay informed of culturally relevant online resources (Cuban 2007, 90–91). Supporting an environment of deep diversity gives us a chance to connect with our patrons in a meaningful way. With budget cuts and the challenges of hiring new staff, creating a multilingual environment is a simple way to add value to existing resources.

WORKS CITED

Chin, Jeff. 2011. "Start the Conversation with Google Translate for Android." Google Translate Blog. October 13. http://googletranslate.blogspot.com/2011/10/start-conversation-with-google.html.

Cuban, Sondra. 2007. *Serving New Immigrant Communities in the Library*. Westport, CT: Libraries Unlimited.

Gilliland, Jordan. 2011. "Breaking Down Language Barriers with Translated English-Language Results." Google Translate Blog. October 25. http://googletranslate.blogspot.com/2011/10/breaking-down-language-barriers-with.html.

Kyrillidou, Martha, Charles Lowry, Paul Hanges, Juliet Aiken, and Kristina Justh. 2009. "ClimateQUAL™: Organizational Climate and Diversity Assessment." Paper presented at the Association of College and Research Libraries, Seattle, Washington, March. http://www.libqual.org/documents/admin/ACRL_Paper_FINAL_20091.doc.

Newseum. 2008. Newseum Press Kit. April 4. www.newseum.org/press-info/press-materials/press-kit.pdf.

Sciweavers. 2011. "Explore State-of-the-Art in Your Research Field." http://www.sciweavers.org.

Part V

Outreach Initiatives

Chapter Twenty-Four

"If You Build It, [They] Will Come"

Actively Inviting Multicultural Users to Academic Libraries by Offering Family Literacy Workshops

Ladislava Khailova

The metaphoric vision of the United States of America as a melting pot of cultures, popularized by Israel Zangwill's drama *The Melting-Pot* (1908), has continued to hold true in the twenty-first century. Between the years of 2000 and 2009, the number of foreign-born individuals residing in the country is estimated to have increased from 31,107,889 (11.1% of the total population) to 38,517,234 (12.5%) (U.S. Census Bureau 2000, 2009). Linguistic diversity has also been on the rise, with 46,951,595 (17.9%) U.S. residents using language other than English at home in 2000 and 57,159,470 (20%) of those older than five years doing so in 2009 (U.S. Census Bureau 2000, 2009). It is essential for academic libraries to respond to such accelerated diversification of American society by actively inviting multicultural users into their buildings. Growing minorities in the area represent an especially desirable focus. By recruiting them, libraries can decrease potential cultural and language barriers in the community. They will enhance these community members' familiarity with the libraries' collections, services, and structures, thus making them feel welcome to utilize and benefit from educational institutions at any time. Family literacy workshops represent a type of library program that provides an excellent vehicle for these outreach efforts.

Northern Illinois University Libraries (NIU Libraries) in DeKalb, Illinois, has developed and implemented such a program for the area's Hispanic/Latino families with children aged birth to five. First launched in the summer of 2010 under the title "Off to a Good Start," the program consisted of two identical workshops and attracted nine local families. The overarching goal was to introduce the demographic group to the academic library's bilingual juvenile collection and to explain the general importance of reading to young children. I, as the program coordinator, together with my English-Spanish translator, Rebecca Martin, also modeled simple, effective reading techniques. Based on the 100 percent positive feedback from parents, the program was offered again in the fall of 2011 under the title "Starting Ahead, Staying Ahead." This elaborated version consisted of three interconnected ninety-minute sessions, with eleven families participating. The focus was newly on continuity and providing immediate feedback to parents on their direct involvement in their children's emergent literacy development. Participants repeatedly voiced their pleasant surprise that community members could utilize the NIU Libraries and expressed their plans to visit the institution again in the future. The feedback confirms our assumption that family literacy workshops are a valuable tool for academic libraries trying to reach out to the area's growing multicultural population.

The development and implementation of the workshop series at NIU Libraries, while ultimately very successful, was not without its stumbling blocks. The following sections provide suggestions about the design, financing, recruitment, retention, and evaluation to help other academic libraries wishing to introduce similar programs for multicultural users.

DESIGNING FAMILY LITERACY WORKSHOPS: RATIONALE, TARGET POPULATION, AND CONTENTS

Library programs for multicultural groups have the important potential of lessening cultural and language barriers. As documented above, multicultural families do not necessarily use English as the first language at home. While this factor alone enhances the country's social diversity, it may also result in children's difficulties with developing adequate early literacy skills if paired with a family's low-income status (Cassidy et al. 2004, 479). As Hyslop (2000) posits, parents of such families may care deeply about their children's education but are also often low-literate themselves and thus believe they lack the ability as well as financial means to support their children's literacy efforts. In addition, if they are recent immigrants, they may be unaware of the American school system's requirements. The language barrier between them and the school only intensifies these problems (Hyslop 2000, 1–3). Consequently, learning to read and write well can represent a higher challenge for children growing up in these families than for children from more privileged, mainstream, English-speaking homes.

Research shows that family literacy workshops can significantly aid in bridging the gap between the literacy achievements of children of different socioeconomic backgrounds. For instance, within disadvantaged social groups, parental involvement in such programs is strongly interlinked with children's literacy accomplishments (Hannon 2003, 102). It is thus strongly encouraged that academic libraries actively provide multicultural parents, especially those who are financially challenged, with the opportunity to enroll in family literacy projects. The interactions can enhance their home literacy environment through library readings and related activities and result in the families' increased awareness of the library as an institution so they feel comfortable using it for educational purposes in the future.

Performing a simple population scan to identify rapidly growing minority groups in the community is always a good idea for libraries planning to offer workshops. Interested institutions can look at recent Census data, rely on their existing user statistics, and/or develop a brief survey to collect new data about the broader community. For example, I analyzed the 1990 and 2000 Census reports for Illinois and DeKalb (county and city) before deciding to focus the NIU Libraries' workshops on local Hispanic/Latino families, who continue to form one of the area's largest groups of families in which English is not the first language spoken at home (U.S. Census Bureau 1992, 2002). Libraries can use a similar strategy to select their target population.

When proceeding to develop the contents of family literacy workshops, academic libraries need to understand that there is no prescribed, one-size-fits-all format. The choice of a specific multicultural population is likely to have some impact on the design in terms of highlighted collections and services. Also, as discussed by Purcell-Gates (2000), there are possible differences based on the emphasis of the program. The scholar mentions the division of family literacy programs into three types, depending on whether instruction is delivered directly to (1) children as well as adults, (2) adults only with anticipated benefits for children, or (3) children only, with expected benefits for parents (Purcell-Gates 2000, 860). Libraries can use this classification to make basic decisions about activities to include. At NIU Libraries, the main instructional focus was on parents because they are, to a large extent, the creators of the home literacy environment. They were the key audience of a mini-lecture on the importance of early parental involvement in young children's literacy development, as well as of a hands-on workshop on practical age-appropriate guidelines for reading to children. In addition, they were introduced to the institution's reference services, catalog system, and English/Spanish juvenile books collection. However, the children also gained from the program. While parents attended the lecture and toured the building, the children engaged in a set of literacy interactions with qualified literacy assistants. They read and discussed books and represented them through art. When reunited with their parents, they participated in two structured lap-sit story times and completed a take-home reading list, which they personalized by selecting fifteen titles. Academic libraries can vary these activities as needed to maximize the benefit their targeted population is receiving from the program.

FINANCING THE PROGRAM: DRAFTING A DETAILED BUDGET AND SEEKING GRANT OPPORTUNITIES

In addition to selecting the target multicultural population and developing a basic program outline, libraries need to make specific plans for financing the events. The programs can be relatively expensive, especially if the library offers multiple incentives—books for families to take home, day-care services, refreshments, and so on—to participants. Therefore, coordinators are strongly encouraged to draft a detailed budget and seek potential sources of financing well before the anticipated launch date of the workshops. Important questions to consider include the following:

- Personnel: Is the program coordinator donating his or her time, or is compensation necessary? Do the workshops require the presence of a translator? Will literacy assistants or babysitters be recruited to provide day-care services?
- Materials: How much will fliers, sign-up sheets, and handouts cost? Play and craft materials to occupy children during workshops may be needed as well. If props (puppets, boards, magnets, etc.) are used for hands-on literacy activities, what will the cost be? Is there a plan to give age-appropriate juvenile books to families to take home? Will other literacy-related prizes be offered?
- Facilities: Will the event venue (room, utilities, etc.) be provided as an in-kind contribution by the library or will there be an associated cost? Will transportation be offered? Is there a plan for refreshments?

Once program coordinators prepare a preliminary budget based on these and similar questions, it is high time to review available sources of funding. The easiest solution is to receive needed funds from the academic institution itself, but in these times of financial constraints, this will not represent a viable option for many. Accordingly, it is often necessary to seek grants focused on libraries, family literacy, and/or multicultural populations. For example, coordinators may consult the Library Grants Center site, which lists hundreds of grants available to libraries of all types; the Institute of Museum and Library Services grants page, which offers information on sources of federal support for libraries and museums; or the Grants.gov site, which provides an interdisciplinary listing of federal grants. It was by searching grant-reviewing resources like these that I learned about the Illinois Reading Council, which graciously agreed to sponsor the NIU Libraries' workshops through its Adult and Family Literacy Grant. Therefore, the value of these sites in trying to locate an appropriate sponsor should not be underestimated.

SUCCESSFUL RECRUITING: NETWORKING, PERSONALIZED APPEALS, TRANSPORTATION, AND DAY-CARE SERVICES

Securing funding for the workshops does not represent the only potential difficulty. When trying to recruit for their programs, libraries may face a surprising challenge in the form of a lack of trust by the targeted group. This applies especially if the intended program recipients have not previously utilized the institution. With multicultural users, immigration policy issues often play a significant role, since some potential participants may worry that they will be stopped by campus police or asked for personal documentation at the institution's door for no specific reason. Consequently, seeking partnerships with local organizations already offering services to the relevant demographic group is vital. They can help portray academic libraries as trustworthy institutions, thus playing an indispensable role in promoting the newly launched library programs.

NIU Libraries' experience with family literacy workshops demonstrates the benefits of such networking. The program targeted a demographic group of which I (the coordinator) am not a member. Therefore, I contacted several of the area's organizations with direct ties to the DeKalb Hispanic/Latino community: churches offering Masses in both English and Spanish, elementary schools with bilingual programs, youth organizations with a multicultural component, and literacy centers. I experienced several relative failures with such efforts until I found great partners in a nonprofit creative education group called smART (in 2010) and in the Kishwaukee College Family Literacy Program (in 2011). The partnerships proved very fruitful, with these organizations being extremely instrumental in advertising and recruiting for the events.

Apart from creating partnerships, it is important for academic libraries to make repeated individual appeals to interested parents to ensure high participation rates for workshops, as documented by current research. For instance, one study noted that after fliers and automated voice-mail messages failed to produce desired results in having parents sign up for a fifteen-week literacy program, more personalized methods such as individual phone calls to potential participants had to be used (Cassidy et al. 2004, 483). Along the same lines, another article, offering advice on overcoming barriers to Latino/Hispanic parent involvement in educational activities, recommends that educators take special efforts to make communication very personable and build on the cultural values of these families (Quezada et al. 2003, 38). NIU Libraries adopted a similar approach after only about a third of the families who signed up for the very first workshop in 2010 actually attended. Following a discussion with the participants, the translator and I concluded that the relatively low turnout could be attributed to the families forgetting about the event altogether or experiencing change in their schedule. To prevent the reoccurrence of the problem, we always made sure that all interested individuals were given a reminder call a few days before the event. The strategy proved to be quite successful, with an average of 70 percent of families that signed up arriving for subsequent workshops.

Providing free transportation and day-care services also increases chances of successful recruiting. As for transportation, not all participants may have a personal vehicle at their disposal; others may have never been to the campus before and may find it challenging to navigate it effectively. Good maps help but are not always sufficient. Therefore, if possible libraries should offer to bring the families to the program venue. Such service may be quite costly, though, unless the academic institution already has a system of buses or vans in place for such purposes. Often, the partnering organization can help as well—for example, one of NIU Libraries' partners, Kishwaukee College, used its own vehicles to bring participants from a central location in DeKalb to the university. Once at the program venue, the families usually appreciate if there is a free day-care service for them to use. To maximize the benefit children receive from attending, I recommend that the day care be made an integral part of the literacy instruction plan, with children participating in literacy activities rather than simply engaging in unstructured play. At NIU Libraries, almost 90 percent of the participating families took advantage of the free literacy-focused day-care and transportation opportunities and reported that their availability made them more inclined to sign up for the workshops. Consequently, in future versions of the program, every possible effort will be made to secure such services again for the purposes of recruiting in addition to focusing on networking and personal appeals.

INCREASING RETENTION BY COMMUNICATING RESPECT AND STRENGTHENING THE SENSE OF A CULTURAL COMMUNITY

In conjunction with adopting measures for recruiting a satisfactory number of families, it is vital for library workshop coordinators to apply strategies for increasing retention. Retention can be defined both in terms of the attendees' continuing participation in workshops consisting of more than one session and of their return to the institution upon the program's completion. Creating and strengthening the sense of a cultural community among participants contribute greatly to their levels of retention because it makes them perceive the library as a place where they are supported. Correspondingly, it is a good idea for coordinators to acquaint themselves with the cultural preferences of the targeted demographic group, while avoiding blunt generalizations in the process. It is always useful to research existing programs offered to the multicultural group by other institutions and learn from their successes and pitfalls in developing and sustaining a culturally welcoming environment. Approaching members of the selected group directly and asking them for suggestions is also constructive. Using this approach when preparing for the NIU Libraries' program, I realized early on that family is an essential component of the Hispanic/Latino culture. Therefore, I decided to incorporate a mini-social with simple refreshments to frame each workshop. In this way, participants were given ample time to get to know one another and to create a bond, as endorsed in literature (Cassidy et al. 2004, 485). Similar bonding techniques can be used with other cultural groups as well.

A related imperative that pertains to workshops for any minority is avoiding any semblance of a remediation program. A number of studies have rightly opposed programs that are based on a deficiency model and try to force practices that seem too foreign to the home culture (Cassidy et al. 2004, 481). At the same time, it is desirable that additional literacy practices are introduced to families, as it is the purpose of the workshop; the challenge is to do so through collaboration and without disqualifying the practices already established in the homes of participants (Hannon 2003, 105). To communicate respect for the established while introducing the new, providers can, for instance, supplement research data during presentations with participants' personal stories about home literacy interactions. Such exchanges help attendees and coordinators learn from one another, in spite of their potential cultural differences. Also, interpreters should be made available to allow attendees to communicate in their mother tongue. Along these lines, families participating at NIU Libraries' workshops were encouraged to use both Spanish and English, both during the program and during their literacy interactions with children at home. They were also introduced to monolingual as well as bilingual books in the juvenile collection. As the immediate feedback provided by parents indicated, these practices contributed to their feeling welcome and respected. At any program, participants' satisfaction with the cultural support offered is likely to encourage them to utilize the institution in the future.

EVALUATING WORKSHOPS FOR IMPROVEMENT PURPOSES

While coordinators tend to receive immediate, informal feedback during the individual sessions, evaluating the overall success of a family literacy workshop objectively can be quite challenging. Measuring positive program outcomes—such as the participants' return rate to the libraries and/or the increased frequency of parent-child literacy interactions in the home—often requires a long-term interaction with the families. However, library workshops can rarely provide that. Also, while direct observations of participants at home are invasive or inappropriate, self-reports from them often cater to the expectations of the questioner (Purcell-Gates 2000, 864–65). Similarly, for the evaluator, it is usually hard to separate wished-for expectations from reality. In spite of these inherent limitations, libraries have to make attempts to collect data about their programs to improve them in the future.

When coordinating the "Off to a Good Start" and "Starting Ahead, Staying Ahead" workshops, I concluded that a brief questionnaire consisting of simple yes/no questions and a final open-ended comment section works very well. Examples of queries can include the following: Did participants become more familiar with a specific collection/service at the library? Do they plan to use the books in this collection in the future? Did the workshop help them understand the value of reading to their young child(ren)? Did it help them determine how to read to their young child(ren)? Based on the program, do they plan to spend more time reading with their child(ren)? The closing, open-ended section can encourage the attendees to comment on the workshop in general, asking them, for instance, to specify what they considered most beneficial and what they would like to see changed. When structured around such learning objectives, the evaluation instrument allows the coordinator to assess the total impact of the program. Yet, because of the brevity and straightforward character of the queries, participants do not tend to find the evaluation tool too cumbersome or time-consuming and are likely to complete and return it—especially if care is taken to use English as well as the native language of the served multicultural population. Based on the collected data, libraries are then able to seek additional funding with grant organizations, adequately target new groups through advertising, and modify the workshop contents.

CONCLUSION

Academic libraries often focus primarily on their institutions' students, faculty, and staff when planning, assessing, and further developing their collections and services. General community members, while also welcome to utilize the libraries, tend to be on the periphery of their interests. However, given the ever-increasing multicultural population in the United States, libraries are strongly encouraged to reach out beyond their immediate user population and engage the broader community. Specifically, it is a good idea to invite the area's growing minorities to the institutions through family literacy workshops or similar programs to enhance their access to educational materials. While such programs require advance planning, they are also extremely rewarding. They have the potential of resulting in an increased frequency of literacy interactions in the homes of participants, thus helping multicultural children acquire adequate early literacy skills and later succeed in school and in life. Personally, I take this to represent one of the most satisfying ways to utilize available resources.

WORKS CITED

Cassidy, Jack, Roberto Garcia, Carmen Tejeda-Delgado, Sherrye D. Garrett, Cynthia Martinez-Garcia, and Roel V. Hinojosa. 2004. "A Learner-Centered Family Literacy Project for Latino Parents and Caregivers." *Journal of Adolescent and Adult Literacy* 47(6): 478–88.

Hannon, Peter. 2003. "Family Literacy Programmes." In *Handbook of Early Childhood Literacy*, edited by Nigel Hall, Joanne Larson, and Jackie Marsh, 99–111. London: Sage.

Hyslop, Nancy. 2000. "Hispanic Parental Involvement in Home Literacy." *ERIC Digest 158.* Report: EDO-CS-00-09. http://www.csa.com.

Purcell-Gates, Victoria. 2000. "Family Literacy." In *Handbook of Reading Research*, edited by Michael L. Kamil, Peter B. Mosenthal, P. David Pearson, and Rebecca Barr. 853–70. London: Erlbaum.

Quezada, Reyes L., Delia M. Díaz, and Maria Sánchez. 2003. "Involving Latino Parents." *Leadership* 33(1): 32–34, 38.

U.S. Census Bureau. 1992. "Table DP-2. Profile of Selected Social Characteristics for Illinois: 1990." http://www.census.gov/census2000/xls/90smp17.xls.

———. 2000. "Profile of Selected Social Characteristics: 2000." http://factfinder2.census.gov/faces/tableservices/jsf/pages/productview.xhtml?pid=DEC_00_SF4_DP2&prodType=table.

———. 2002. "Illinois: 2000. Table DP-2. Profile of Selected Social Characteristics: 2000." http://www.census.gov/prod/2002pubs/c2kprof00-il.pdf.

———. 2009. "Selected Social Characteristics in the United States: 2009." http://factfinder2.census.gov/faces/tableservices/jsf/pages/productview.xhtml?pid=ACS_09_1YR_CP2&prodType=table.

Chapter Twenty-Five

Community Family Literacy Programs at the Azusa City Library

Maria A. Pacino

In this chapter, I will outline the importance of literacy development and share examples of library programming centered on literacy skills during challenging times of budget cuts. These specialized programs, serving children of very young ages through senior citizens, were initiated through grants, private donations, and/or volunteer services from partnerships and collaborations with area schools and other community agencies. The information shared in this chapter comes from library documents available to the public, conversations with library staff, commissioner reports, and grant proposals from the Azusa City Library.

Literacy proficiency has been an ongoing topic of concern in many countries, especially in the United States. We frequently hear that Americans appear to lag behind other Western democracies in terms of schooling, especially regarding literacy rates and skills. Test scores seem to be the primary indicators of low literacy skills among many of America's children. This apparent literacy crisis is not just an American concern; it is a global issue across pluralistic democracies with implications for the labor market.

The promise of literacy is a right of individuals in global, democratic societies, so that citizens are able to make informed decisions and participate in the democratic process. Libraries, particularly public libraries like the Azusa City Library, are instrumental in keeping the dream of literacy competency alive by providing essential literacy skills and services to children and adults in diverse communities. In an effort to increase literacy rates around the world by 50 percent by 2015, the United Nations initiated the United Nations Literacy Decade (UNLD) in 2003 with a commitment of education for all (EFA); literacy is viewed as a freedom and a human right. According to the UNLD, one in five adults worldwide cannot read; many of them are women; around 40 percent of the population in poor countries is illiterate (United Nations Educational, Scientific, and Cultural Organization n.d.).

Although literacy rates in developed countries, including the United States, are relatively high, the reality is that a significant number of Americans have low literacy skills. The National Assessment of Adult Literacy (n.d.) reports that approximately 15 percent of the U.S. population falls below basic literacy levels, has great difficulty with reading and writing comprehension, and can be defined as functionally illiterate (Literacy Education n.d.). According to the National Center for Education Statistics (n.d.), approximately 23 percent of adults in California lack basic literacy skills (in Los Angeles County the number rises to 33%). High illiteracy rates have an impact on communities and society, especially in a global, digital world. Illiteracy leads to high unemployment, poverty, and a less competitive workforce.

According to *The Urban High School's Challenge: Ensuring Literacy for Every Child* (DeLeon 2002), literacy in the United States has given advantage to the upper middle class, leaving women and minorities on unequal footing in terms of educational access and resources. Such a disadvantage has resulted in high dropout rates, especially for Latinos and African Americans. A *Dateline NBC* Television report (Brokaw 2003) revealed that more than 15 percent of adults living in the United States are functionally illiterate. These adults are unable to read a work application, instructions for medication, or bank statements. Although statistics indicate that modern democratic countries have eliminated illiteracy, many citizens seem unprepared for the demands of technology-oriented, global democracies. In addition, functional illiteracy in families creates a culture of poverty that can become cyclical, especially in some immigrant populations. Many parents are unable to read to their children or help them with homework. Although literacy development is part of schooling, public libraries are the community agencies that take on the responsibility for adult literacy development.

Preparing individuals for twenty-first-century citizenship for pluralist, global democracies means redefining literacy and acquiring skills that go beyond reading and writing, especially in the digital age. Western notions of literacy have been primarily text based and tend to devalue and exclude cultures that emphasize oral tradition, observational skills, and non-Western modes of discourse, often characteristic of immigrant populations. Libraries can help create meaningful literacy environments that help individuals connect literacy to life experiences, allowing them to make meaning of the world.

The definition of literacy for a digital, global society includes interpreting print and nonprint materials; academic ability in numeracy, science, and economics; quantitative and qualitative research skills; information access and management; computer and digital technology; social media interaction; critical thinking; cultural awareness and cross-cultural communication, including bilingual and/or multilingual expertise; analysis of issues from multiple perspectives; understanding of families and communities in the world; character development; conflict resolution; and moral/ethical decision–making skills for participatory democracy (Rafferty 1999).

Gilster (2005) writes about the definition of digital literacy for effective communication in global democracies. He stresses the need for Internet users to become knowledgeable consumers of information, using critical thinking and metacognitive skills to assess the validity and credibility of online information. Literacy for the twenty-first century requires proficiency in digital technology, which includes the ability to access information through multiple platforms from computers and digital devices. In less affluent neighborhoods, there is the potential for a digital divide, in which some citizens may have limited access to digital technologies and, thus, be unable to acquire the necessary skills to compete in a global job market.

"New Literacies and Twenty-First-Century Technologies," a position statement from the International Reading Association (2009), says:

> The Internet and other forms of information and communication technologies (ICTs) are redefining the nature of reading, writing, and communication. These ICTs will continue to change in the years ahead, requiring continuously new literacies to successfully exploit their potentials. Although many new ICTs will emerge in the future, those that are common in the lives of our students include search engines, webpages, email, instant messaging (IM), blogs, podcasts, ebooks, wikis, nings, YouTube, video, and many more. New literacy skills and practices are required by each new ICT as it emerges and evolves. (1)

Libraries like the Azusa City Library become the hubs in diverse communities, bringing families and other community members together to seek information and engage in various other literacy activities. Public libraries offer the hope of literacy in democratic societies.

The public library in the city of Azusa serves a population of approximately 46,360 people (67.6% Latino, 20% Caucasian, 3.2% African American, and 7.1% Asian). Fifty percent of the population is Spanish speaking (Los Angeles Almanac n.d.). According to library statistics, Azusa is one of the least affluent communities in the area, with over 15 percent of the population living below the poverty line and nearly 14 percent unemployment. A majority of students in local schools in grades 2–5 are considered underprivileged; approximately 10 percent of these children are homeless. Given the predominance of Latino community members, some library services are bilingual, such as selected story times (*cuentos bilingues*) and movie nights in Spanish and English.

PROGRAMMING

Children's and young adult literacy programs in the Azusa City Library include

- Azusa Reads, Azusa Writes, Azusa Counts, and Azusa Calculates programs (after-school tutoring services for K–12 children by local university students)
- Bark for Books (children read stories to specially trained dogs)
- Book to Films (films based on novels, autobiographies, or other books)
- Bookmobile services for children and adults
- *Cuentos Bilingues* (Spanish) story time with crafts
- Family Fun series (child performers, puppet shows, arts and crafts), sponsored by United Mexican American Youth and Parents of Azusa (UMAY-PA)
- Family Place (parents/families with babies and toddlers; English language)
- Moonlight Story Time and Craft Hour (children attend wearing pajamas)
- Movie Nights in English and Spanish
- Read with Me Parent/Toddler Bilingual Spanish Story Time
- Story times in English with arts and crafts
- Summer Reading Program (serving babies through older kids)

Literacy programs for adults include

- Arts and crafts and cultural events
- Bookmobile outreach services to the community, including schools
- Canyon City Book Club (community members discuss relevant fiction and nonfiction books, some on local history)
- Lunch at the Library, providing an opportunity for Azusa citizens to participate in discussions on topics that impact the city's residents
- Technology instruction in computer, Internet use, and other digital technologies

Other adult literacy programs and services, funded by the Canyon City Foundation, specifically designed for maturing adults (the boomer generation and senior citizens) include

- Book delivery through a partnership with Meals on Wheels
- Bookmobile stops at senior centers throughout the city
- Taming Technology program for the baby boomer generation

The Azusa City Library has a close relationship with the community and has several established partnerships with community agencies: Azusa Pacific University (tutoring of K–12 students); Azusa Unified School District (promotes library literacy services to enhance student academic performance); Foothill Family Services (offering classes on nutrition and child well-being, and the bilingual Read with Me baby and toddler program); the Azusa Wellness Center (which provides health information to families on nutrition and fitness); and the United Mexican American Youth and Parents of Azusa (UMAYA); this organization sponsors the library Family Fun series and coordinates cultural and informational events throughout the community.

Following are descriptions of selected literacy programs, funded either by grants, local agencies, or private donors.

Azusa Reads, Azusa Writes, Azusa Counts, and Azusa Calculates Programs

Azusa Reads, Azusa Writes, Azusa Counts, and Azusa Calculates are after-school programs. The public library partnership with the local university, Azusa Pacific University (APU) and the Azusa Unified School District (AUSD), has been in existence for over ten years. Undergraduate student volunteers provide Monday–Thursday after-school tutoring services to elementary and secondary students from the school district. This is an opportunity to assist K–12 students with homework and literacy skills. Approximately 250 students from thirty-five local schools take advantage of these programs. This reciprocal partnership allows university students to fulfill their community service hours. At the end of each academic year, the city library has a thank-you reception for the university students. The reception is attended by the library staff, the mayor and other city council members, university officials, school district officials, K–12 students, parents, and other community members. K–12 students and parents feel that this tutoring service is essential to the academic success of the children.

Adult Literacy Program

The purpose of the Adult Literacy Services (ALS) program, funded by California Library Literacy Services (CLLS), is to provide critical literacy services to English-speaking adults who lack the literacy proficiency and skills needed to function effectively in society. Volunteer tutors are English-speaking adults, trained by a literacy specialist and given teaching and learning materials. Instruction in the Adult Literacy Program is delivered one-on-one to establish a relationship between instructor and learner. It is important that volunteers understand their role in dealing with adult learners. Adult learners are defined as those at least sixteen years old; seeking literacy services for themselves; completing the process to qualify for services; establishing literacy goals; and attending the tutoring sessions. Most learners seek literacy services for job improvement, to become active in their children's school, or to participate fully in the community and society. Tutors and learners meet regularly, a minimum of once a week for at least ninety minutes. Adult learners are also introduced to community resources and services that may benefit them or their families. Participants in the Adult Literacy Program report a very positive experience for both learners and volunteer tutors. The Adult Literacy Services website of the California State Library (http://libraryliteracy.org/about/als/index.html) shares videos depicting many rewarding stories of program participants in different libraries.

Bookmobile

Bookmobile Service (library on wheels) was funded by a grant from the Canyon City Foundation in 2008 to purchase a van and customize it for an itinerant library. During Bookmobile stops, patrons can get library cards and check out books. There are also story times for children. The Bookmobile travels throughout the city, with daily scheduled stops at schools without libraries, parks, and senior centers. Another Canyon City Foundation grant enabled the Bookmobile to expand library services to a larger group of senior citizens by increasing the number of stops at senior centers. Bookmobile users often tell the driver how grateful they are that library services are brought to them, since for many of them a trip to the public library would be impossible.

Family Place

Family Place is a program for public libraries funded by a grant from Family Place Libraries within the California State Library. This program is especially designed to encourage families in the literacy development of infants and toddlers. The goal of the Family Place Libraries program, established in 1996, is to enable public libraries to become the literacy centers of communities by expanding the role of children's services in promoting healthy child and family development from birth, parent and community involvement, and lifelong learning. Core components of Family Place Libraries include a collection of appropriate materials for babies, toddlers, parents and service providers; parent-child workshops; coalition building with community organizations and agencies; developmentally appropriate programming; library staff trained in family support; and outreach to new and nontraditional library users. Family Place Libraries incorporate toys, books, music, multimedia, and other resources for child development and parenting workshops. Library spaces are redesigned to accommodate age-appropriate furniture and materials to provide library service to infants, connect families with community resources and service agencies, and reach out to nontraditional library users.

These family community connections nurture children and prepare them for school readiness. Family Place Libraries, part of a network of public librarians who oversee these children and family services, provide a wide range of resources on parenting and child care; early childhood development, literacy, and education; health, safety, and nutrition; books and toys for young children; bibliographies; demographics; and reading resources (Family Place Libraries n.d.).

The Azusa City Library is already an established meeting place for families in and around Azusa. Offering numerous story times, as well as tutoring and reading programs, the library is a year-round focal point for this community. The Azusa City Library has molded its programs and collection to reflect a community with a large bilingual/Spanish monolingual population that naturally embraces the concept that the library is for the whole family. Since the library is already heavily used by families, we believe that an innovative program establishing a connection to learning and literacy from early childhood that also addresses the concerns of schools, parents, and community advocates will be well-received and well-used in Azusa. Establishing a connection with the family as a whole to learning and literacy from early childhood is an effective way to combat the declining academic performance that has bedeviled Azusa schools in recent years. Helping parents and caregivers become their children's first educators fits accordingly with our strategic plan to promote early literacy. Family Place relates to this plan by helping us provide Azusa's families with the tools necessary for a learning environment and making developmentally appropriate books and toys readily available. Consequently we can establish the groundwork for school readiness.

The Family Place training institute helps reinforce the fact that education begins at birth and reminds us of the importance of play in early childhood development. Including infants and toddlers with their families in a child-appropriate setting with available books, manipulatives, and user spaces ensures an integrative approach in the promotion of early education. As we said in our 2010 grant application, literacy, knowledge, and cultural awareness are the very tools that are necessary for our residents to become members of tomorrow's work force. The Family Place grant provided furniture, toys, books, and materials for parenting workshops. A grant from Target was used for creating in-house, early literacy thematic kits for the program (baby and toddler softcover books, toys, finger puppets, and other storytelling props; some kits include a CD with music). Parents are allowed to check out the kits after attending the Family Place parent workshops.

Taming Technology

The Taming Technology Program was funded in large part through a grant and statewide initiative from the California State Library called "Transforming Life after Fifty," a technology initiative for individuals age fifty and above, with an emphasis on those recently retired or nearing retirement. Technology services include access to computers, basic computer instruction, and introduction to digital technologies and devices, such as iPhones, iPods, and iPads, as well as navigating the complexity of the Internet world. The Taming Technology Program provides the boomer generation with some basic training in digital technologies.

FUNDING

Funding for many of the literacy programs at the Azusa City Library came from California Library Literacy Services (http://libraryliteracy.org) of the California State Library (http://www.library.ca.gov); the Canyon City Foundation (http://www.canyoncityfoundation.org); and Target, which has a local store (http://sites.target.com/site/en/company/page.jsp?contentId=WCMP04-03176). (A Gates Foundation grant was used to expand broadband services for Internet access.) Other literacy funding sources are the Friends of the Library, local businesses and other community agencies (like the local Rotary Club and the Women's Club), and private donations.

CONCLUSION

The Azusa City Library literacy programs described in this chapter demonstrate that even in times of severe budget cuts, public libraries can continue to make a difference in diverse communities by expanding literacy services to their constituents of all ages—from babies, children, teens, and adults to those nearing retirement and senior citizens. These programs are successful because of grant funds from the California State Library, local organizations like the Canyon City Foundation, Friends of the Library, and other community agencies and partnerships that provide ongoing funding, as well as volunteer services from community members. These literacy initiatives are possible if we tap resources that include

- Grants from local, regional, or national foundations
- Partnerships with local K–12 schools, universities, businesses, and other organizations

- Volunteer community members

Public libraries fulfill the promise of literacy for citizens in pluralistic, democratic societies. A recent *Los Angeles Times* article reminds us of the critical need for libraries: "Even in the Internet age, libraries perform a vital service to society. Libraries are a public good and a civic responsibility. They are about our future as much as they are our past" (Lopez 2011).

I would like to thank Nancy Johnson, director of the Azusa City Library, as well as all other staff members who oversee the various literacy programs, for providing the information needed to complete this chapter.

WORKS CITED

Brokaw, T. 2003. "Tom Brokaw Reports on Adult Illiteracy in the United States." *Dateline NBC*, August 8.

DeLeon, A. G. 2002. *The Urban High School's Challenge: Ensuring Literacy for Every Child.* New York: Carnegie.

Family Place Libraries. n.d. http://www.familyplacelibraries.org (accessed January 3, 2012).

Gilster, P. 2005. "Digital Literacy." In *Jossey-Bass Reader on Technology and Learning*, 215–28. San Francisco: Jossey-Bass.

International Reading Association (IRA). 2009. "New Literacies and Twenty-First-Century Technologies." http://www.reading.org (accessed January 3, 2012).

Literacy Education—Teaching Literacy. n.d. http://www.caliteracy.org (accessed January 3, 2012).

Lopez, S. 2011. "Librarian's Binding Words." *Los Angeles Times*, November 11. http://articles.latimes.com/2011/nov/09/local/la-me-1109-lopez-libraries-20111108.

Los Angeles Almanac. n.d. "City of Azusa." http://www.laalmanac.com/cities/ci06.htm.

National Assessment of Adult Literacy (NAAL). n.d. http://nces.ed.gov/naal/kf_demographics.asp#3 (accessed January 3, 2012).

National Center for Education Statistics (NCES). n.d. http://nces.ed.gov/naal/estimates/StateEstimates.aspx (accessed January 3, 2012).

Rafferty, C. D. 1999. "Literacy in the Information Age." *Educational Leadership* 57: 22–25.

United Nations Educational, Scientific, and Cultural Organization (UNESCO). n.d. http://www.unesco.org/new/en/ (accessed January 3, 2012).

Chapter Twenty-Six

An Oral History Guide

Mark Donnelly

"Oral history" refers both to a method of recording and preserving oral history testimony and to the product of that process. It begins with an audio or video recording of a first-person account made by an interviewer with an interviewee (also referred to as narrator), both of whom have the conscious intention of creating a permanent record to contribute to an understanding of the past. A verbal document, the oral history, results from this process and is preserved and made available in different forms to other users, researchers, and the public. A critical approach to the oral testimony and interpretations is necessary in the use of oral history.

Oral history is distinguished from other forms of interviews by its content and extent. Oral history interviews seek an in-depth account of personal experience and reflections, with sufficient time allowed for narrators to give their stories the fullness they desire.

The content of oral history interviews is grounded in reflections on the past as opposed to commentary on purely contemporary events. Oral historians inform narrators about the nature and purpose of oral history and of their interviews specifically. They ensure that narrators voluntarily give their consent to be interviewed and understand that they can withdraw from the interview or refuse to answer a question at any time. Narrators give this consent by signing a consent form or by recording an oral statement of consent prior to the interview. All interviews are conducted in accord with the stated aims within the parameters of the consent.

THE BAYSIDE AND OZONE PARK PROJECTS

This chapter is based on my work as an outreach librarian for the Special Services Department of Queens Library in New York City. Intergenerational projects were created and carried out in the local communities of Bayside (2006–2007) and Ozone Park, Queens (2008–2009). The memories of older adults from the Bayside Senior Center and the Ozone Park Senior Center, both affiliates of Catholic Charities Services, were collected and recorded through partnerships with public and private schools in those communities.

The intention behind this oral history guide is to help librarians and leaders of various organizations gain a better understanding of how to develop, conduct, and complete oral history projects within their own communities. The steps provided are drawn from my coordination of the above-mentioned projects in Bayside and Ozone Park. Some of this was trial and error. We partners learned from our experience in the Bayside project and were able to make improvements as needed. For one, we learned the importance of location—having the school and senior center relatively close to one another in order to make traveling to do the interviews easier for both the students and adults. The Bayside Senior Center was about a mile away from Marie Curie Middle School (M.S. 158), where the student interviewers came from. With the Ozone Park project, we focused on a Catholic elementary school, St. Mary Gate of Heaven, located only a block from the senior center. We also learned that using a Q&A format worked better for a more comprehensive print document. And we added a video documentary component to the project in Ozone Park.

In the Bayside project, the students were mainly Asian American, a large demographic group in Bayside in recent years. The older adults were more of a mix—two were German Jews who survived the Holocaust; others were of Irish, Italian, and Asian heritage. One was from the Philippines. Two of the eight seniors were men, which is reflective of the smaller number of men compared to women that one finds in senior centers in Queens. One of the most touching moments in the Bayside project occurred when the two Jewish women told their separate stories of escape from Nazi Germany as girls in the late 1930s via the Kindertransport, a rescue mission to help children flee safely by ship and train before the outbreak of World War II. What powerful history told firsthand!

On the lighter personal side, we heard from interviewee John, a Chinese American, about the newspaper route he had in Queens as a teenager and also how he spent part of his growing years back in China. Mary, an Irish American, talked about going to the 1939–1940 New York World's Fair in Queens and then the delight of taking her children to the 1964–1965 World's Fair on the same site.

With the Ozone Park project, it turned out that all the older adults were of Italian heritage and all were women. Three men who originally signed up withdrew before the project got under way. (In both the Bayside and Ozone Park projects, the older adults volunteered. The students were selected by teachers, but these students were volunteers also.) The students from the Catholic school were of South Asian heritage, often Indian and Bangladeshi. Their grandparents lived in this community that had been populated by Italian immigrants in the late nineteenth and early twentieth century. It was particularly exciting to see these students interact with and question people from a different cultural background than their own. Two of the seniors had emigrated from Italy as adults, and in the case of a woman in her late nineties who spoke little English, her close friend translated for her in responding to the student questions. This was arranged beforehand by the manager of the Ozone Park Senior Center, who knew all of the women and the dynamics among them.

Besides our experience with oral history I have included a list of resources at the end of this article that can support you in your own projects. Hearing an older person tell his or her story can be very moving. It can help us better understand how our lives were influenced by the people who came before us. What events shaped them, and what events did they help shape? These questions can inspire us to explore our own family histories. The following is part of mine:

> As a boy, I was always interested in hearing stories about the past from my fraternal grandmother, parents, and other relatives. (My maternal grandmother died when I was five, my fraternal grandfather died when I was a baby.) They lived through some very big events—the Great Depression and World War II, for instance. I was known for my curiosity about our family history and all that went with it.
>
> Some stories weren't easily forthcoming. Both my parents came from poor families on the East Side of Manhattan, but my mother's family was even worse off. Her father died when she was twelve, and her older sister left high school to go to work as a waitress. They had to go down to a factory by the East River at six in the morning and break up crates for scrap wood, bring the scraps home, and put them in the pot-bellied stove to heat the apartment.
>
> My father was a gunner and radioman on a B-24 in the Army Air Force in the Pacific during World War II. When my brother and I were growing up, my dad never talked about the bad experiences of combat, only the adventure of travel and the comradeship in the service. I used to love to go through his memorabilia folder of photographs, letters, and medals. It was only when I was an adult that my mom told me how my father would wake up screaming in the middle of the night when they were first married, screaming from nightmares about the war. A family friend whom my dad confided in also told me this. My dad did tell me that he used to go to Catholic Mass on the airbase before every

combat mission and received Holy Communion; whenever he shot down a Japanese plane he would say a prayer for the pilot. My dad flew forty missions and was discharged from the military on his twenty-first birthday in 1945.

My mother's contribution on the home front in World War II was to work for Liggett & Myers Tobacco Company at a plant in New York City. Her job was to box cartons of cigarettes to be sent free to U.S. servicemen overseas.

This was a lifetime ago, and both my parents are deceased, as are their siblings and most of my other relatives of that generation. I never chronicled formally the stories in our family. I talk to my brother and my cousins and we remember them. And their children have heard some of these stories. But what about actually recording the stories so that they are preserved? These stories can have an impact beyond our immediate circle.

I've known older adults who met both Eleanor and Franklin Roosevelt; who fought in the Battle of the Bulge during World War II; who served in the American Red Cross in India; who survived the Nazi occupation of Belgium.

You have your own family and friends with stories, no matter how big or small those stories are. Preserving these memories is important to our collective history as a nation and as a world population.

STARTING OUT

If you're interested in starting a project at your community library, you need interested people. Try to network at your library with students, adults, and older adults you are friendly with. They can put you in touch with organizations such as schools and senior centers. You may be doing this on a very grassroots level with individuals. But if you decide to approach organizations, use these people as sources. Ask the students what schools they go to; check with your young adult librarian about teens she or he works with. Ask the older adults what groups they belong to. In a multicultural community, identify people who can serve as translators if needed.

Suggested Steps

- Identify an organization with older adults, and a school group or youth club to partner with. These might be senior centers, nursing homes or assisted living facilities, hospitals, and public or private schools. Additional organizations to look at might be local historical societies, colleges or universities, government (town, city, county), arts councils, religious and civic associations, and veterans groups.
- Identify administrators at the sites.
- Have voluntary signups after talking up the idea for the project.

- Have participants bring an old or favorite photograph to jump-start discussion.
- Get committed administrators on board at both the school or youth club and the senior site.
- Determine what type of end publication you want (written, audio, video, or a combination of these) to document the personal stories of the interviewees.
- Identify resources and equipment.
- Determine your budget and possible funding.
- Coordinate interview schedules. Have back-up dates in the event of bad weather.
- Set up a production schedule. Allow for extra time.
- Have a culminating event to celebrate the publication or documentary.
- Catalog the print or media document(s) you produce and have reference and circulating copies in your library.

The Interviewing Process

- The willingness and eagerness of participants in the interviews is important. All involved should desire to listen and learn.
- Preface your longer questions with "Describe . . ." or "Tell me about . . ."
- If you get a one-word answer, follow up with another question.
- Don't pressure people. Let them know that they do not have to say or reveal anything they don't want to. Nothing about the interview process should feel threatening for a participant. Help the participants feel that what they have to contribute is important. They are living history.
- Encourage participants to bring in any mementos from the past that they'd like to talk about: photographs, letters, documents, or objects such as a baseball glove, a doll, or a cherished article of clothing.
- Be prepared for the possibility that someone might become overwhelmed when answering a question. Allow people to take their time. Stop if necessary. Move on to another topic if something is too sensitive. Also, let people feel comfortable enough to expand beyond the question you asked.

Sample Questions

- Where were you born and where did you grow up? Describe your childhood, including any significant events. Describe your family life.
- Describe what your education was like.
- Tell us about a significant person(s) in your life and why that person(s) was important to you.
- Describe your work either outside or inside the home.
- Did you raise a family? Describe this.

- What important national and international events took place in your lifetime? How were you affected by these?
- Was there a particular time in your life that seemed to play the most important role in shaping you? Describe.
- What types of physical objects, if any, do you keep as memories of your past?
- What major changes have you witnessed in society in your lifetime? How did these changes affect you?
- What were you involved in as a young person? What were you involved in during your middle years?
- What kinds of activities are you involved in today? Is there something you'd like to do now but can't? Is there anything else you'd like to try?
- What differences do you see between when you grew up and when your children grew up and/or your grandchildren? Were these differences positive, negative, or both? Describe.
- What would you tell the children of today about life when you were growing up?
- What is appealing to you about society today? What is not so appealing?
- How would you feel about being a young person today? What advice would you give today's younger generation?

PROJECT NOTES

When we did the Bayside project, a funny story came out. Flora, an Italian-American, had told the students interviewing her that she grew up in the 1930s in New York with radio but without television. The students interpreted that to mean that Flora's parents couldn't afford a TV and wrote this. I corrected the statement when editing the written material. The students didn't know that commercial TV was not available until after World War II in the later 1940s. In a subsequent meeting of the people who administered the project, we realized the students could have used a timeline prep lesson about major historic events and inventions in the twentieth century. When we went on to the Ozone Park project, I discussed this with the teachers appointed to oversee the student interviewers. The social studies teacher went over a timeline with the students in the fall before the students conducted the interviews that winter. He showed me the timeline from the history textbook he was using and even gave me a copy to borrow. I felt this overview of the twentieth century helped the students in preparing for the Ozone Park interviews. We didn't experience any surprises there like the TV example I mentioned before.

I want to mention a follow-up event with the Ozone Park project: We went beyond the premiere of the video at the Ozone Park Senior Center in June 2009. The following school year, the half-hour video/DVD was shown to the general student body at Robert H. Goddard High School. Four of the women interviewed for the project were on hand at the school that day for a Q&A after the film. This idea came from Janet Fash, the high school media and communication arts teacher who directed the film. She felt that all the students at Goddard would benefit from seeing the film and getting a chance to interact with the older adult participants. And it would also give the high school camera crew a chance to speak about their involvement. An additional touch of emotion was supplied when the overall student body viewed childhood photographs of the women interviewees and then saw these women, now in their late seventies and eighties, in person.

Also, John Hyslop, the digitization manager of the archives at Queens Library, put together a PowerPoint presentation on the history of Ozone Park using digitized historic photographs and maps from the collection. I had used some of the photographs for the print publication of the interviews and supplied them to Janet Fash for the video. Now we were able to see even more images in this virtual walk through the history of a community.

I thoroughly enjoyed spending time doing computer searches on the database of digitized historic photographs of the Bayside and Ozone Park communities. A shot of a Long Island Railroad train in winter snow in 1905 as it headed east from the station looked like a very rural scene. The southwest corner of 35th Avenue and Bell Boulevard in Bayside taken by surveyors and dated February 1949 showed a tree-lined street and a small corner store with a big Coca-Cola sign on top. Today the trees are gone and there is a Gulf gas station on the corner with a Dunkin' Donuts concession inside.

Looking through the digital bank for period Ozone Park photographs, I came across a 1910 shot of the St. Mary Gate of Heaven School marching band. The all-boy band members were in uniform and stood on both sides of a big bass drum with the school name on the front. I saw a photograph from 1916 of a milk wagon, complete with horse and driver. On the side of the wagon were the words "Aqueduct Farms." In later decades, the Aqueduct name was associated with Raceway (for horse racing). Today there is a gambling casino on that site. I saw a photograph of the St. Mary Gate of Heaven Church in the early twentieth century, before the steeple was added, and a photograph from the same period of Broadway in Ozone Park when the street appeared to be a dirt road.

These are all treasures I unearthed. I'm sure similar jewels are out in your own communities, just waiting to be found. I encourage you to begin the journey. These objects will complement the living history you will discover through the spoken words of the people you interview.

I remember the late Irish writer Frank McCourt being interviewed on PBS by Charlie Rose. The author of the acclaimed memoir *Angela's Ashes* told Rose that everyone has a story. We can help people tell those stories through oral history.

RESOURCES

Texts

Best, L. 2007. *Genealogy for the First Time: Research Your Family History.* New York: Sterling.

Donald, R. 2003. *Doing Oral History: A Practical Guide.* New York: Oxford University Press.

Frommer, H. 2008. *Remembering Yankee Stadium: An Oral and Narrative History of the House That Ruth Built.* New York: Abrams.

Larson, M. C., ed. 2008. *Heroes among Us: Firsthand Accounts of Combat from America's Most Decorated Warriors in Iraq and Afghanistan.* New York: New American Library.

Queens Library, Ozone Park Senior Center, St. Mary Gate of Heaven School, and Robert H. Goddard High School of Communications, Ozone Park, New York. 2009. *Ozone Park Oral History Project.* New York: Queens Library.

Sommer, B. W., and M. K. Quinlan. 2009. *The Oral History Manual.* 2nd ed. Lanham, MD: AltaMira Press.

Williams, H. R., ed. 2004. *Weren't No Good Times: Personal Accounts of Slavery in Alabama.* Winston-Salem, NC: John F. Blair.

Organizations

The American Memory Historical Collections from the Library of Congress

The Institute for Oral History at Baylor University, Waco, Texas

The Oral History Association

Smithsonian Center for Folklife and Cultural Heritage

The Southern Oral History Program of the University of North Carolina, Chapel Hill

StoryCorps (stories archived at the Library of Congress and broadcast weekly on National Public Radio)

The University of Santa Cruz, California, Library

The Veterans History Project of the American Folklife Center of the Library of Congress

Chapter Twenty-Seven

Librarians' Role as Educators in Promoting Library Resources for Multicultural Patrons while Advancing a National Health Initiative

LaVentra E. Danquah and Wendy G. Wu

COLLABORATING WITH HEALTH-CARE PROFESSIONALS TO TEACH NATIONAL LIBRARY OF MEDICINE RESOURCES AT AN INTERNATIONAL CONFERENCE

At its core, the National Library of Medicine (NLM) provides trusted information services that promote health literacy, improve health outcomes, and reduce health disparities worldwide (National Library of Medicine 2006). More precisely, "Health literacy is the degree to which individuals can obtain, process, and understand the basic health information and services they need to make appropriate health decisions. But health literacy goes beyond the individual. It also depends upon the skills, preferences, and expectations of health information and care providers" (Nielsen-Bohlman, Panzer, and Kindig 2004). Similarly, *Healthy People 2020* defines health disparity as "a particular type of health difference that is closely linked with social, economic, and/or environmental disadvantage. Health disparities adversely affect groups of people who have systematically experienced greater obstacles to health based on their racial or ethnic groups" (United States Department of Health and Human Services 2012).

For years librarians have fostered value-added partnerships with health-care providers and community users to encourage library use and improve access to resources. Just as the Internet and Google have changed patient-physician dynamics, librarians continue to play their role in educating health-care providers on the limits of solely using Google for clinical decisions, and in teaching consumers how to locate reliable health information amid voluminous web resources (Giustini 2005; Waksman 2012). To effectively participate in efforts to address national health initiatives, librarians should explore various approaches to (1) promoting awareness of ubiquitous health information resources to health-care providers and consumers alike, (2) advance consumer-focused programs for underserved populations domestically and abroad, and (3) work to reduce health disparities experienced by minority populations. This chapter describes two unique experiences used in promoting NLM health resources and encouraging further library usage for health-care professionals and consumers. One experience involves selected librarians conducting health information research training and assistance at an international conference for health-care professionals. A different experience led to developing a website and arranging instructor-led courses for multicultural health-care consumers.

The NLM web portal offers a wealth of refereed health information to aid in advancing biomedical research, training, and global health initiatives. The platform provides access to biomedical literature, molecular biology tools, medical terminologies, information on drugs and diseases, clinical trials, environmental health and toxicology, health services, public health, an e-book collection, and more. MedlinePlus, NLM's consumer health website, contains extensive information on health and wellness, conditions and diseases, drugs and supplements, medical and surgical procedures featured in interactive tutorials, and surgery and anatomy videos, which patients can view in multiple languages. Interactive resources like Tox Town allow consumers to locate information on potentially hazardous chemicals contained in household products, along with other environmental health concerns or risks found throughout most neighborhoods and industrial areas.

Reportedly, health-care professionals indeed use the basic search features in PubMed (http://www.ncbi.nlm.nih.gov/pubmed) to identify research and patient care information. Anecdotal evidence suggests that these busy professionals may be unaware of (1) the variety of NLM resources such as the consumer health portal, specialized databases, and newly developed tools, and (2) the most efficient method of locating clinical decision support information among an extended list of search results.

The National Network of Libraries of Medicine Greater Midwest Region (GMR) selected one of us along with other librarians to promote NLM health information resources at the annual Radiology Society of North America (RSNA) conference. The RSNA conference is the largest medically related, international meeting in North America, with nearly sixty thousand health-care professionals and vendor service providers in attendance. This is an opportune event for librarians to utilize their expertise to help advance a national health initiative. For one week, librarians manned GMR's Informatics Booth. Cohorts designed and delivered interactive continuing education sessions, as well as short talks and demonstrations. More specifically, healthcare professionals learned of advanced and newly updated features for PubMed, how to execute effective search strategies, and tips for managing scholarly citations.

Previous conference data suggested that international participants may have experienced communication and language barriers during training sessions, and they were less likely to practice newly acquired information-seeking skills. As a result, whenever possible librarians with bilingual skills actively conversed with international participants in their native language. Participants were encouraged to visit the Informatics booth for additional follow-up and individual consultations. Librarians were careful to communicate and provide demonstrations at a slower pace, along with translating NLM's basic information in participants' native language (e.g., Chinese). Librarians with bilingual skills provided a valuable service during the event.

According to conference evaluations, participants learned efficient search strategies and identified new tools and/or improved features to aid in their research and clinical decision-making efforts. Reportedly, the demonstrations and sessions were relevant for identifying patient care information and academic research. Participants expressed plans to alter their health information–seeking strategies based on the new search tools and features they had learned. In addition, several attendees provided recommendations for future workshops and expressed their willingness to recommend NLM health information sessions and services to fellow colleagues.

A LIBRARY PROJECT AIMED AT REDUCING HEALTH DISPARITIES FOR MULTICULTURAL PATRONS

Eliminating health disparities for multicultural patients continues to be a primary health concern, as recently noted on the National Conference of State Legislatures (2012) website:

> Many factors contribute to racial, ethnic, and socioeconomic health disparities, including inadequate access to care, poor quality of care, community features (such as poverty and violence) and personal behaviors. These factors are often associated with underserved racial and ethnic minority groups, individuals who have experienced economic obstacles, those with disabilities and individuals living within medically underserved communities. Consequently, individuals living in both urban and rural areas may experience health disparities. Despite ongoing efforts to reduce health disparities in the United States, racial and ethnic disparities in both health and health care persist.

Libraries with a mission to provide consumer health information can play a pivotal role in helping patrons make informed health-care decisions. For example, Shiffman Medical Library at Wayne State University's Community Health Information Services (CHIS) initiative provides the following services and programs for community members: (1) customized consumer health information packets, (2) reference and research services, (3) instructor-led library workshops, and (4) topical programs and exhibits through its *Community Conversations on Health* series. Extending such services has significantly increased the library's visibility and patrons' use of library resources.

A special library project targeting multicultural patrons entailed developing a website dedicated to health disparities information on African Americans. The fundamental goal is to demonstrate how health information can be applied in making informed health-care decisions. The website was supplemented by instructor-led library workshops, which taught participants how to locate and make use of the information. The sessions were conducted at a partnering public library where patrons were also introduced to other CHIS services. The website, *African American Health Disparities Information* (http://www.lib.wayne.edu/sites/aah/), brings attention to primary health disparities affecting this patron group. The contents of the website reflect information that reinforces healthy lifestyle modifications. CHIS (http://www.lib.wayne.edu/sites/chis/) is a model community service that provides customized programming and health information services for multicultural groups.

CONCLUSION

The 2011 Horizon Report captures how technology continues to change the dynamics of the profession with the following statement: "The abundance of resources and relationships made easily accessible via the Internet is increasingly challenging us to revisit our roles as educators in sense-making, coaching, and credentialing" (Johnson et al. 2011, 3). Opportunities abound for librarians to engage in service initiatives targeted toward multicultural users. The simple examples set forth in this chapter describe methods used to influence multicultural patrons to increase their use of library resources and services. Collaborating with local, regional, and national partners to achieve these goals can significantly improve a library's chances of success. Librarians ready to emerge as information experts and educators can use these models as a framework for charting their course of action. Start off by exploring how the following services or strategies can be expanded or customized for selected patron groups: (1) creating and promoting online resources, (2) providing training and research assistance at professional conferences, (3) attending and highlighting relevant information resources at community events, (4) communicating with patrons in their native language during service interactions, and finally (5) continually expanding your knowledge about how your users learn, work, and play, along with best practices used within and beyond the profession to meet their needs.

WORKS CITED

Giustini, Dean. 2005. "How Google Is Changing Medicine." *British Medical Journal* 331(7531): 1487–88.

Johnson, L., R. Smith, H. Willis, A. Levine, and K. Haywood. 2011. *The 2011 Horizon Report.* Austin, TX: New Media Consortium.

National Conference of State Legislatures. 2012. *Disparities in Health.* http://www.ncsl.org/issues-research/health/health-disparities-overview.aspx (accessed March 15, 2012).

National Library of Medicine (NLM). 2006. *Charting a Course for the 21st Century—NLM's Long Range Plan 2006–2016.* http://www.nlm.nih.gov/pubs/plan/lrp06/report/default.html (accessed March 12, 2012).

Nielsen-Bohlman, Lynn, Allison M. Panzer, and David A. Kindig, eds. 2004. *Health Literacy: A Prescription to End Confusion.* Washington, DC: National Academies Press.

United States Department of Health and Human Services. 2012. *Healthy People 2020.* http://healthypeople.gov/2020 (accessed March 15, 2012).

Waksman, Ron. 2012. "Google Medicine." *Cardiovascular Revascularization Medicine* 13(1): 1–2.

Chapter Twenty-Eight

Programs, Signage, and the Kitchen Sink

Attracting Multicultural Patrons to School Libraries

Kris Baughman and Rebecca Marcum Parker

Attracting multicultural patrons to your library can be challenging—language, cultural, and educational differences can challenge both prospective patrons and library staff. Attracting multicultural patrons depends on building trust and relationships; the patrons you seek need to feel welcomed, comfortable asking questions, and assured that they belong. Excellent staff development on customs, practices, and even in language, plus careful communication techniques (such as maintaining eye contact with non-English speakers even when communicating through a translator), will show the community you want to reach that your library is a welcoming place to work, read, and enjoy.

Great signage can help draw patrons initially, as well as help patrons who are reluctant to ask questions. Programs that include and appeal to those of the culture you hope to draw will attract patrons and show your library's interest in having their patronage. Pertinent programs and carefully created signage in libraries serving multicultural patrons can attract those who need encouragement to enter the library. Both will show patrons that their needs and interests matter, and will encourage patrons to use the library.

THE BEGINNINGS OF A GREAT RELATIONSHIP

Our experience with multicultural patrons began fifteen years ago in a school library with a Latino population well over 65 percent. Most of our school population was low-income. The school had been restructured, so this was a new experience for staff and students. We found our way; within three years we earned Missouri's Gold Star Award for the success that the school community achieved.

A crucial first step was asking for help from Latino parents and students, plus partnering with organizations that also served them. These students, parents, and organizations were eager to form a committee and ask others for help. We brainstormed ideas for initial programs and asked for opinions regarding any ideas we had. Our most valuable partnership was with an eager parent volunteer who was very invested in the school. Her enthusiasm was infectious! She was exceptional at selling other parents on our program—finding volunteers was easy with her at the helm. These initial meetings even corrected our use of the term *Hispanic*—an okay English term long used by the community. The committee preferred *Latino*, the Spanish equivalent, which was much more accepted in the Latino community.

One initial issue we needed to tackle was the many differences between our patrons. While all spoke Spanish, our students were from Mexico, Central America, and South America. We had to be sure to understand that there were many differences between countries; after all, could one lump Americans and Brits in the same cultural categories because both speak English? Next, we secured help with translations. A good translator needed to be familiar with term differences between different Latino countries, and also to realize that commonly used terms might not be correct. *Librería* was often the word our parents used for library, but we discovered that this word really meant "bookstore." Our great translator told us the correct term was *biblioteca*, and we educated all in the use of this term.

MULTILINGUAL COMMUNICATION IS CRUCIAL

The committee and staff decided that it would be crucial to have all library documents published and distributed in English and Spanish. We started with the library contract; one side was in English (table 28.1) and the other side in Spanish (table 28.2). Our school translator provided the Spanish translation, and we tested it with our bilingual parents, who helped us make additions, subtractions, and corrections.

The parents and staff liked the combination of behavior expectations and library book guidelines in our library contract. We posted large copies to help students remember what our expectations were, and this helped nearly eliminate the number of student discipline problems. Bilingual and Spanish-speaking parents and students appreciated the Spanish translation, and students were proud to tell me each year as their parent was able to read and sign the English side. Distributing bilingual documents became the standard for the school; parents and students appreciated having information easy for all to read.

Improved Signage

After reviewing and adding English signage in our library, we reviewed these signs and asked our committee if any additional signs were needed. We added some additional English signs, and then worked to translate and hang the new Spanish signs. We used fadeless construction paper that we laminated for all of the signs—very effective and inexpensive. Initially we used die-cut letters and numbers, but we found that signs created in Microsoft Word were faster to make, and we could vary the font and size quite a bit. We color-coded areas and types of materials; for example, nonfiction signs were blue, fiction signs were yellow, reference signs were red, magazines signs were purple, and easy/everyone fiction signs were green. We posted our color code in various places in the library—at the entrance, the circulation desk, and in larger aisles in the stacks—to help our patrons find what they needed.

Table 28.1. Library Contract in English

Room: _____
Library Contract
In the library I will:
- speak so that only those who need to hear me can,
- listen carefully and follow the directions,
- respect others, and
- respect all library materials, furniture, and equipment.

While using books library and school books I will:
- be careful with books so others can enjoy them,
- return any book I find, even if it is not mine, and
- be responsible with my library book.

I understand what is expected of me. I accept the consequences of my actions.
_____, Student

I will help my child in keeping this contract, ask my child about any overdue books, and pay for any lost library books.
_____, Parent

Table 28.2.   Library Contract in Spanish

Sala de clase _____
El Contracta de los Libros
Dentro de la biblioteca hare:
- hablare de modo que solo estos quien puedan necesitarme escucharme,
- escuchar cuidadosamente y seguir las instruciones,
- respetar a otros, y
- respetar todo el equipo, muebles, y materiales.
Mientras usas los libros de la escula:
- yo cuidare bien los libros de modo que otros puedan disfrutarlos a ellos,
- regresare cualquier libros que yo encuentre sin embargo si ellos son mios, y
- quitar responsabilidades para libros y uso de la biblioteca alquilar los libros con migo.
Yo entiendo que esto esperare de mi y yo aceptare las consequencias de mis acciones.
_____, Estudiante
Yo ayudare a mi niño a conserver el contracto, incluyendo el pago de los libros.
_____, Padres

AN INVITING LIBRARY ATMOSPHERE

Making the library welcoming and warm was important, too. It was originally bare and offered no alternative seating or pillows. To add color, we backed
bulletin boards and drab areas with colorful wrapping paper. We combed
garage sales, thrift stores, and stores for pillows, beanbags, lamps, and decorations; we especially looked for decorations from the countries our students
were from. We shamelessly begged for donated materials, and we were sure
to publicly thank donors. We appealed to organizations serving the same
clientele for donations they could not use in their organization, and likewise
we gave them donations we couldn't use. Students and parents loved the
library's new warm atmosphere, and we were often busy at any time of day.
We began playing classical music to support the music curriculum, then
added traditional music from Spanish-speaking countries.

DEVELOPING RELATIONSHIPS

We then kicked off the year by having a Read-In and chili dog supper for our
students and families. Unfortunately, we were a bit behind on planning, and
the notices needed to be out by the end of the day. Our translator was ill and
consequently could not help. To get by, we depended on a semester of
Spanish and a free translation website. The morning after the notices went
out, the amused "barking" of parents gave us the hint that maybe our transla-

tion was lacking! Yes, our translation of "chili dog" meant an actual, barking dog with chili on it. Amused students began questioning us about supposed missing pets! Fortunately, the parents and students were really amused by our mistake, and it created a strong camaraderie among us. The effort we had made to reach out left a positive impression, even though our translation was horrible! It's not a mistake we recommend, but it did cement a strong relationship between us and the parents. And no one missed the Read-In and chili dog supper—it was another chance to bark at us! Even fifteen years later, we will hear barking behind us and turn to see the smiling face of a former student or parent.

GROWING OUR PROGRAM

As a group we brainstormed future programs showcasing the skills of our students and parents, plus programs educating us all in cultural traditions, stories, and history. We began a library newsletter called "In the Pink." (The library was pink, plus it was a good way to teach English idioms to students!) The newsletter was always presented in English and Spanish, and, along with news, it gave tips for reading at home with children. Students began to contribute to the library news going home and loved being recognized (any suggestion used in the library was always publicly credited to the creator). Our reading buddies contributed news about their readings and progress. We partnered with the public library and presented their program information in the newsletter, too. We published new acquisitions in the newsletter so that all would know what was available.

The library signage led to school signage, and parents really responded positively to this. At all school meetings, we began actively advertising that translators would be on-site and recruited parent officers to plan and run the meetings. We found from the beginning that we needed to allow twice as much time for translations and questions. We realized that only the most important items should be addressed; since a four-hour-plus meeting might turn off parents, we pared down topics, and everyone appreciated this change. Our first meeting was not as well attended as we had expected, so we surveyed the parents and found that, since many could not afford child care, some who had hoped to attend did not. Providing child care gave us a huge boost in attendance, and that became a permanent part of our parent meetings. Serving meals was a great way to attract parents, and some of our best discussions happened during informal mealtime conversations.

STAFF DEVELOPMENT HELPS EVERYONE

As a staff, we continued to seek staff development to help us understand our clientele better. At the same time, our parents wanted to cook their specialties for us. We combined this into a dinner and a chance to hear about cultural beliefs and views. It was a bit daunting to see the spread and to hear that a polite guest tries a bit of everything, but I was glad to know what to do to best honor these parents who took so much time to provide information and delicious food. We learned to eat less for a couple of days before celebrations!

Even though a semester of Spanish from the local community college was helpful, we wanted to learn more. After exploring programs and costs, we realized that the best programs were too expensive and didn't necessarily address our needs for library- and school-specific vocabulary. Since our large district included Spanish programs taught by native speakers, we begged for funds to pay these experts already in place throughout the district to teach Spanish classes specific to our needs at no cost to any teacher or librarian who was interested. The classes were fabulous; we learned language to help us discuss difficult situations with parents, specific vocabulary, and ways to help our newest students who had no English skills. An added benefit was hearing from these native speakers what it was like walking into a new school with no understanding of anything said or written. Plus, we learned more about the school cultures and beliefs about learning in the native countries of our students. It was a great perspective that really changed and shaped our dealings with our newest students and parents, plus the programs and structure of our library. Our instructor even role-played with us; she would speak in the fast cadence of an upset or excited parent, and this greatly helped us improve our listening and language skills.

OPENING THE LINES OF COMMUNICATION

We found immediately that our Latino parents were very interested in learning English, and we found outside groups who were experienced in teaching English language classes to provide them at our school in the library. Our parents loved this; many had limited education and liked coming to classes in a place where they already felt comfortable. English language classes led to a heart-warming request by a group of native English-speaking parents: could classes be offered in Spanish? Our English-speaking parents were eager to communicate with other parents; I never heard a parent insist that conversations should be in English at school, and I loved that all of our parents were eager to communicate no matter the language.

A Nontraditional Solution

At this point, we tallied the successes and planned for future steps. We found that our committee of parents and interested community members took us in great directions that we would have never headed without their help. At the beginning of our second phase, we looked to restructure the library collection. We had a limited number of simple bilingual books, but we found that we had many needs that these books could not serve. Our patrons had multiple needs: some wanted to be able to read popular American books in Spanish with a Spanish-speaking relative, some Spanish-speaking parents and grandparents wanted to share Spanish favorites from their childhood with the children in their family, some bilingual parents wanted to read with their American-born children in order for them to master Spanish as well as English, and some of our students wanted to maintain their Spanish as they learned English. Buying translations of American books in Spanish was becoming much easier at this time, and we were able to find Beverly Cleary, Harry Potter, and many favorites in Spanish. Buying traditional Spanish literature and popular Spanish literature was more challenging. Parents and community had some suggestions, but we found that many of these were out of print or possibly only available in anthologies which with we were not familiar. Fortunately, other schools in our district were facing the same challenge, and a native Spanish-speaking district librarian was willing to travel to an international children's book fair to evaluate, plan, and order books for us. It is always great to know that one can find help from experts instead of blindly playing hit-and-miss in an area in which you have no experience! We were all excited when these books arrived—adults in the community found old favorites and new interests. We found so much interest in these new books that we created a project in which students and their team members (some were their family members, neighbors, or other interested adults) shared reviews of these new books. The reviews helped new Spanish language learners; it was easier to decide what to read and what they'd have the most success with.

We surveyed students as to how to organize the new materials so that our patrons could more easily find materials. We ended up reorganizing the library; we wanted our new collections to not feel like an afterthought, and we wanted the organization to make sense to our patrons. We shelved the translations of American and original English language books with the regular fiction section, and made a separate section for the Spanish books originally in Spanish and color coded them orange. We created displays to advertise the new offerings. An added benefit was that the library floor plan had better flow and was easier to keep organized.

IMPORTANT IDEAS TO REMEMBER

Sadly, due to budget constraints, the librarian position became a part-time one. Fortunately, the funding did not decrease much and the library staff was able to continue to provide great, specific resources. After a couple of years, despite protests from the community served, the school was closed due to a district-wide decrease in students. Thankfully, librarians of schools remaining open were able to select books from the collection, and other Latino students were able to enjoy these resources.

We learned rules to live by as librarians of a multicultural school:

- Assume most of what you know of another culture is not correct, especially if you learned it in a traditional American school or college setting. We went into this using the term *Hispanic* and are grateful that a brave soul corrected us!
- Maintain eye contact with those with whom you are communicating, especially if you are communicating through a translator.
- Ask questions always! Question what you do not understand, because once you get the concept, you can possibly apply it to other situations.
- Attend community programs for and created by your target community so that you can continue to expand your knowledge.
- Attend the in-school and out-of-school programs your students perform in. It's a great way to get to know your families better.
- Learn at least a bit of the language of the culture you serve. This will show your library's interest in the patrons you wish to attract and retain.
- Know that you will make mistakes, and be prepared to laugh at yourself and to apologize and learn from them. A great sense of humor can guide you well!
- Never hesitate to ask for help. We all like to be experts, and most are flattered and eager to help.
- Always look for new avenues of help and resources.
- Double check your work and translations!
- Plan ahead so there is plenty of time to catch mistakes and problems.
- Ask students and parents for their opinions and suggestions. Your best ideas and most successful plans often start with ideas from others.
- Be prepared to change direction when necessary; don't become so married to a plan that you cannot see a better one when it presents itself.

An open mind and heart can take your library program from one with new challenges in attracting new multicultural patrons to a successful library where all feel welcome. The benefits are many for librarians and library staff willing to take the plunge!

Part VI

Programming and Events

Chapter Twenty-Nine

Raising Awareness in Academic Libraries with Multicultural Exhibits, Installations, and Decorations

Fantasia Thorne and Kimberly Williams

Libraries may partner with other units on campus to create exhibits or displays to showcase multicultural issues and celebrations. Sometimes the exhibits can be controversial, but the library is one of the only buildings on campus that is a neutral site—one wherein every student and staff member should feel free to display aspects of their heritage. This chapter will discuss the benefits of encouraging students and staff to use library space to display multicultural exhibits, and also the collaboration between the library and the office of multicultural affairs to create such exhibitions.

EXHIBITS AT BIRD LIBRARY

Syracuse University Library's Learning Commons (LC) is defined as a user-driven and user-centered space, and this model has manifested itself in a number of ways. The Fiber Sculpture and Fiber Arts and Architecture courses often exhibit class projects around the three floors of the Learning Commons. The innovative and creative artwork is something library patrons enjoy, and the student artists appreciate using the library as an exhibit space, since it provides a larger audience than their classroom setting or their department's exhibit space. The art and exhibits in the library have prompted more groups to use the space to express themselves as well, be it to celebrate

259

a specific time of the year (e.g., Chinese New Year, Black History Month) or to draw attention to a specific racial issue (e.g., local and national Asian hate crimes).

For the past two years the Chinese Student and Scholar Association (CSSA) has decorated the first floor of the Learning Commons with a number of ornate and attention-grabbing objects. In 2011, the CSSA, the library, and the Folk Arts, Festival, and Public Display anthropology class decorated the first floor of the Learning Commons with items such as zodiacs, Chinese red lanterns, and a knot wishing tree. The decorations, as well as most exhibits, have been documented in the Syracuse University Learning Commons Flickr account, unrestricted and able to be viewed by all.

Since 2010, an exhibit has been displayed during the month of February for Black History Month. One of the ways we celebrate African American history and life is by displaying books written by and about African American people. For staff working in the library, exhibits and new book projects require structured collaboration. Members of the staff in the Learning Commons locate the books in the catalog and retrieve them from the shelves; then the Access Services and Sharing Department changes the holding locations and places the books on a new bookcase. A table has been placed near the circulation desk containing flyers advertising events sponsored by the office of multicultural affairs, also including colorful Black History Month calendars available for patrons. With the exhibit positioned next to the circulation desk, it is inevitable that a large number of patrons will be able to view and enjoy the materials on display.

Student groups and staff appreciate the willingness of the library to serve as a supportive space to exhibit aspects of their culture. Items displayed reach a wide range of patrons from many cultures, disciplines, majors, and socioeconomic backgrounds. The director of the Learning Commons, Lesley Pease, in an e-mail communication on March 5, 2012, revealed her hopes that the library be seen as an ally that provides students and staff an avenue through which to communicate something important to them. She also feels the exhibits, installations, and decorations serve as "a means to educate, sources of inspiration, consciousness-raisers, springboards for further inquiry, ways to break down barriers, encouragement for others to bring their exhibit ideas forward, and a way to show users that the LC is open to doing things and trying things out." Having such a supportive Learning Commons director has been pivotal in making many of the exhibition ideas come to life.

CONTROVERSIAL EXHIBITS

In April 2010, the library partnered with the office of multicultural affairs to create the Anti- Asian Hate Crime exhibit. The exhibit was designed by staff, faculty, and students to bring awareness to the microaggressions and violent hate crimes that Asian American people face. Asian and Pacific Americans are often seen as the "model minority," which is a term used to describe those people from underrepresented groups who excel in ways that other underrepresented groups do not excel. As a result, when violent crimes are committed against Asian and Pacific Americans that are directly related to their race/ethnicity, these crimes are dismissed and not recognized as hate crimes. For example, in 1997, the staff in a Syracuse Denny's restaurant refused to serve a group of Syracuse University Asian students because of their race/ethnicity. This year is the fifteenth anniversary of that incident, and many people, including current Syracuse University students, are unaware that it happened. The Anti-Asian Hate Crime exhibit brought light to this incident and other hate crimes committed against Asian- Pacific Americans. The exhibit was placed in the library for a month in the lower level of the Learning Commons. For the opening reception, an Asian American activist spoke, and others shared their stories and experiences with hate crimes committed against Asian Americans. The library display of this exhibit exposed staff, students, faculty, and other patrons of the library to the myth that exists about the "model minority."

Some institutions exhibit controversial topics with the hope of creating dialogue among the student body, as well as educating the public to very sensitive issues. In 2003, the American University Library installed an exhibit titled "Sorrow and Hope in the Holy Land: Palestine and the Palestinians" as described in the article titled "Multiculturalism and Library Exhibits: Sites of Contested Representation," by Gwendolyn J. Reece (2005). Cosponsored by the Library's exhibits team and Students for Justice in Palestine, the purpose of the exhibit was to alert library patrons to the political struggles in Palestine. The exhibit displayed images, maps, cultural items, and books. A comment book was also placed near the exhibit in order to document the remarks made by the viewers. A number of patrons applauded the library's effort to provide a venue for such a controversial topic, but many were upset and made numerous negative comments, with some even accusing the library of promoting racism. The comment book was an ingenious method that provided patrons the anonymity to leave their honest opinions and reactions to such a controversial exhibit.

In December 1995, an exhibit was curated by George Washington University American Studies professor John Michael Vlach, titled "Back of the Big House: The Cultural Landscape of the Plantation," and was contracted to be displayed in the Library of Congress. The exhibit was removed only three-and-a-half hours after its installation due to complaints from African American staff members. The incident, described in an article by Gordon Flagg (1996) titled "Bowing to Staff Protests, LC Removes Slavery Exhibition," explains that the exhibit had already traveled for a year and was displayed in four other locations without complaints. The Martin Luther King Jr. Library in Washington, DC, installed the exhibit shortly after its removal from the Library of Congress. A follow-up article titled "D.C. Lib. Picks Up Closed LC Exhibit" (1996) briefly addresses the aftermath of the exhibit's controversial move, which outraged many individuals. Similarly, at Syracuse University, we created in the spring of 2011 the controversial exhibit about anti-Asian hate crimes. Libraries sometimes are the source of contentious materials, and although the Syracuse University library did not experience controversy on the same level as the Library of Congress, the idea that libraries are places of contention is one that we would like to highlight in this article.

Exhibits such as "Sorrow and Hope in the Holy Land: Palestine and the Palestinians," "Back of the Big House," and the "Anti-Asian Hate Crimes" exhibit address controversial issues and should be handled in sensitive ways. Reece's article describes the channels the exhibitors followed to ensure the library was aware of and supported the content of the exhibit. When the library finds itself in a space of controversy there are measures that may be taken to eliminate the issue. Precedent has been set with altering controversial content, because in the case of the Palestinian exhibit, the content of the exhibit had to be modified so patrons would be enlightened and not outraged. While creating exhibits, it is advantageous to include other departments such as the office of multicultural affairs in order to determine whether or not content and images may be considered insensitive or inappropriate.

FUTURE PLANS FOR EXHIBIT COLLABORATIONS

Creating exhibits for the celebratory months, such as Black History Month or Asian Pacific American Heritage Month, is a good way to begin displaying multicultural exhibitions in libraries. Plans are being developed to create an exhibit for Latino Heritage Month and Native American Heritage month in the Learning Commons. Exhibit proposals accepted by the Learning Commons are presented to the library exhibitions committee, chaired by the director of communications. The committee is responsive and communicative when reviewing proposals, ensuring timely installation dates and any other support needed to create professional and engaging exhibits.

CONCLUSION

Although the collaboration between the library and many offices appears seamless, while creating exhibits dialogue, keeping an open mind, and perhaps making compromises on both sides must occur. If an exhibit is considered controversial, it is crucial that the appropriate procedures are followed to ensure support of the exhibit committee, the library, and the university. If done well, everyone benefits, and the library is seen as a site for activism and not just passive learning and research.

WORKS CITED

"DC Lib. Picks Up Closed LC Exhibit." 1996. *Library Journal* 121(2): 15. http://search.ebscohost.com/login.aspx?direct=true&db=lxh&AN=9602017724&site=ehost-live.

Flagg, Gordon. 1996. "Bowing to Staff Protests, LC Removes Slavery Exhibition." *American Libraries* 27(2): 10. http://search.ebscohost.com/login.aspx?direct=true&db=llf&AN=502850072&site=ehost-live.

Reece, Gwendolyn J. 2005. "Multiculturalism and Library Exhibits: Sites of Contested Representation." *Journal of Academic Librarianship* 31(4): 366–72. doi: 10.1016/j.acalib.2005.04.006.

Chapter Thirty

Bridging the Gap

Exploring the Racial Divide in Louisiana

Derek Mosley and April Grey

The Ernest J. Gaines Center at the University of Louisiana at Lafayette is an international center for scholarship on Ernest J. Gaines and his work. As part of the Edith Garland Dupré Library, the Gaines Center honors the work of the University of Louisiana at Lafayette's writer-in-residence emeritus and provides a space for scholars and students to work with the Gaines papers and manuscripts. The Ernest J. Gaines Center has become an African American heritage center and a hub for community activities related to diversity and multiculturalism. Programs from around the academic community have found a safe and open environment to bring all races together for discussion and reflection on a shared past.

Born in 1933 on a plantation near New Roads, Louisiana, Gaines based his award-winning novels on the African American experience in the rural South. Ernest J. Gaines's literary works include *The Autobiography of Miss Jane Pittman* and *A Lesson before Dying*, both later produced as award-winning films. His generous donation of his early papers and manuscripts and a multitude of artifacts to Edith Garland Dupré Library provides the foundation for the center's collection. The mission of the Ernest J. Gaines Center is to foster research and scholarship on the life and works of Ernest J. Gaines. The Gaines Center has hosted a number of events relating to Gaines's experience in southwest Louisiana and explores sociologically intense themes such as racism, stereotypes, and discrimination in the historical context and in the present day.

TYPES OF PROGRAMS

The Gaines Center hosts many guest speakers from a variety of backgrounds. These speakers have unique perspectives relating to race and the impact of race on modern society. To provide our academic community with a truly multicultural series of events, the Gaines Center hosts lectures and readings by international speakers and scholars on the topics of race in literature, film, and society. A variety of events also keeps the programming interesting. Not only do we rely on guest lecturers for our programs, we also screen movies and hold discussion groups, art shows, and musical performances.

THEMED EVENTS

One of our recent speakers was Dr. Wilhelmina J. Donkoh, senior lecturer and Fulbright scholar from Kwame Nkrumah University in Kumasi, Ghana. She was invited to speak on the topic of slavery and slave tourism in Ghana. In anticipation of the lecture by Dr. Donkoh, the Gaines Center, in collaboration with the History and Geography Department, hosted a screening of a documentary about slave castles and the slave tourism industry in Ghana. The film *Through the Door of No Return* gave viewers background information about the topic that Dr. Donkoh would present to the community. We wanted students and community members to get an understanding of what the Ghana slave tourism industry was, before they would have an opportunity to ask questions and discuss the topic.

At the lecture, Dr. Donkoh discussed her research with the audience of about seventy guests and then opened the floor for questions and discussion. For over an hour a group of diverse strangers maintained thoughtful respectful discussion about the slave trade and the slave tourism industry. Audience participants from a variety of racial and ethnic backgrounds were able to question the morals of a country profiting from a horrendous part of history, how this type of tourism came to be, and how people from all over the world knew about it.

Documentary films, lectures, and discussion programs are popular at the Gaines Center and always well attended by students and community members. We feel this program about race tourism in Ghana was successful and can be replicated at other libraries. One question asked during the discussion pondered whether or not African American tourists would be accepted in Africa if they visited the continent because of a common heritage or due to the money that African Americans bring to the tourism industry. One student who was of a mixed racial heritage asked what ethnicity she would be perceived as in Ghana. This led to a discussion about racial culture and who had historically been considered black. Other libraries can use race as a way to engage their discussion participants. There is much success to be had from exploring our cultural differences, and libraries should actively seek new perspectives for topics and programming.

AUTHOR READINGS

Collaboration is the best way to bring in a diverse audience for discussion of the racial divide. The Gaines Center has a strong relationship with the Creative Writing Program. We partnered with them to host a series of readings by ethnically diverse authors. The readings drew in large crowds and presented to our students and local community the literary works from a variety of people of multicultural backgrounds. It also afforded the Gaines Center another venue for discussion of race in literature and culture. Novelist Lily Hoang and South African Poet Laureate Keorapetse Kgositsile are two of the authors who highlighted their racial experience in their literary works and shared their writing with an audience at the Gaines Center.

SOCIAL MEDIA

To open a dialogue about the perceived racial divide in Louisiana and the southern United States, the Gaines Center also utilizes social media platforms. The archival collection and the writings by Ernest Gaines have such a rich and detailed picture of slavery and the civil rights movement that there is a huge potential for outreach on the topics of slavery and segregation. The Gaines Center has a website, a Facebook page, and a Twitter account to publicize the events at the Gaines Center. These online media platforms help to attract students and community members to the programs we are offering at the Gaines Center. By posting thought-provoking quotes from Gaines's works on Facebook and Twitter, we are able to engage online participants in discussion.

MOVIE NIGHT

The Gaines Center partners with the History Department to show a monthly film series relating to the African American experience. In the past year we have screened *Amistad*, *The Color Purple*, Disney's *The Princess and the Frog*, Ernest Gaines's *The Autobiography of Miss Jane Pittman*, and the miniseries *Roots*. Members of the university community and the public are invited to come to the screenings. Films have been a great tool to explore themes and get more people to visit Gaines Center to learn about the research opportunities available there. After the movie is finished, a chosen moderator leads a discussion with the audience. We have invited professors, students, and staff to lead the discussion as moderator. Choosing a variety of moderators keeps the discussions fresh and forward thinking. For example, when a student leads the discussion, he or she tends to talk about current topics and try to relate them to the film they have just seen. Moderators usually have a passion for the film or subject matter and theme surrounding the film. Professors who have written scholarly articles on the film or the book if it has been turned into a film are asked to moderate the discussions of their particular interest. Having an authority on the film or someone who has a background regarding the matter positively influences the discussion. Though the films are about African American themes, the audience tends to be very diverse.

The most-attended movie night followed by great discussion occurred with the screening of the Disney movie *The Prince and the Frog*. Since this is the first Disney film about an African American girl and the story is based in Louisiana, many students and faculty members showed up for this screening. The student discussion leader centered the lively discussion on the racial stereotypes in the movie. The stereotypes were not just those relating to African Americans but also the Louisiana Cajun and Creole cultures. The audience discussed the gender stereotypes of women and gender roles in cultures throughout the United States. The discussion participants were diverse culturally, and this led to a long discussion about stereotypes of different students on campus. We believe that the movie night program can be replicated at other libraries to have meaningful conversation about the state of race in film and culture.

Discussion participants usually ask tough questions about race, and the audience responds openly and honestly. Many moderators pull out themes and want to engage the audience about the depiction of African Americans historically and in the current landscape. One of the most controversial movies shown in this series has been the television miniseries *Roots*, based on the book by Alex Haley. The entire series was shown in the Gaines Center throughout Black History Month, with one episode being shown a week. Though the crowd was small, they were dedicated to screening the miniseries and discussing the themes that were brought up each week. Many of the students had never seen or even heard of this landmark series. It was important to the Gaines Center and the History Department that the students have the opportunity to view the film. A film series can be a very easy and economical way to engage a community and explore racial issues. Each movie screening typically has ten to thirty-five people. The Gaines Center provides snacks and drinks. A local pizza restaurant donates six large pizzas to the monthly program. Since the inclusion of pizza at the film screenings, more students attend. It also gives a local business the opportunity to support the Gaines Center and advertise the restaurant.

CONCLUSION

Not only does the Ernest J. Gaines Center have events, they also let other organizations on campus and in the community hold events that relate to our programming goals. This also helps bring new visitors and spreads the word about the Gaines Center. There are many ways to attract a diverse and interesting group of people to your center to participate in multicultural programming. Libraries must think outside the box and use new ideas to engage a dialogue and discussion across the racial divide.

Chapter Thirty-One

Café a las Siete/Coffee at Seven

Cross-Cultural Programming at a Public Library

Diana J. Lennon

PROGRAM IDEA AND PURPOSE

Café a las Siete/Coffee at Seven is a series of bilingual Spanish-English events designed to promote cross-cultural understanding and to build positive community relationships. Each program attracts a mix of native Spanish and English speakers and offers a place to interact and share an appreciation for educational and cultural offerings, both musical and artistic. Latino patrons are attracted to the library when interesting and enjoyable community events highlight their culture and the talent and work of other Latinos living in Westchester County, New York. The resulting dialogue and interaction creates an improved rapport among the residents of Greenburgh and provides a welcoming environment for all community members, including new immigrants and those seeking to learn about Latino culture.

For two years, and with a third year scheduled, Café a las Siete has highlighted the cultural arts from Latin America in weekly sessions over four to six weeks. A guitarist from Argentina and another with Dominican roots have entertained library patrons; a Mexican woman has led an intergenerational workshop on how to make traditional tissue-paper flowers; and a Peruvian woman has taught beading techniques, learned from her grandmother, to patrons of all ages and backgrounds. An exciting cooking demonstration led by an Ecuadorian sous-chef gave everyone a "taste" of Latino culture. Isabel Allende's novel *Island beneath the Sea* was the focus of a well-attended book discussion group. A vibrant concert presented by a local group whose members are from Ecuador, Peru, and Chile closed the series each year with much acclaim. Their music created a special fiesta atmosphere, with patrons and staff dancing and enjoying coffee and desserts. We first envisioned this project and planned it as a one-time series. Now with two years of experience, and a third year planned and funded, we foresee an annual event built on foundations established through careful planning and presentation of excellent and popular programs.

STEPS TO SUCCESS

Identifying a Need

While there were no apparent issues or negative feelings among the different ethnic groups visiting the library, we did notice that there was little interaction among them. Latinos in particular did not seem to take advantage of programs and the services offered at the library. We asked ourselves what steps we could take in order to (1) bring various ethnic groups together, and (2) bring more Latinos into the library. Our answer was to create a rich cultural program that would attract a variety of people while also introducing Latinos to the library by showcasing their own artistic heritage. We named it Café a las Siete/Coffee at Seven because each program would start at seven o'clock in the evening and we would offer coffee and light food. It was the idea of a café, however, that seemed most fitting: a comfortable social gathering place with entertainment and the opportunity to meet new people and greet old friends. With this goal in mind, we began to investigate the practical issues of finances, artists, and public relations.

Funding

The Café a las Siete project was funded for 2010 and 2011 by a grant from the ArtsAlive program of ArtsWestchester, which receives some funding from the Decentralization Program of the New York State Council on the Arts. We learned of the grant opportunity by subscribing to the ArtsAlive newsletter, frequent visits to their website (http://www.artswestchester.org), and attending their grant information sessions. The grant required that we provide matching funds, which came from our adult programs budget. For the first year of the program, the library and ArtsAlive each provided $1,200; for the second year, $1,600; for 2012, the amount is $1,000 each, as both organizations' funding has been reduced by high percentages. This has forced us to shorten the length of the program from six weeks to four, yet still plan an impressive program. Much of this is due to our ability to build on the success of previous years by cultivating our relationships with area artists and musicians, who have been quite generous in performing at a reduced rate.

Another important resource we called upon was the Friends of the Greenburgh Library; they generously provided money for refreshments. Additionally, area restaurants donated food each year, and when we explained our program and its purpose, they were happy to donate food in exchange for the free advertisement at our programs. The relationships we have built with them over time have made it easy for us to request food donations, especially when we also pointed out the overall benefits to the community that the café atmosphere and cultural heritage programs would offer. We also were lucky enough to have as a library board member a retired chef from Spain, who volunteered to make delicious tapas for the final programs, the culinary highlight of each year.

Performers

To find the artists for the first year's program, we searched the ArtsAlive Westchester database of performers and spoke with a number of area librarians who work with the Latino community. With the database contacts and through recommendations, we selected musicians and artists to approach regarding our program. All of the performers recognized the importance of attracting Latinos to the library and showcasing local Latino talent. We chose those musicians who recognized their own influence in the community, embraced their Latino background, and wanted to promote this heritage by sharing their artistic talent. Each graciously charged us a reduced fee to show their support of the library and the program; we thanked them publicly for this at their performance. Their professional networks also brought people, many for the first time, into the library to see them perform, and allowed us to promote the library to these newcomers.

We decided to arrange a series of programs that offered music every other week, with a movie, book discussions, a family health night, and a cooking program on alternate weeks. The variety of programs made the series attractive to more people, as very different interests were showcased, and allowed patrons to attend some or all of the programs.

Public Relations

An important factor in promoting the programs was that all flyers, posters, and announcements (website, LCD screens) were in both Spanish and English. Flyers had Spanish on one side and English on the other; posters used different fonts for each language. It was very important to ensure that the Spanish used was grammatically correct and did not use colloquial language from one specific country, as the Latino population encompasses people from many nations. A library must locate and create an ongoing relationship with a person who can appropriately compose or translate the information to be provided into Spanish. We are lucky to have Spanish speakers on staff, but other libraries may want to contact high school Spanish teachers and others who frequently write in correct Spanish to assist them.

Another significant contribution to the program's success was the colorful and symbolic logo created for the series by our public relations assistant. A partial view of a classical Spanish guitar, with "Café a las Siete" in black set against a red background with yellow details, caught everyone's eye and sparked interest, while making the program familiar from year to year. This logo was on posters, flyers, programs, and the library's LCD screens, and was prominently displayed on our website for the duration of the series. After each program, a librarian created posters using pictures taken by local amateur photographers, and hung them up around the library in order to continue the buzz created at each program.

In the program's first year, printed bilingual invitations were sent to patrons, community members, professional contacts, and other library personnel from a mailing list created specifically for this project. Due to budget restrictions in the second year, printed invitations were not sent, so an increased effort was made to promote the series. Library personnel and volunteer patrons distributed flyers throughout the area, especially to locations frequented by Latinos. Flyers also were readily available throughout the library.

Each year, press releases were sent in both languages to area bilingual, English, and Spanish newspapers and radio stations. The local online newspaper included a story on the series, which also contributed to bringing patrons into the library to enjoy these programs. At the time of the first two series, the library did not have a Facebook page or Twitter account. For subsequent years, it is expected that these social networking tools will announce the series to a wider and ever-growing audience. The use of both these traditional and newer advertising formats will reach an audience of varied age, ethnicity, and linguistic background and will likely spread the word faster and with greater impact.

Indeed, a major factor for the success of Café a las Siete was the development of a strong word-of-mouth network among patrons. As momentum grew, so did program attendance, and the buzz that quality programs were taking place at the library spread throughout the community. It is very important to note that this was not left to chance; a concerted effort by all library staff and key patrons was critical to its success. At every opportunity, staff spoke with patrons about Café a las Siete, pointing out posters, flyers, and the website information while patrons were checking out materials, asking reference questions, in computer classes, and during casual conversations. Latino patrons whom the staff knew well were asked to spread the word and invite their friends and contacts; some made announcements and posted flyers at their churches, organizations, and workplaces. Librarians also sent flyers via e-mail, as well as weekly reminders, to personal and professional contacts, and requested that these be forwarded to anyone who might be interested in the series of programs. This continual reminder was an important form of advertisement that became apparent as the number of library contacts increased through the partnerships we created with each weekly program.

Community Partnerships

In an effort to both reach new audiences and present lesser-known aspects of the Latino culture to our patrons, the library partnered with the Westchester County Chamber Music Society, whose members are well-respected and very talented musicians. Their program, "Classical Music with a Latin Flair," was very well received by the audience, and for many, it was their first experience with classical music by Spanish composers such as Manuel de Falla and Isaac Albéniz. Both classical music fans and those who like Latin music were brought together in a unique affiliation to share their love of music.

We also worked with the Chamber Music Society in presenting a film titled *Tocar y Luchar/To Play and Fight*, which documents the development of the Venezuelan Youth Orchestra (now known as the Orquesta Sinfónica Simón Bolívar/Simón Bolívar Symphony Orchestra) by following some of its members from local music lessons to international performances. Many attendees were unaware that the program existed and commented on the importance of showing this type of entertaining and educational film at the library.

The library also partnered with the Westchester Photographic Society, a local group of professional and amateur photography enthusiasts, in a mutually beneficial arrangement. The photographers enjoyed unusual and interesting subjects and venues, while allowing the use of their outstanding photos by the library, the artists, and ArtsWestchester for promotional purposes. Some of their work, in fact, was shown in photo exhibits both at this library and other libraries in the county. The photos were used in a series of posters designed to attract patrons to the events and were displayed prominently in the library in both Spanish and English. The Westchester Photographic Society's professionalism and generosity added a distinctive and personal touch to the Café a las Siete series, while offering their members an opportunity to photograph exciting artists and a unique setting in which to practice their craft.

A variety of restaurants in the area also contributed to the success of the Café a las Siete series. An Argentinean restaurant donated food, as did a Caribbean bakery and the local deli. Some of the library's regular patrons brought in dishes from their native countries, and the former library board member/retired chef made a *tortilla española* for one program in addition to tapas for another. Having food as another focal point of many of the programs attracted patrons and added to the fun and camaraderie shared by participants.

One of the 2011 programs centered around food and was presented by an Ecuadorian sous-chef who created colorful and delicious salsas. He also sings and plays the guitar and the *charango*, a small Andean stringed instrument of the lute family, so the attendees learned about food, ate well, and were serenaded all in one program, much to their delight! This program turned into a family-like affair, as participants helped prepare and serve the food. Recipes for the salsas were copied and handed out, and an extensive cookbook display encouraged beginner and advanced cooks to try their hand at preparing Latino dishes.

This particular program also resulted in very positive feedback, and patrons began requesting more programs that focused on Latino cooking. As a result, our former board member and retired chef offered to present a series of programs on cooking techniques and Spanish cuisine, which resulted in a Conversations with Chef Tomás series, now in its fourth month. Being able to create new programs from others, and quickly bringing ideas to fruition, has been a key element in the library's overall programming success.

Another important offshoot of the Café series was the creation of the library's Spanish-English conversation group, a weekly event for those learning both languages. Two of the first year's programs focused on conversation, and while we had been hoping to create a language group for quite some time, the impetus truly came from the patrons who had enjoyed Café a las Siete. They wanted to continue the conversations year round, and with minimal work by library staff, and at no cost, this group now has met weekly for over a year. Native speakers of both languages support and encourage each other by practicing their Spanish and English conversation skills. Friendships have formed and deeper cultural understanding has resulted, key goals of the library and the Café series. Additionally, this enthusiastic cohort of language learners has become a key promoter of the Café a las Siete series, with many enjoying every session along with their families and friends. The library is a pleasurable part of their lives, and the library is enriched because of their presence in our building and our community.

Programs and Performers

As mentioned earlier, the musicians charged reduced fees for their performances, not only because of their kindness, but because we clearly explained our program goals and stated our financial constraints. One musician even invited his fellow Argentinean, a very accomplished and widely known guitarist (who happened to be in the area), to perform with him at the library, to tremendous acclaim. Fostering friendships that bring about this type of generosity is critical to finding quality performers who will donate their expertise to the library. Knowing the key members of your Latino community, and continuous networking, will create an environment of mutual support that will make library programming enjoyable and successful. We also remain in contact with our artists throughout the year, not just during the Café a las Siete month(s). We join their mailing lists and follow them on social networks, as well as attend their other area performances, shows, and classes, as much as possible. This mutual respect gives us confidence that each year we will be able to find quality musicians and artisans to take part in our series. Many of them, in fact, ask to be included in the following year's programs!

Each year it is important to find the balance between offering new programs and keeping audience preferences in mind. The following outline of three years of Café a las Siete will show how the programs have changed enough to attract newcomers and maintain interest, yet also keep audiences satisfied with returning favorites. The 2010 series consisted of eight events: the movie *Tocar y Luchar/To Play and Fight*; five musicians from the Westchester Chamber Music Society offering "Classical Music with a Latin Flavor"; a tango concert featuring Argentinean guitarist Pedro Baez; a family health night and bilingual stories and songs, a fair with bilingual health professionals, and a story time program with our bilingual librarian; "An Evening of Mexican Paper Art" with local artist Aurelia Fernández Marure; two English-Spanish conversation sessions led by Spanish-speaking library staff; and an evening of Andean music featuring the group Runahurco, a seven member group who play music from Peru, Ecuador, and Chile.

In 2011, we began with the cooking program, during which the audience helped make two salsas, and sous-chef Jesús Chuquitaipe added a touch of music to the program. This was followed by the return of Pedro Baez, accompanied by another Argentinean guitarist, Federico Díaz, both of whom captivated and enthralled a large crowd. We then hosted a discussion (in English) of Isabel Allende's *Island beneath the Sea*, copies of which were made available at the library a month prior to the discussion. Next, a well-established musical group, the Ricardo Gautreau Trio, joined us for the first time, and was very well received. A local artisan, Blanca Medina, presented her beading skills and taught a class of all ages how to make lovely jewelry with traditional techniques. The series ended on a high note as Runahurco, renamed Jilatanaka (meaning "brothers" in the Aymara language of South America), returned to perform another incredible concert, once again proving to be an audience favorite.

The 2012 program will open with a guitar concert by Pedro Baez, the Westchester-based musician from Argentina, who will select another Latino guitarist to accompany him for the performance. A book discussion on a

Latino writer's fiction (title to be decided) not generally known to U.S. readers will be the second program. Next, former library board member and retired executive chef Tomás Saez will present a cooking program that will focus on Spanish tapas. The last program of the series again will feature the very popular Andean band Jilatanaka, which consists of seven talented local musicians, all originally from South America. While challenging budgets may force difficult decisions about how many programs to have and which artists to invite back, it is important to keep in mind which programs have been the favorites of patrons and the community. These continual balancing acts, and always fostering friendships and contacts, are critical components of library programming.

The strong foundation established in 2010 will allow us to continue to offer the Café series regularly, even when faced with budget issues or fewer library staff, two current challenges many libraries are confronting. As libraries undergo change in the current economic and political atmosphere, we will continue to promote the library's services, collections, and other programs to our Latino patrons, bringing them further into the library community by offering culturally enriching, educational, and entertaining programs that acknowledge and respect their heritage.

When we first envisioned this project, we planned it as a one-time series. With two years of success, and recently having received the ArtsAlive grant for a third year, we know that we can offer a continuing program. We have formed a network of generous people who will continue to believe in our goal of creating a mutually beneficial and nurturing artistic environment at our public library that welcomes people of all ethnic backgrounds. We will continue the series in order to build upon the conversation we have started, and our future programs will be culturally enriching, educational, and continue to serve as a conduit between the English- and Spanish-speaking communities in our area.

TITLES FOR FURTHER READING

Alire, C., and J. Ayala. 2007. *Serving Latino Communities: A How-to-Do-It Manual for Librarians.* 2nd ed. New York: Neal-Schuman.
Byrd, S. M. 2005. *¡Bienvenidos! Welcome! A Handy Resource Guide for Marketing Your Library to Latinos.* Chicago: American Library Association.

Chapter Thirty-Two

So You Think You Can Write?

Programming That Encourages Creativity

April Grey and Derek Mosley

How can you get a diverse group of participants into your library for a month-long program? Choose a topic that will appeal universally to all people. Libraries are all about sharing the written word, and writing a novel holds esteem across every culture. We wanted to get the University of Louisiana at Lafayette and the surrounding community involved in an international program that celebrates creative writing and promotes authorship, friendship, and community. We did just that by opening the doors of the Ernest J. Gaines Center to aspiring novelists during NaNoWriMo.

WHAT IS NANOWRIMO?

National Novel-Writing Month (NaNoWriMo) is a month-long writing program run through the Office of Letters and Light (http://www.nanowrimo.org). The goal of the program is to write a fifty-thousand-word novel during the month of November. Participants from all over the world join in the celebration of creative writing during the program by feverishly writing their way to the word count goal. People from all cultures and backgrounds are interested in sharing their creativity through storytelling. Libraries, schools, and independent bookshops can get involved in NaNoWriMo by hosting a write-in session where workspace is available for program participants to sit down and write their novels. Participants will work on their novels alone or can engage the group with questions or ask for help from the group. Tables and chairs are all you need to welcome the writers to your library. It is helpful to have outlets for everyone to plug in their laptops too.

WHY SHOULD YOUR LIBRARY GET INVOLVED?

As libraries we should take every opportunity to actively promote literacy by inviting people from diverse cultures into our space to see what our library has to offer. Most of the participants in this program love reading and writing. Offering an inviting environment for writing will be great publicity for your library. In exchange for participating in this program you will get a group of enthusiastic readers in your library to make friends, write something they enjoy, and create a sense of community. All your library needs to do is to offer time and space to have a great program that includes diverse people of all walks of life.

THE ERNEST G. GAINES CENTER

Housed within the Edith Garland Dupré Library at University of Louisiana at Lafayette is the Ernest J. Gaines Center. The center highlights scholarship on Ernest Gaines and his works. The center honors the work of UL Lafayette's writer-in-residence emeritus and provides a space for scholars and students to work with the Gaines papers and manuscripts. Ernest Gaines's generous donation of his early papers and manuscripts and many artifacts provided the foundation for the center's collection. Many cultures are interested in the human condition portrayed in Gaines's novels; the books are translated into seventeen languages, which touch a multitude of worldwide readers. The décor includes a huge collection of awards, photographs, and Ernest Gaines's typewriter. The study tables and a lounge area with comfortable reading chairs and a couch are inviting to students and allow for a centerwide view of the accomplishments of this great African American writer.

To celebrate creative writing during NaNoWriMo, Dupré Library hosted a write-in at the Ernest J. Gaines Center each Tuesday in November from 4 p.m. until 6 p.m. The Ernest Gaines Center was open to all writers so they could work on their novels. We invited students, faculty, and community members through three different means of publicity. First, we posted fliers around campus and at local coffee shops. The fliers highlighted the date, time, and location of our write-in sessions, along with the NaNoWriMo logo and website information. Next we had articles about the write-in sessions in the student newspaper, *The Vermilion*, and local community newspaper, *The*

Advertiser. Finally we used online venues to promote the NaNoWriMo program. The University of Louisiana at Lafayette, Edith Garland Dupré Library, and the Ernest J. Gaines Center's websites posted information about the program, and information was added to the Facebook page of the Ernest J. Gaines Center to promote the program to Facebook followers. The Facebook post was then shared on the Edith Garland Dupré Library Facebook page and the University of Louisiana at Lafayette Facebook page. Promotional information about the write-in sessions was posted on the NaNoWriMo website and discussed on the message boards with the regional municipal liaison, a NaNoWriMo-appointed local volunteer.

CREATIVE WORKSPACE

The Ernest J. Gaines Center provided the creative environment for writers to come and work on their novels. Comfortable seating encouraged students, faculty, and community members to relax, mingle, and talk about their creative processes. It also gave the opportunity to bounce ideas off each other. Extension cords and power outlets allowed participants to use their laptops, but some chose to write their novels longhand while seated at tables. The seating on the couch was always the first to be taken by a novelist in need of comfort from the looming deadline of fifty thousand words in thirty days. Coffee and snacks were provided by the Friends of the Library. Coffee breaks were an important time for participants to discuss their progress with each other. Dictionaries, thesauri, pencils, and erasers were set up on a coffee table and were available for participants to use during the writing sessions. You can choose to provide as little as a workspace or as much of a smorgasbord as you want during your write-in sessions.

PUBLICIZE YOUR WRITE-IN

The most important thing you must to do to have a successful NaNoWriMo session is to publicize it as much as possible. Once you get participants in the door, they entertain themselves. Collaboration with the public library, academic departments on campus, and community interest groups is the key to get the word out about your write-in sessions and publicize your event to diverse groups of participants. Giving flyers to faculty in the creative writing and English departments also helped boost our participant numbers. Student organizations on campus included the student newspaper, the undergraduate writing club, Writer's Bloc, and the campus literary journal, *The Southwestern Review*. They were each sent notification on the upcoming write-in sessions to create buzz about NaNoWriMo across campus. Community groups were also contacted to publicize the program. The Writers' Guild of Acadiana and the Bayouland Storytellers Guild of Southwest Louisiana were contacted to publicize the sessions. Acadiana author Cheré Dastugue Coen publicized the write-in sessions at the Ernest J. Gaines Center on her Facebook page and the Louisiana Book News blog.

FUTURE ENHANCEMENTS

In the future we would like to expand NaNoWriMo programming at the University of Louisiana at Lafayette to include a writing contest. One possible scenario is a juried competition of all the completed novels submitted on or before November 30. There are logistical concerns that would have to be addressed before this contest can occur. How would we keep track of when the author started the novel? Who can participate in a university-sponsored contest? These questions and more would have to be decided before a contest was implemented.

Another way to expand the NaNoWriMo would be to invite local authors to come to the Ernest J. Gaines Center to discuss creative writing, participate in write-in sessions, and work side-by-side with student, faculty, and community participants. Professors from the English Department's creative writing program would be ideally suited to assist NaNoWriMo participants with creating an outline of their novels, teaching the basics of plot development, and providing other assistance that may be needed to finish writing a novel within the one-month deadline. The concern would be that participants are there to write a set goal of words and don't have time to learn about the writing process, and perhaps it wouldn't be beneficial for participants who are there for fun instead of lectures.

In future years we would like to partner with the academic library at South Louisiana Community College in Lafayette to increase the amount of write-in sessions offered. Additional write-in sessions would give participants even more opportunities to work on their novels and will create a larger community of writers to interact with during the program. Individually each institution posted information on the NaNoWriMo message board to promote our respective write-in sessions, but we didn't take the initiative to work together on publicity. Further collaboration with the community college would benefit both libraries and may garner additional publicity from increased exposure of the writing program.

One final idea to enhance our NaNoWriMo would be to have an event to close the month down and celebrate the accomplishments of the novelists. Challenges to a wrap-up party may be the timing of the end of the program falling the week after Thanksgiving break and at the beginning of study week before final exams. Academic libraries may choose to collaborate with the public library to host a completion party, and that would be a good time to have participants share a bit of their novels during a reading.

CONCLUSION

NaNoWriMo is a proven program to get diverse people into your library and participating as a multicultural community with a common love for creative writing. It brings together a diverse group of community members due to the popularity of writing universally across all cultures. This program has general appeal to all ages, genders, and races. You will find that community members come to hear stories from other writers, and the participants encourage each other in the writing process. We had a diverse group of participants at the Ernest J. Gaines Center write-in sessions. We believe that this is due to the appeal of writing and creative storytelling throughout cultures and the publicity of the event through traditional and online social media. Whether you can only offer the novelists one write-in session or can offer them a space for weekly sessions, they will benefit from meeting others interested in creative writing and cheering each other on to give it their all to write a fifty-thousand-word novel in thirty days.

Chapter Thirty-Three

English Conversation Clubs at the Charlotte Mecklenburg Library

Staci Falkowitz

In these times of scarce resources and lean budgets, librarians nationwide are seeking creative, cost-effective ways to introduce their resources to nontraditional users. English conversation clubs offer an informal, fun, and safe learning environment where participants can practice their English speaking and listening skills; they also provide an essential service to an underserved population, while promoting cross-cultural understanding in our increasingly diverse community. By reaching out and promoting your program to local churches, Latino-owned businesses, apartment complexes, and nonprofits that serve non-English speakers, your library system gains a new source of library users, volunteers, and advocates.

English language learners attend ESL classes in a variety of places, including community colleges, churches, and a variety of nonprofit agencies. However, classes tend to focus on reading, writing, and grammar. Students continually express a need to practice speaking the language, an opportunity they don't usually get at home. Where can they find a relaxed, tolerant atmosphere to do this? What better fit than the public library, an institution dedicated to providing equal access to information for all people, regardless of who they are?

OBJECTIVE

To provide an informal, fun, and safe learning environment in which participants can practice their English speaking and listening skills, Charlotte Mecklenburg Library decided to create an English Conversation Club. Our aim is not to lecture, but to facilitate conversation among the members and encourage active participation in speaking and listening. In addition, we encourage discussion, learning about and respect for the many countries and cultures represented in our community. We hope to promote and increase the use of library services among populations who don't traditionally utilize public libraries and their resources. Finally, we strive to foster relationships with these potentially lifelong library supporters and advocates.

PROFILE

- We host weekly one to one-and-a-half-hour meetings at several library locations.
- In addition to typical learning activities, cultural events such as potluck luncheons featuring food from many countries are held.
- Over two hundred members have joined and participated since we started in January 2008.
- There are typically between ten and twenty members present; the average attendance is fourteen.
- Over twenty countries have been represented, including Mexico, Cuba, Puerto Rico, Colombia, Peru, Bolivia, Venezuela, Argentina, Nicaragua, Brazil, Tunisia, Iran, Armenia, Vietnam, Japan, South Korea, and China.
- Participants are encouraged to bring in topics they would like to share with the group. They often share newspaper articles, family photos, and other keepsakes when telling their stories. This practice has proved to be extremely effective in creating a bond among the group, increasing the comfort level enormously.

GROUP PLANNING AND PREPARATION

We use a variety of online and print resources that offer guidelines, tips, and ideas for discussion topics. Popular topics include current events, navigating the local school system, holidays, movies, sports, and idioms. For some of the best websites for discussion ideas, see textbox 33.1.

Textbox 33.1: Best Websites for Discussion Ideas

East Side Literacy Talk Time Topics
   http://www.eastsideliteracy.org/tutorsupport/ESL/ESLTalk-Time.htm

---

ESL Speaking Activities
  http://www.eslgo.com/resources/sa.html
Easy Conversations for ESL Beginners
  http://www.eslfast.com/easydialogs/index.html
Dave's ESL Café
  www.eslcafe.com
Conversation Questions for the ESL/EFL Classroom
  http://iteslj.org/questions
ESL Gold
  http://www.eslgold.com/speaking/topics_conversation.html
Compelling Conversations
  http://compellingconversations.com/blog/ESL/conversation-class
ESL Conversations @ Your Library
  http://eslconversationclubs.blogspot.com

PROMOTIONS

The groups are promoted using several methods, including the library website and flyers posted in the library. Blurbs are placed in the local media (including local Spanish-language newspapers and radio), and the group is listed on Craigslist and social media networks like Facebook. We visited local community groups offering ESL classes, including local community colleges, nonprofit agencies, and churches, to promote the group and other library resources. We notified our personal and professional e-mail contact list, and we identified and shared with key individuals in our local international community. Of course, word of mouth is often the most effective tool of all.

TRACKING/EVALUATION

An intake form was used to gather basic information, including name, contact information, native country/language, English-speaking level (beginner, intermediate, advanced), and interests. A spreadsheet was used to track members with information gathered from the intake form. This is a helpful tool for keeping statistical data. We created before-and-after surveys related to literacy levels of participants before and after predetermined periods.

CHALLENGES

- Lack of child care and space. Many of the participants have small children, so planning a simultaneous program for children is helpful if you have staff or volunteers available.
- Time of day. You may need to try different days and times before you find the best one for your particular community. Weekday mornings have worked the best for us.
- Varied levels of ability. When faced with this issue, divide the group (if there enough participants) and recruit a more advanced member to assist you in facilitation.
- Difficulty with evaluation. Outcomes are difficult to measure, but we look at the differences based on self-reported comfort levels in speaking the language collected through our intake forms and later with follow-up questions.

BENEFITS AND OPPORTUNITIES

- Develops a new source of library users, volunteers, and advocates.
- Provides additional programming resources when participants become volunteers.
- Promotes cross-cultural understanding in our increasingly diverse community.
- Provides a new service to an increasingly underserved population.
- Increases library use.
- Aligns with the library's vision of creating opportunities for personal success in reading and learning for everyone.

USE OF VOLUNTEERS

After a severe budget shortfall in 2010, a reduction in force took place, and almost half of the staff at Charlotte Mecklenburg Library was lost. Some branches were closed; all underwent a reduction in hours. As a result, remaining staff became flexible and creative in order to continue providing valuable library service. Thanks to a huge rally within the community, the library managed to recruit a record number of volunteers, which made a huge impact on the library's ability to provide effective services. Our conversation groups were no exception. Bill Mirrielees is one of those volunteers. A dedicated participant in one of the library's groups since 2009, this native

English speaker became part of the group because of his interest in different cultures. When the staff member facilitating the group was transferred, Bill graciously offered to become a volunteer facilitator for the group and has continued to do so, in addition to starting a second group at another library location.

Another participant, a native of Ecuador, was an active member of the group for several months. Always a lively participant within the group, she always managed to bring the quieter participants out of their shells. Not only did she become a regular user of the library, she also volunteered her time to teach a series of basic Spanish classes at our library, an extremely popular program with patrons.

LESSONS LEARNED

- This group self-morphed into a high-beginner to high-intermediate level group. Those at the very beginning and very advanced levels tend to seek alternatives and benefit less. At the very least, it is a good idea to break into groups with similar ability levels.
- The child-care challenge limits the potential adult participation, especially during the summer months. It may be a good idea to consider taking a break if your class size dwindles noticeably.
- Flexibility is important. Some sessions need to be more structured, while other times things can be more informal. I recommend having some structured activity planned for each meeting, but being willing to go with the flow depending on the group you have that day.
- The members love participating in food-related activities such as our luncheons. It gives them yet another opportunity to share something of themselves, their country, and their culture through their native foods.
- The icebreakers and idioms are big hits. Taking about ten minutes at the beginning to use one of these goes a long way in encouraging people to speak.
- Depending on the community you serve, offer day, evening or even weekend meetings.

INCREASED LIBRARY USE

Hosting English Conversation Clubs at your library puts you in a unique position to bring new users into the library. Be sure to introduce the members to library programs, materials, and services, and sign up those without them for library cards. Our participants heavily utilized a variety of ESL materials, especially CDs and DVDs; books about grammar, idioms, and citizenship; and dictionaries. Our Reader Development collection has also been a big hit, as are TOEFL books and the bilingual materials for children.

CONCLUSION

By preserving the value of libraries as the cornerstone of free access to information, we continue to fulfill our original mission. We open our doors to any individual in our community regardless of race or ethnic background to ensure that every individual will be able to pursue a full life filled with opportunity and will be able to make well-informed decisions due in part to the use of library materials, services, and programs. In doing so, we expand our base of support for the library, resulting in a special kind of patron in the future who will remember the impact the library had on his or her life and highly regard us as a vital institution in our society.

Part VII

Reference Services

Chapter Thirty-Four

Active Listening without Visual Cues

Phone Reference Tips for ESL Learners

Erin Brothen and Erika Bennett

Phone conversations pose unique challenges, no matter the student on the other end. Without visual cues or the ability to see what the student is looking at, there is increased opportunity for misunderstanding and frustration. When the student is not a native speaker of English, the interaction can be even more difficult to navigate successfully. Are you understanding what the student is asking for? Does the student understand what you are saying?

Librarians are not the only helping professionals or service providers who encounter phone confusion. Any industry with callers from around the globe runs into the very same issues and difficulties. Customer service literature provides some insight into the ways you can improve phone interactions when there is a language barrier. Nancy Friedman (2000), also known as the "Telephone Doctor," provides five points of general advice for working with people who have limited English proficiency:

1. "Do not pretend to understand." Ask for clarification and admit when you have missed something.
2. "Do not rush." Allow the other person time to think and speak. Let him or her finish speaking before you begin.
3. "Do not shout." Raising your voice is a common habit when there is a communication barrier, but try to avoid doing it.
4. "Do not be rude." Be careful about how you phrase your requests for repetition or clarifying information. "I'm sorry, but I missed what you just said" or "My phone connection is bad, can you repeat that?" is better than "I can't understand you."

293

5. "Keep a job aid available." Friedman recommends a job aid with common phrases in the languages your callers most often speak, but other aids can also be beneficial. (28)

This advice, originally meant for customer service operators, is also relevant for librarians engaged in phone reference. While these may seem obvious, and dovetail with existing reference interview practices, they can be difficult to put into consistent practice. The success of your phone interaction often lies in more intangible characteristics: "Interpersonal meaning is not only made through verbiage but also voice quality" (Forey and Lockwood 2010, 121). It is important to make a conscious effort to follow phone best practices during the call. Smile as you begin the conversation and continue to do so throughout, regardless of your emotional state. A physical smile will warm your vocal quality, perhaps alleviating any negative emotions that are welling.

Of course, reference calls are not synonymous with customer service. Library users have unique needs and characteristics, and librarians frequently provide instructions over the phone. Doing everything for a caller just because they have an accent won't help them build the skills they need for long-term academic success. This means that there are some specific words of advice relevant to librarians. Following these tips can help you learn what the student really needs and can give the student the resources necessary to be successful.

- Let the student talk. This doesn't just mean that you shouldn't rush him or her. If a student has a particularly strong accent, it may be impossible to understand every word he or she says. But chances are good that he or she is asking questions that are very similar to the questions you get every day. Sometimes it helps to just relax and let the student's words flow. You can develop an understanding of the gist of the question without understanding every word. Then succinctly repeat what you think the student is asking.
- Accent does not necessarily mean lack of understanding of English. Adult learners of English often have a strong accent but also have a good command of English. In an academic setting this may mean that they are very familiar with the technical language of their field. The structure and complexity of their spoken English will help you determine if they simply have an accent or actually struggle with their knowledge of English. Getting this right can keep you from talking over the head of your caller or sounding too condescending.
- Don't forget that you have an accent as well. If you typically talk with library users from your own region, you may not realize how strong your accent is. Try to tone down your own regional dialect, use of idioms, and

filler "ums" and "ahs." Foreign speakers of English are likely familiar with the bland accents they hear on television and in movies. Mimicking that can aid their understanding of what you say.

- If possible, look at whatever they are looking at. If a student doesn't know the specialized vocabulary of publishing or libraries, or is worried about pronouncing the technical terms found in scholarly literature, he or she may be relieved to have you look at it as well. If the course is online, try to access the course room or assignment. If it's a question about a database or other online resource, ask the student to walk you through how to get there. Simply say, "It might help if I look at X as well."
- Send a written follow-up by e-mail, if possible. Speaking abilities in a foreign language often lag behind reading comprehension, and a written documentation of what you did allows students to reread, look up words, or consult with a friend. Adding screenshots means that they will have a personal job aid to refer back to as needed. If you send video tutorials, try to include closed captioning or a transcript. This will allow students to pause the video and look up any vocabulary that is confusing.
- Beware the super-polite student! The effusive use of "thank you" may be hiding an actual lack of understanding. The student may not realize what is considered a standard level of service from a reference librarian, and he or she may not know much help or the amount of time you can offer them. Others may be embarrassed by their lack of understanding and use appreciation to hide it. Don't be afraid to state exactly what you are willing to do. They may not know that you can walk them through an entire search, or that you are willing to remain on the phone until they have printed out the article they need. And if you suspect they don't understand something you said, offer to explain again or to send them some backup information.

What should you do if you simply cannot bridge the communication gap? Two common reasons for this are interpersonal breakdowns and language barriers that are too large to overcome. You may not be able to completely make up for either of these problems, but you can try some tactics to mitigate the damage.

If the level of frustration becomes too great and you are no longer having a real conversation, it may be time to get off the phone. If you think you have a good idea of what the student is trying to do, offer to send written documentation. If it's possible for the student to come on-site, it may be better to talk in person so you know that you are both looking at the same things. Admit that you aren't able to help, and offer to have another librarian work with the student.

When the problem is one of basic communication, it is often best to work off of the same documentation. Try to see the assignment they are working on, or look at citations they are trying to locate. You may be able to spot the words or phrases you are struggling to understand when spoken. Screen-sharing tools, e-mailed documents, and even an in-person appointment can give you a text-based backup to the spoken word. When callers lack the depth of vocabulary to accurately describe what they need, working off of a shared written document may be the only way to be sure that you are accurately answering their questions.

Finally, you must accept that you won't be perfect. Sometimes a call will just go badly. English language learners can have all the imperfections of native English speakers: they can be impatient, angry, confused, or terrified. So can you! All of this can add to the difficulties of understanding an accent or being understood by your caller. Even though librarians are used to having a few bad reference calls, it's the ones involving accents that seem to cause the most grief. Do your best, try to learn from any mistakes you make, and remember that we're all human.

It may also help to have a workshop with other reference librarians at your institution regarding phone reference with foreign speakers of English. If you are able to listen to a recorded call or conduct some mock calls that use the strategies outlined above, you can build your confidence when faced with the next call that suffers from a lack of communication. Calls from students with particularly thick accents may be rare in your library, so it's important to become familiar with these strategies in advance. The first time you try some of them, it may feel unnatural. If you are used to speaking quickly or use your accent to build rapport with local students, it may be very difficult to switch to a different persona on the phone. In fact, actively practicing your phone skills while on reference calls with native speakers of English can be beneficial.

These strategies are not just applicable to calls with speakers of foreign languages. Communication barriers can occur between any two individuals. In a library setting, even native speakers of English can encounter vocabulary or processes that are entirely new and confusing. Native English speakers can also have accents that are unfamiliar to you. Following these best practices can improve phone reference regardless of the home country of your caller.

WORKS CITED

Forey, Gail, and Jane Lockwood, eds. 2010. *Globalization, Communication, and the Workplace: Talking across the World.* New York: Continuum.

Friedman, Nancy. 2000. *Telephone Skills from A to Z: The Telephone Doctor Phone Book.* Menlo Park, CA: Crisp Learning.

Chapter Thirty-Five

The Culturally Relevant Reference Interview

How to Enhance Reference Transactions in an Era of Diversity

Erin Brothen and Erika Bennett

Librarians, like members of other helping professions, are committed to serving the needs of diverse populations. Public libraries perhaps hold the stereotype for serving refugee and minority populations. Yet, as businesses become more global, corporate librarians serve a broader multicultural audience, and as colleges and universities enroll a growing number of international students, all librarians must increasingly display cultural competence.

Cultural competence represents a new and evolving practice goal among therapists, counselors, and psychologists. Curriculum that fosters cultural competence requires intense self-reflection on the student's part. The student must develop self-awareness, sensitivity, and demonstrate a skill for dealing with client differences. Notably, the counseling cycle can be very similar to a reference interview. The counselor establishes rapport, analyzes situations, addresses needs, and then closes the session in a set fashion. This means there may be room for parallel skills with cultural responsiveness.

What would a culturally responsive reference interview look like? The answer should be a part of all library school course work. While a number of articles talk about the burgeoning need for multicultural awareness, few use the same understanding of cultural competence at the same level of codification as medical and behavioral help professions. Most psychology and client-facing help professions require dedicated courses that foster cultural competence.

Without the guidance of practice, librarians are left to their own devices to determine the main components of a culturally competent reference interview. However, three components are logical: the culturally responsive collection, understanding our own limitations and development needs, and the epistemology of otherness.

THE CULTURALLY RESPONSIVE COLLECTION

Librarians need to build fertile soil for culturally competent reference services by having a culturally supportive collection. As a baseline, we must acknowledge that diverse backgrounds suggest diverse approaches to information seeking. By including a wider array of resources in our collections and being well-versed in them, we can provide help to diverse students without pigeonholing them. We can move beyond simple understanding to effective interactions.

In academic libraries, two related forces are pushing libraries toward building broader collections. Faculty are more likely to emphasize personal passion, relevance, and leadership in student work, which encourages students to look to their own experiences and communities for their research topics. Similarly, as students from more diverse backgrounds enter degree programs, they are bringing a desire for social change in their own communities to their studies. This can cause friction with library resources when those communities have received scant scholarly attention in the past.

It's important to acknowledge that research literature itself reflects dominant cultural values when consulting with patrons of all backgrounds. All sociological academic theories are, to some extent, culture-bound. Research focus and funding can create an imbalance in a topic area. Research articles may portray diverse groups as being culturally deficient rather than culturally situated.

Regarding the library collection:

- Build your knowledge of the library's publications that focus on other cultures. Even if you don't speak the language of the publication, your students may. ALA's *Policy Manual: Section 60, Diversity* states that budgeting should be allocated equitably to address multicultural populations.
- Connect with multicultural librarian professional associations.
- If you have a significant population that speaks a specific foreign language, try to provide some instructional resources in that language.

- Keep track of situations where the collection was too limited. This can help you figure out where to build your multicultural or international collections.
- Look at your student demographics. If you find a large population of students in a particular field from a single region, you may want to build your collection in that area.

UNDERSTANDING OUR OWN LIMITATIONS AND DEVELOPMENT NEEDS

Another challenge is the great diversity contained within multicultural populations. This broad term covers everything from populations within the United States to recent immigrants to international students who are attending a U.S. institution but planning to return to their home country. Navigating the great differences between and among these populations can be complicated. Librarians should include goals for improvements with all the different diverse library populations in their annual professional development goals.

Librarians can proactively increase their ability to help diverse patrons by staying aware of exclusive tendencies. Librarians should provide easy access to major reference works, journals, or other publications that focus on specific populations, so that patrons and students can quickly move from a personal interest to a workable research topic. This can be done with topical guides and pathfinders. When librarians create guides and help for your patrons, they should take care not to forget to provide similar help for multicultural topics. For example, as they create guides for current events, they need to make sure they include some for regional events from around the world. When they collect links to Internet sources, they shouldn't forget to include links to international or foreign organizations and governments.

Beyond sensitivity and awareness, librarians need to recognize the various learning and communication styles of others. We need to be able to adjust our interview habits based on those style differences. We can also gain understanding from multicultural textbooks and reference books for counselors, therapists, and other helping professions.

EPISTEMOLOGY OF OTHERNESS

Librarians have increasingly been interested in improving services to outgroups: patrons who for cultural or social reasons may not feel comfortable navigating a library. While they might not always put it in social psychology terms (e.g., "outgroups"), librarians are part of a larger trend. The ethics of serving the unique needs of multicultural groups is a current emphasis of many helping professions like psychology, counseling, and social work, as mentioned. In the absence of our own course work, we can turn to theirs to discover better culturally sensitive reference practices.

Curriculum and standards are very clear that it's not enough just to *avoid discrimination*, but all staff members need to work toward multicultural *competence*. The professional literature and standards make it clear that it is also not enough for libraries to have a single librarian responsible for diversity (e.g., Mestre, 2010). Minimal acknowledgement of the existence of diverse values and populations is not sufficient.

Library visitors from ethnically diverse backgrounds may feel particularly "other" in the library. There are many ways to help fix this by making the physical library more inviting and marketing strategically to specific demographics. Still, the core of our service itself—the reference interview and collections—could also use some adjustment. This can make the library both more comfortable and more relevant to people from different ethnic or national backgrounds.

This can be a touchy area, since acknowledging the differences between groups could be seen as pejorative or based on stereotyping. In other professions, discussions of cultural universality versus cultural relativism persist. From a culturally universal standpoint, "good librarianship is good librarianship." Equity means that one's approach should not change from student to student. A reference interview follows the same recipe regardless of the audience. From a relativist standpoint, all norms, values, and attitudes are culture bound. A good librarian adapts her or his approach to meet the culture of the student. There are nonetheless things we can do to improve the situation.

First, it's important to acknowledge some of the barriers that diverse and international patrons face when coming into the library:

1. Patrons from foreign cultures may be unfamiliar with the role of the librarian or support services. What do they do? What kinds of help can you receive? If they are coming from another country, there may be differences between what is considered appropriate levels of service from a librarian.
2. Different conceptions of plagiarism and citation may confuse students. Academic honesty policies tend to emphasize individualism over collaboration, which could conflict with cultures that value collectivism.
3. They may struggle with languages, accents, or social norms that are new or different. Friendliness and patience are required.

4. They may be expecting an inhospitable environment with little help from librarians or few resources for their areas of interest. Do not personalize any suspicions or seeming derision for services or collections. Reflecting negative emotions will only diminish your effectiveness.

5. They may not realize that their difficulties in the library are actually common to all students, no matter their background. Both high- and low-achieving students may be afraid of admitting confusion.

There are some simple actions that librarians can take to help mitigate these issues. Other solutions may take more time and expense, but are also well worth the effort.

During direct interactions with patrons, such as reference:

- Don't be afraid to clarify what you can do for a patron. Offer help proactively, since patrons may not realize when they can ask for help.
- Encourage the patron to return with follow-up questions. Emphasize the hours and modes of service.
- Let patrons know that their questions are not unusual or too basic. "We get this question a lot" can ease some of that anxiety. Offering up the number of reference questions that are answered per semester can provide encouragement.
- Be patient. Language barriers can increase the time it takes to provide appropriate help. Follow up with supplemental help, such as written guides or instructions, that patrons can use later on their own or with a friend.
- Admit limitations when there may not be a lot of available resources on students' topics. Help them come up with ways to work around or adjust the topic. For example, there may not be a lot of research on the country they are interested in, but you may find more information about the larger region. The skill of widening search terms can fuel an instructional moment.
- Try to figure out what is most important about the topic to the user. They may be most interested in focusing on the study population, which is helpful to know if you need to help them shift their final topic.
- Express enthusiasm for the topic. Allow patrons to talk about *why* they want to pursue a particular research topic. A little bit of verbal approval goes a long way.

As college populations become more diverse, student needs and interests will diversify as well. It is within the power of academic librarians to make these students more comfortable and at the same time connect them with the resources they need to be successful—likewise, with increasingly global businesses and diverse public libraries.

Above all, change will start in library school course work. Cultural competence needs to be a mainstay in the same fashion as any other helping profession. It's not enough to simply demonstrate awareness and serve effectively, but we must demonstrate a specific skillset in regard to multicultural patrons as a required component of the curriculum.

WORKS CITED

American Library Association. *Policy Manual: Section 60, Diversity*. http://www.ala.org/abou-tala/governance/policymanual/updatedpolicymanual.

Mestre, Lori S. 2010. "Librarians Working with Diverse Populations: What Impact Does Cultural Competency Training Have on Their Efforts?" *Journal of Academic Librarianship* 36(6): 479–88.

Chapter Thirty-Six

Risk Looking Stupid

Michael Buono

On busy days, I sit at the reference desk and I patiently listen to people explain to me their need in the sparse amounts of English they know. I do all the things they teach you to do in library school to convey I'm listening. I nod my head, smile, and make affirming noises. Then I try to help them the best I can. My answers are stitched together English and Spanish. They involve hand gestures. It helps, and I'm Italian so it happens anyway. I apologize profusely, and I find myself in their shoes.

I find myself trying to convey what may be a simple message with elaborate amounts of effort. I feel foolish, isolated, and like I'm under some microscope. I feel like people are staring at me. But in that instant, there is a connection. A moment where the language barrier is forgotten, and we are two people figuring something out together. The process can be draining, but the moment you succeed at forming that connection is a sweet thing.

The same connection happens when I manage to truly engage a person of another culture, age group, or some other specific minority group.

PAY EXTRA ATTENTION TO GOOD CUSTOMER SERVICE

Good customer service is rare. It is especially uncommon for minority groups and those who do not speak English. Cultural barriers that prevent easy communication can often fluster even experienced librarians. When people become flustered, the tenets of good customer service break down. Of those cultural barriers, the language barrier is the hardest to bypass. This makes the other elements of customer service more important. Make eye contact, smile, nod, and use nonverbal indicators. You may wish to practice smiling. It is important to create an internal checklist to review whenever you feel flustered. Because you *will* feel flustered, and that is okay.

There are two keys to maintaining a strong standard of customer service in frustrating situations. One, always maintain a positive attitude. A positive attitude is like armor against tense situations. It is difficult to do this all day, every day. It can be difficult to maintain in really stressful situations. Even when a positive attitude is impossible to maintain, smile. Smiles are like weapons. In literature they say a lot about a character, and people really do pay attention when you bare some tooth. Practice in a mirror to remind yourself what muscles you use to smile, or focus on smiling when you encounter a frustrating situation in your own life. As simple as it is to smile, it is the first thing we forget to do when our equilibrium is thrown off.

Two, their needs are more important than your own. It sounds simple, but humans have a tendency to get defensive when we get frustrated. Once we start getting defensive, it is difficult to change gears. It becomes an "us versus them" mindset, and it can ruin a reference interaction. When I encounter a difficult customer service situation, I remind myself silently that this is not a power struggle. It allows me to maintain my positive attitude and keep a clear head in even the most trying situations.

ASK QUESTIONS

It is always better to ask questions than to make assumptions. It can be difficult to understand exactly someone who speaks a different language, speaks with a heavy accent, or speaks with culture-specific terms. It can be easy to confuse their request for one material with an unrelated material. In library school, they teach us to use the reference interview to get to the heart of a request. These same tactics are useful to navigate cultural barriers that confuse requests, but the importance of asking questions goes beyond the reference interview. Banter can be an important part of dispelling stereotypes and understanding your patrons. This must be done with some cultural sensitivity, but people generally like talking about themselves. It feels better to be given the opportunity to explain something rather than have assumptions made about you. You risk making a faux pas or looking stupid. But it is better to look stupid and appear to care than to look intelligent and appear cold.

WALK PATRONS TO THEIR MATERIAL

Walk all patrons to their material. It can provide many opportunities for positive patron interactions. For people who generally get poor customer service, it also gives you the opportunity to make them feel special. It takes the desk, which some find intimidating, out of the equation. It shows them that your focus is on their need, and that the phone and computer don't matter. For non-English speakers, this strategy also allows you to verify visually that the patron has found the correct item. If the patron is willing, this is also an excellent time to engage in banter and build a rapport.

USE THE LANGUAGE YOU DON'T KNOW

When dealing with non-English speakers, it is better to use the little of their language that you know. Even if, like me, you sound like a fool as you cobble together a sentence with the little bit of this or that you know, it is important to try. It will not feel like you are accomplishing much, but you are. You are laying the foundation for a relationship. This moment of struggle can lead to a connection.

There are two reasons this connection forms. First, the person you are speaking to sees that you may be trying to learn. As non-English speakers, they can probably empathize with that. The second reason is respect. You are showing them respect by trying to meet them on equal terms. Yes, you may mangle their language or make inadvertent gaffes. But if you stay calm and show humility, it conveys a tremendous amount of respect. They may stop you and tell you not to worry about it, but that is okay. That just shows they understand your position and that you've developed a basis for your understanding of one another.

KEEP A LIST OF KEY PHRASES

Develop your own list of words and phrases you will commonly hear or use. I took a six-session Spanish course with a librarian named Will Salas, who handed out a sheet of commonly used terms and phrases. It has been a great resource. However, I have begun to develop my own sheet for several reasons. The first is placement. I put my more frequently used phrases at the top. The second is content. I use some phrases; I don't use others. Plus I have had to add some. You don't need to know Spanish to do this. Other librarians have developed their own sheets of commonly used non-English phrases.

JUST IN CASE, HAVE A TRANSLATION SITE OPEN

Don't be afraid to use Google Translate, Babblefish, or some other translation site. Translation sites are not a perfect solution, because they do not always translate things well. Sometimes though, they do the job when someone has a complex question. Make sure to include the phrase for "Can you write your question down" on your list of phrases.

AVOID USING CHILDREN AS TRANSLATORS WHEN POSSIBLE.

It is understandable for non-English-speaking parents to ask their children to translate for them. It can often make a person's difficult situation a lot easier. Children may be used to translating for their parents, but that does not mean they like it. Avoid using them as translators if possible. It can get annoying to constantly be asked to interpret for people. In addition, the parents may feel levels of guilt and shame for putting their child in that position.

THANK THE CHILD, BUT ANSWER THE PARENT

At times, it will be impossible to avoid using children as translators. Sometimes, there is a nuance to the language unless you truly understand it. In these times it is important to make eye contact with the parents when they are explaining their request to the child, and it is important to make eye contact with the child when he or she is explaining it to you. It is equally important to regularly make eye contact with both the child and the parent when answering the request, with greater focus on the parent. Before the reference transaction ends, be sure to thank the child and apologize for your inability to speak the language.

IT ALL BOILS DOWN TO RESPECT

I encourage you to try to learn the most common non-English language used in your area, but this article isn't about learning another language. It is about respect. Even though I do not speak any language other than English, the fact that I am trying has improved my relations with minority clients. My Spanish is a horribly mangled mess of half-remembered verbs from my education and a six-session course taught at my library, but people's faces light up when I use it. I am willing to compromise my own image of authority by looking stupid for the sake of helping them. It's not the use of the language that makes them happy. It is the fact that they are being respected. Respect works, whether it's the language they speak, the color of their skin, or their age that separates you from them.

Chapter Thirty-Seven

Genealogy Reference for Diverse Customers

J. Wendel Cox and James K. Jeffrey

Genealogy is one of the most popular hobbies in the United States, and each day it brings legions of researchers to public, academic, and private libraries and archives in search of information about previous generations. Yet there is little genealogy reference instruction offered in today's graduate programs in library and information science, nor is there much written guidance for librarians charged with genealogy reference. Of those librarians who do offer genealogy reference, many derive their knowledge from their own research or the accumulation of experiences with customers. While librarianship itself is increasingly diverse, our customers often are more diverse than our profession or the librarians they meet at reference desks. Lack of instruction, lack of resources, and the limitations of our own experiences create a distance between ourselves and customers seeking assistance with the resources and tools available to unlock the lives and experiences of previous generations. Added to this mix is a widespread misconception extraordinary for its pervasiveness and power: that those with ancestors outside Europe will have difficulty finding relevant information. This misconception is held by librarians. It is held by researchers, including those who visit libraries like our own, where they express these convictions. It is held by prospective researchers who never visit libraries because of it. And, in our experience, it is a conviction librarians have expressed to researchers, even as they have referred them to us, with assurances of inevitable disappointment.

In what follows, we address this conviction, which we know to be mistaken—and, frankly, pernicious and destructive—and provide guidance for those who serve a diverse genealogical community. We offer basic principles to bear in mind and to relate to customers when providing genealogy reference service. In most instances, these principles are indistinguishable from those we would extend to anyone, regardless of family origins, and this similarity is itself our first, foremost, and guiding principle: the research process will be similar for almost every patron, even as it will inevitably draw on different resources. Accordingly, this is a primer concerned with process, rather than a comprehensive description of sources relevant to peoples of various national origin or ethnic identification. In fact, given the diversity of people patronizing almost any contemporary library, an attempt to provide a comprehensive account of relevant sources would be perverse. When we suggest particular resources, it is because these are aggregations of resources, rather than anything especially apt for a particular community.

THE PUZZLE OF ONE

Regardless of family origins, every genealogical researcher begins his or her first or next step with an individual who is the object of research. At the beginning of research, this is likely to be the researcher, while for others with more experience it is often an individual from an earlier generation about whom the researcher would like to know more. This is the puzzle of one. Genealogical research works with one individual at a time and proceeds from a review of what is known, what is unknown, and what knowledge is sought. Researchers come to us in two forms: (1) those with an interest, but little research accomplished; and (2) those with research accomplished, but a problem or next step that has escaped them. In either instance, genealogy reference begins with the reference interview. A basic reference interview is essential, even with a researcher who is familiar to us personally, whenever someone approaches seeking direction and assistance. Every reference librarian will recall instances where a hectic day has led us to neglect the reference interview and rush a customer to a source, if only to assuage them, to avoid a customer's—or librarian's—frustration, or to avoid the uncomfortable fact that we may not have known how to offer assistance. Instead, we should slow down, start a conversation, and arrive at the puzzle of one. Who is the object of research? What is it about this person the researcher wishes to explore? What does the researcher know? What does he or she want to know?

Individuals lead us to previous generations. What line to follow, whether to a maternal line or a paternal line, is the researcher's prerogative. It may be the case that the researcher is uninterested in or unwilling to pursue a particular line, or uninterested in or unwilling to pursue relations beyond a certain degree. Again, what constitutes family is itself a matter of difference among us, and the reference librarian must be alive to the fact that not all researchers are interested in the genealogy of biological relations, reckon relationships as we might, or assign similar priorities to particular family members. Indeed, we have had occasion to include pets as coequal family members, and the power of such connections, for young and old alike, deserves to be respected and honored. Anyone who thinks animals an unusual object for genealogy need only consider the carefully documented pedigrees of thoroughbred horses and the passion and material interests they excite, to see the error of his ways.

Our refrain with all researchers at the beginning of their efforts is first to gather information from their family, howsoever defined, or those familiar with their family but not part of it, such as longtime friends or constant figures from a faith community. This effort does more than simply gather information. It often begins conversations within families about origins, identity, and the experience and influence of previous generations. Such conversations frequently define the scope and direction of subsequent research. And such conversations, of course, can be painful. The librarian can provide a measure of encouragement to pursue such conversations, and note that these conversations may continue for years and ebb and flow as comfort, reflection, and willingness to discuss the past dictates. Our personal and professional experience affords numerous instances where a family member declined to share experiences of war, loss, poverty, or other hardship with spouses and children, only to willingly and candidly share their lives with grandchildren, nieces or nephews, or otherwise perfect strangers who offered the courtesy and respect of listening intently to a story of obvious importance. In many instances, such conversations serve to strengthen families and friendships and afford individuals the comfort of what becomes a shared experience and common past through conversation.

MATCHING QUESTIONS TO SOURCES

Researchers who gather information from memory, family members, or those associated with a family, eventually will turn to the librarian to move beyond memory or records immediately at hand. Here begins the effort to identify, explore, and use a world of records and information about the human experience. We describe these sources broadly and do so intentionally because of the extraordinary range of sources available for genealogical research. Some of these sources may be familiar, and their relevance more obvious; others are an almost constant surprise to even seasoned researchers.

Borrowing from historians, we distinguish between primary and secondary sources. Primary sources are those documents, records, or traditions immediate to the events they record, such as a census schedule, a marriage license, or parish register. Additionally, these items distinguish themselves for not having been created to serve the purposes of genealogists, though they frequently provide information invaluable to genealogical research. Such sources of information almost always have their origin with a secular or sacred authority, and the question is often one of where and when to look for information with origins in a particular level of governance or a faith community and its records.

Secondary sources are those that cast an eye on a topic, often at a remove in time if not space, and recount, examine, or analyze events, experiences, or individuals of the past. These are the publications genealogical researchers have created in a variety of different forms, including histories of particular individuals and their descendants, guides to research, or even indexes or guides to the use of primary sources. This literature is invaluable, and researchers should be introduced to it early, encouraged to make frequent use of it, and returned to it whenever a question about the next step or source arises. It is unlikely the frustrated researcher at the reference desk is the first to struggle with a particular question or challenge, and other researchers who have successfully addressed these questions write articles, offer classes and seminars, or comment online about their experiences.

We also extend our scope for secondary sources to the body of scholarship written by historians, anthropologists, sociologists, geographers, and other students of the human experience. Here we make a passionate plea to librarians and genealogical researchers alike not to neglect relevant scholarship from many fields that will variously inform their research and aid immeasurably in understanding diversity. Such scholarship affords context, insight into relevant sources, and, for the researcher and the librarian, a check on ignorance, assumptions, or misunderstandings about other places and times. Frequently, the most fruitful genealogical research is a conversation between primary and secondary sources, where researchers find clues to the lives of previous generations and insights into, and context for, the contours of specific lives and the experiences of communities, regions, peoples, and nations.

With the puzzle of one posed, the question becomes where to direct a researcher for information for previous generations. Guides for research on particular peoples, places, and periods abound, and often librarians can quickly identify, via their own library's catalog or WorldCat, a handbook, guide, or manual for research relevant to a researcher's needs, or suggest a periodical or newsletter with interesting content. An investment in the exploration of such guides pays dividends for the researcher and librarian alike, and we encourage researchers to make themselves familiar with the guides available for particular research interests. We are continually astonished by the number of genealogists who have devoted years to research but have never consulted reference works for their area of inquiry. Researchers new and seasoned alike must be encouraged to identify, use, and return frequently to such works as their specific puzzles change over time, and as new reference works become available.

There may be a temptation to turn to resources assumed to be relevant to the researcher's previous generations because of a religious or ethnic identification, needlessly setting aside other resources of great value. In our experience, librarians have directed researchers with connections to the Hispanic communities of the San Luis Valley of southern Colorado and northern New Mexico to difficult-to-use church records. In fact, the essential first source for this long-established community is the U.S. federal census and its decennial enumerations stretching back to the establishment of American dominion after war with Mexico concluded in 1848. Census records will form a backbone for many researchers with previous generations living in the United States in 1940 or before. Likewise, researchers with previous generations living elsewhere in the world should be directed to any relevant national, state, or regional census available to them.

Other researchers may not find previous generations in a census because condition or political status precluded or shaped their enumeration. For example, researchers with ancestors held in slavery may be discouraged with the disappearance of an earlier generation into bondage and their remove by name from the U.S. federal census prior to 1870, but this merely turns the researcher to other records, and to the challenges of research in new areas. For those researchers with connections to indigenous peoples, the unique political condition of most American Indians as members of domestic dependent nations (to use the phrase of Chief Justice John Marshall in his 1832 decision *Worcester v. Georgia*) sees previous generations enumerated in earlier censuses only if they lived apart from a tribal community. Conversely, the control and disposition of tribal peoples generated extensive records. The so-called Indian censuses of reservations are readily available, indexed, and often reflect enumeration on an annual basis. A few hours with these records can provide a customer with ties to a reservation with several generations and opens the door to staggering volumes of primary sources maintained by federal authorities as well as a rich body of secondary sources from various fields of inquiry.

DIGITIZATION AND ONLINE RESOURCES

Digitization and online resources have revolutionized genealogical research, and whether available through personal subscription, library subscription, or open access databases, digital records facilitate unprecedented access and searching. Commercial enterprises have an interest in creating and meeting a demand for sources, which bodes well for the continued growth of resources. With a similar result, although from different motivations, the Church of Jesus Christ of Latter-Day Saints (LDS) actively preserves and digitizes sources relevant to genealogists the world over. Given the LDS mission worldwide, the growing numbers of LDS adherents and the theological motivation for genealogical research, there is every reason to believe resources will continue to grow at an astonishing rate.

Ironically, even as digitization has created an expectation of online access, so much material is now available that relevant digital content is likely to elude librarians and researchers. Seasoned researchers scramble to stay abreast of new additions to subscription or open access resources; new researchers express surprise when led beyond the census and a few other frequently used sources. Access does not equal awareness, and librarians should routinely share discoveries with each other and researchers, and make a concerted effort to ask adept and forthcoming researchers about their latest online finds. In many instances, we learn about new resources from our researchers, and those researchers using new databases and areas of inquiry are likely to become extraordinary resources in their own right, able to explain their experiences and insights to librarians and fellow genealogists alike. This is especially true with resources from elsewhere in the world, and it is likely the researcher encountered today with a passion for research in a distant land will become the instructor of a special genealogy subject program offered tomorrow at your library.

It is, of course, a mistake to believe all records are digitized and available online, even at a fee. Librarians must encourage researchers to explore materials available only as print or microform. What is less frequently appreciated is how many databases reflect only a portion of a collection of records, and librarians and researchers must read database descriptions and notes to understand the limits of particular databases, especially limitations of period, place, and particular religious or ethnic community included in or excluded from the records. In many instances, librarians and researchers alike can anticipate the advent of a digital resource, or better understand its strengths and weaknesses, by consulting guides to records created by researchers, national archives and libraries, or posted on genealogical wikis and online forums. Likewise, many print volumes previously available only in a handful of libraries are available online as digitized books. We have answered any number of calls from researchers and librarians alike where the request for research in a volume held in our collection was answered with a referral to Google Books and a complete text available online without cost or delay.

THE ETHNIC IDENTITY ASSIGNMENT

In recent years, we have encountered students with assignments on ethnicity, often with a requirement to research the student's family and its origins. These assignments have come to us from middle school classes, high school classes, and college and university courses. At their best, these assignments afford an opportunity to examine self-identity, community, and significant questions of ethnicity and race in the American experience. At their worst, poorly constructed assignments, often with arbitrary requirements to research three, four, or five or more generations deep into a student's past, have confused students and librarians alike, and led to frustration, anger, and even tears. We have wondered if the instructors involved in such assignments have themselves undertaken a similar effort, for it would surely demonstrate to many the impossibility of what has been required. Instructors should not be dissuaded from such assignments, but they must understand what students have been asked to research, the process it involves, and the value of close collaboration with librarians to ensure a viable assignment.

In our experience, the best of such assignments have focused on self-reflection and the research process, rather than an accumulation of an arbitrary number of generations, the identification of an original immigrant perhaps removed a dozen or more generations from the student, or other tendentious or ultimately meaningless or impossible objective. We understand the impulse for instructors to set such requirements to encourage substantial research, but the concern for substance can be realized with requirements at once more germane and flexible enough to recognize diversity in contemporary classrooms and the varied experiences students will have with their research. We especially encourage the use of research journals, where students can describe a process and sources used and find in the course of keeping such a journal an element of focus and self-reflection on the research process itself. Our most successful experiences with instructors have yielded moving research reports, deposited in our collection and shared with other researchers, and proudly presented as examples of what is possible to other instructors, students, or researchers in search of inspiration.

LETTING GO, GETTING CONNECTED, AND GIVING BACK

In addition to the numerous interest groups active online, and the many local, state, national, and international genealogical societies to join or follow for the benefit of researcher and librarian alike, it is important to remember how community and networks are built by careful cultivation of each researcher, one encounter at a time. As with any area of reference, there is a fine line between assistance and doing research for researchers. You are not a personal researcher, unless hired to be one outside of your duties as a librarian. Your purpose is to connect researchers with relevant information, not to undertake the work of examining sources, understanding them intimately, and locating the crucial relationship that has eluded a researcher. No one is owed genealogical research. And, ultimately, historical research is not easy, and there is no way to simplify the reality that researchers must invest time and effort in their exploration of the past. The librarian need not become mired in simplifying where there is no simplification to be had. Similarly, realize when to let go and afford researchers the strength and pleasure of their independence. We fail researchers when we do not empower them to make new discoveries themselves, and we deny ourselves and other researchers the opportunity to benefit from the insights gained and shared by their own efforts.

Here we turn to the extraordinary opportunity to cultivate community at your library, and see your researchers and the connections you and they make with each other become your library's greatest asset for genealogical research. Connect researchers with similar interests in a casual and ethical manner, respecting always their privacy and time, and watch how interest, expertise, and community flourish. Provide meeting space, facilitate volunteer projects of interest to the genealogical community, and bring together the leaders of different interest groups to explore common and concerted action and advocacy. Avid genealogists readily share their time, passion, and ideas with others. Today's novice, asking you questions about an unfamiliar land and its people, may become your ally, teacher, and resource for a legion of others to follow.

Index

317

About the Editors and Contributors

Kim Becnel, assistant professor of library science at Appalachian State University in Boone, North Carolina, received her MLIS and PhD from the University of South Carolina in Columbia. With experience in public libraries in Louisiana and North Carolina, she now teaches and researches in the areas of public library management, youth services, and children's literature. Her work has appeared in *Middle Management in Academic and Public Libraries* (2011), *Library Management Tips That Work* (2011), *Diversity in Youth Literature: Opening Doors through Reading* (2012), and *Public Libraries*.

Carol Smallwood received her MLS from Western Michigan University and an MA in history from Eastern Michigan University. She has recently edited the ALA anthologies *Writing and Publishing: The Librarian's Handbook*; *Librarians as Community Partners: An Outreach Handbook*; and *Pre- and Post-Retirement Tips for Librarians*. Some releases outside librarianship are *Lily's Odyssey*; *Women Writing on Family: Tips on Writing, Teaching, and Publishing*; and *Compartments: Poems on Nature, Femininity, and Other Realms* (a 2011 Pushcart nominee). Her library experience includes school, public, academic, and special libraries, as well as being an administrator and a consultant.

Barbara Stripling is an assistant professor of practice at the School of Information Studies, Syracuse University. Until January 2012, Stripling was director of library services for the New York City schools, with fifteen hundred schools and an extremely diverse population of students. Prior to New

York, Stripling was a classroom teacher, school librarian, library grant director, and director of instructional services in Colorado, North Carolina, Arkansas, and Tennessee. Stripling is the author or editor of numerous books and articles. She is president-elect of the American Library Association and will serve as president in 2013–2014.

CONTRIBUTORS

Oriana Acevedo is the multicultural consultant for the State Library of New South Wales (NSW), Sydney, Australia. In her role, Acevedo provides advice on the establishment and development of multicultural services, coordinates research into multicultural issues, and facilitates education and training programs for public library staff in NSW. Acevedo is responsible for the overall management of Cooperative Multicultural Purchasing and Cataloguing, a partnership agreement between NSW public libraries and the State Library to rationalize and improve multicultural services.

Zoia Adam-Falevai, reference paraprofessional at the Brigham Young University, Hawaii, Joseph F. Smith Library in Laie, Hawaii, obtained her bachelor's in Pacific Island studies from the Brigham Young University of Hawaii. She did her internship at the University of Hawaii with the Hamilton Library's Special Collection under the supervision of Karen Peacock in 2006. Adam-Falevai is a member of the Hawaii Library Association. She is currently a student at the University of Hawaii's Library and Information Science Program, and she plans to graduate in 2013.

Frans Albarillo, assistant professor, is the business and sociology librarian at the Brooklyn College Library, City University of New York. He received his MLISc from University of Hawaii at Manoa in 2009, in addition to his MA in linguistics (2007). His undergraduate training includes a BA in French and applied linguistics and a certificate in teaching English as a second language from Portland State University. His research interests include multicultural librarianship, business librarianship, and language and cultural rights.

Judy Anghelescu is adult collection manager at Omaha Public Library, Omaha, Nebraska. She received her MLS from Texas Woman's University. She has worked in a wide variety of libraries: Department of Defense elementary and high school libraries in England, a military base public library in England, British libraries in Cambridge, and a small-town Carnegie library in

Nebraska. She became interested in improving library services for underserved populations after attending a literacy program at a Florida public library.

Ashley Ansah, teen specialist for two branch libraries of the Des Moines Public Library system in Des Moines, Iowa, obtained her bachelor's in anthropology and international studies from the University of Iowa. She received her MLIS from Drexel University of Philadelphia. She has worked with English language learners (ELL) from a variety of countries and age groups for almost ten years. She currently resides with her husband, Josh (who graduated from ELL class as a second grader), their two sons, Kai and Tae, and their daughter, Janiya, in their hearts.

Audrey Barbakoff is an adult services librarian at Kitsap Regional Library in Bainbridge Island, Washington. In her previous position at Milwaukee Public Library, she developed and implemented services and programs for Hispanic and Latino families. Currently, she serves as an intern on the American Library Association Committee on Diversity. Her articles on public librarianship have appeared in *American Libraries*, *Public Libraries*, *Library Philosophy and Practice*, and *In the Library with the Lead Pipe*. She received her MLIS from the iSchool at the University of Washington in 2010.

Kris Baughman, MLS, received her master's in library science from the University of Missouri, Columbia. She taught middle and high school and was circulation department supervisor at Rockhurst University, Kansas City, Missouri, before becoming a media specialist with Raytown, Missouri, C-2 schools. Baughman is a member of Missouri Association of School Librarians, Greater Kansas City Association of School Librarians, and past chair of the GKCASL KC3 Reading Award Program for third-grade students in the Kansas City area. She is a contributing author in *Library Management Tips That Work* (2011).

Theresa Beaulieu, education and outreach librarian at the University of Wisconsin, Milwaukee since 2009, obtained her MLIS from the University of Arizona. Beaulieu is a member of the American Library Association and the Wisconsin Library Association. Beaulieu has worked in libraries and education for many years. She has worked for her tribe as the director of education and cultural affairs and has taught children's literature courses to undergraduate students. She is currently writing a children's book about Electa Quinney, Wisconsin's first public school teacher.

Erika Bennett, MLIS, MS, is the information literacy and instruction librarian and liaison to Schools of Education and Business at Capella University. Capella is an online, primarily graduate-degree institution, serving adult and nontraditional students. Capella has a strongly diverse learner population, with over 50 percent students of color. Bennett has presented at LOEX, ACRL Virtual, Off-Campus Library Services, and Library Technology Conference. She has also published papers in the *Journal of Library Administration* and various book chapters.

Nicky Lo Bianco is executive officer of myLanguage at the State Library of Victoria, Melbourne, Australia. Her particular interest has been working on outreach services, ensuring that libraries are accessible and relevant to the needs of all members of the community. In 2003, when working with the Australian Capital Territory public libraries, she undertook a major review of multicultural services in the territory, resulting in significant changes to service delivery and a major improvement in library use by multicultural communities.

Erin Brothen, MLIS, is education librarian at Walden University in Minneapolis, Minnesota, where she provides reference and instruction services to nontraditional students from diverse backgrounds. Walden University is entirely online, and it serves undergraduate through doctoral students located around the world. Brothen's research and publishing interests include using data to improve reference services and information literacy for adult students. She has recently presented at the fourteenth Off-Campus Library Services Conference and at the ACRL 2011 Virtual Conference.

Michael Buono is a young adult/adult reference librarian in Suffolk County, New York. He received his MLIS from CUNY Queens with a certificate in Youth Services in 2012. He works for two large suburban libraries, and he is an active member of several professional organizations. He is serving on the 2012–2014 YALSA Membership and Promotion Committee and the YALSA Continuing Education Committee. He believes that if you empower youth, then you empower us all. His website is www.michaelpbuono.com.

Allan Cho is program services librarian at the Irving K. Barber Learning Centre at UBC Library in Vancouver, B.C. As a librarian, his work supports community engagement initiatives, arts and cultural programming, and emerging technologies at the Learning Centre. Cho has worked in public and health libraries before joining UBC Library and was a reference librarian at the Humanities and Social Sciences Division at UBC Library. He has published in the areas of emerging technologies in the digital humanities.

Danielle M. Colbert-Lewis, MLIS, reference librarian at the James E. Shepard Memorial Library at North Carolina Central University in Durham, holds the MLIS degree from the University of Pittsburgh, the MEd degree in education leadership and policy studies from Virginia Tech, and the BA degree in anthropology from the University of Virginia. As a reference librarian, Colbert-Lewis instructs classes for diverse populations of students, faculty, and staff. Her research interests include mentoring new librarians of underrepresented cultural backgrounds and legal issues in librarianship and higher education.

Sean C. D. Colbert-Lewis Sr., PhD, serves North Carolina Central University in Durham as assistant professor of history and the history department's director of the secondary social studies teacher certification program. Colbert-Lewis holds BA and MA degrees in history from Virginia Tech and MEd and PhD degrees in education from the University of Virginia. As a 2011 National Board Certified Teacher, he has extensive experience in conducting research and diversity workshops for librarians, principals, superintendents, teachers, and university faculty on how to incorporate multicultural education in their respective occupations.

Ada Con is the library programs coordinator for the Fraser Valley Regional Library, Abbotsford, British Columbia. A graduate of the University of British Columbia, Con has worked in various capacities including that of a reference librarian, area coordinator, library manager at Terry Fox Library, and the diversity services and programming coordinator. She focuses on systemwide multilingual collections, services, and programming. Con has served many years on the British Columbia Library Association's Diversity and Multicultural Services Committee.

J. Wendel Cox is senior special collection librarian in the Western History/ Genealogy Department of the Denver Public Library in Denver, Colorado. He holds a doctorate in American history from the University of Minnesota and an MLIS from the University of Wisconsin, Milwaukee. He has taught and worked at the University of Minnesota, Arizona State University, the University of Minnesota, Morris, and the University of Kentucky. His current research concerns rabies and the politics of dogs in Denver.

Elizabeth Cramer is lead catalog librarian and collections librarian for foreign languages and literatures at Appalachian State University in Boone, North Carolina. She teaches French at the university and enjoys collaborating with university colleagues to improve library resources/services to international students and scholars, as well as domestic students studying abroad. Cramer is active with ALA International Relations Round Table. She has an

MLS from Kent State University, an MA in French from Appalachian State University, and a doctorate in educational leadership from Appalachian State University.

LaVentra E. Danquah, librarian at Shiffman Medical Library, Wayne State University, in Detroit, Michigan, obtained her MLIS from Wayne State University. She has peer-reviewed publications in *Medical Reference Services Quarterly*, *Journal of Consumer Health on the Internet*, *MLA Forum*, and has served as a reviewer for *Journal of the National Medical Association*. Her most recent publication, "Achievements of Selected Twenty-First-Century African American Health Sciences Librarians," appears in *The Twenty-First-Century Black Librarian in America: Issues and Challenges* (2012). Danquah is a consumer health information advocate and speaks frequently at professional meetings.

Becky DeMartini graduated from BYU-Hawaii in 2001 and continued on to receive her MLISc from the University of Hawaii, Manoa in 2005. She returned to BYU-Hawaii in Laie as the reference technology librarian for the Joseph F. Smith Library in 2006. DeMartini creates and maintains the library's website and online presence. She is also responsible for continued access to all electronic resources. She teaches various classes and workshops and participates in marketing the library. She has enjoyed serving as the president of the Hawaii Library Association.

Nyssa Densley worked as a teen and adult services librarian with the Pima County Public Library in Tucson, Arizona, focusing on refugee and immigrant services. At the time of publication, she has accepted a position as assistant branch manager with the Salt Lake County Library System, in Utah. She obtained her MLIS from the University of Arizona and is a member of the American Library Association. She has presented at library conferences about multicultural programming. Her joint presentation at the Arizona Library Association's 2010 conference received the President's Program Award.

Mark Donnelly was a senior outreach librarian for Queens Library in New York City from 2000 to 2011. He is a writer of poetry, plays, and short stories, with numerous publication credits. He holds an MLS from C. W. Post College of Long Island University and an MFA in creative writing from Brooklyn College of the City University of New York. He is a member of the Dramatists Guild of America and of Irish American Writers and Artists.

Nicole Eva has been a librarian at the University of Lethbridge since graduating with her MLIS from the University of Western Ontario in 2008. She also holds a bachelor of commerce with a major in marketing. She currently works at the University of Lethbridge Library in Lethbridge, Alberta, where she is the chair of the student engagement team as well as subject liaison for the faculty of management and departments of economics and religious studies. She teaches both subject-related and general information literacy classes, as well as working on the reference desk.

Staci Falkowitz is the manager of the Scaleybark Branch of the Charlotte Mecklenburg Library in Charlotte, North Carolina. She received her MLIS from the University of North Carolina at Greensboro, where she served as president of LISSA. She is a member of Beta Phi Mu, ALA, PLA, and REFORMA. She has served on several ALA/PLA committees, including the Advancement of Literacy Awards Jury, the Basic Education and Literacy Resources Committee, and as the OLOS Delegate to the ALA Advocacy Coordinating Committee in 2009.

Kristina Gomez is a reference librarian at Milwaukee Public Library in Milwaukee, Wisconsin. She assisted in the development and implementation of a Spanish language virtual reference service for Wisconsin residents. She received her MLS from the University of Wisconsin Madison School of Library and Information Studies, where she received the Diane McAfee Hopkins Diversity Award. Gomez is a member of the American Library Association, Wisconsin Library Association, and REFORMA. She was a 2011 American Library Association Emerging Leader and has appeared in *Public Libraries.*

Alice Graves is a solo career college librarian in Tampa, Florida. She received her MLIS from the University of South Florida. She is a member of the American Library Association, the Association of Research and College Libraries, and the Florida Library Association. Graves is also a member of Beta Phi Mu, the library and information science honor society. Before becoming a librarian, Graves taught college English and worked as a writer for several print and web publications.

April Grey is the head of cataloging at the University of Louisiana at Lafayette. Her hometown is North Tonawanda, New York. After completing her master's of library science at the University at Buffalo, Grey cataloged for Coutts Information Services and Ingram Content Group. Grey served as catalog librarian at Medaille College in Buffalo, New York. Her degrees include a bachelor of arts in psychology and master's in education. Grey serves on the Louisiana Library Association Literary Award Committee and the ALCTS CCS/PCC Committee on Continuing Education Training Materials.

Cynthia Houston is an associate professor of library media education at Western Kentucky University in Bowling Green. She received her MLIS from Clarion University and her PhD in curriculum and instruction from Southern Illinois University, Carbondale. She teaches courses in cataloging, children's literature, and information services. Her research interests range from exploring the dynamic world of digital resources, to bilingual children's literature, international comparative librarianship, and monitoring the status of school libraries in Kentucky.

Amy Hughes, MS, MLS, is an academic programs librarian at Northern Arizona University's Cline Library in Flagstaff. Previously she worked as a librarian and assistant professor at Fairmont State University in Fairmont, West Virginia. She currently works with and provides course support to the College of Social and Behavioral Sciences and the College of Education. Her interests include resource management and library services to rural populations and American Indian tribal communities, including distance education opportunities.

James K. Jeffrey is special collection librarian for genealogy in the Western History/Genealogy Department of the Denver Public Library in Denver, Colorado. He graduated from Marshall University with a BA in history. His graduate studies have included history and geography at Marshall University; archives and local history at the University of Denver; church history at the Iliff School of Theology in Denver; and information sciences at Emporia State University in Emporia, Kansas. He was the 2004 recipient of the P. William Filby Award for Excellence in Genealogical Librarianship from the National Genealogical Society.

Ladislava Khailova, PhD, is an associate professor at Northern Illinois University in DeKalb, Illinois, serving as the university libraries' humanities and social sciences subject specialist and coordinator of services for students with disabilities. Her research interests gravitate toward the historical and cultural factors that shape constructions of the social other, be it in terms of disability, race, ethnicity, or gender. Khailova has published articles on various genres of twentieth-century American literature, as well as on the implementation of ADA in libraries and classrooms.

Diana J. Lennon provides services and programs to the Latino community at the Greenburgh Public Library in Elmsford, New York. Currently enrolled in an MLIS program at Long Island University, Lennon was named the American Library Association's 2010 Miriam L. Hornback Scholar and received a 2010 New York Library Association/Public Libraries Section Conference Scholarship. Her reviews of children's and young adult books are in *Partes de Un Todo (Parts of a Whole)*, published by the Fundación Germán Sánchez Ruipérez in Spain. She received a master's degree in Spanish literature from Vanderbilt University.

Meryle A. Leonard is the outreach manager for Charlotte Mecklenburg Library in North Carolina, coordinating the design, development, and evaluation of a centralized delivery of outreach services for the twenty-branch system. Leonard was a 2007 Lifelong Access Institute Fellow. In 2009 she contributed two articles in the ALA book *Librarians as Community Partners: An Outreach Handbook*. Her library received the 2006 National Award for Museum and Library Services, John Colton Dana Library Public Relations Award, and the 2008 Mora Award. Charlotte Mecklenburg Library's outreach efforts are visible throughout the library's service area.

Joyce Martin is curator of the Labriola National American Indian Data Center, Department of Archives and Special Collections, University Libraries, Arizona State University. She earned a master's in anthropology and museum studies from Arizona State University in 1997 and a master's in information and library science from the University of Arizona in 2007 and is Phi Beta Kappa. Martin edits the *Labriola Center Newsletter* and holds memberships in the Arizona Library Association and the Society of Southwestern Archivists, where she is on the publications committee.

Kelly Rhodes McBride is the lead librarian for information literacy in Belk Library and Information Commons at Appalachian State University in Boone, North Carolina. Her primary responsibilities are in the development and assessment of the library's information literacy and instruction program. She has published and presented on topics covering information literacy, instruction, and assessment at the American Library Association, the Library Orientation Exchange, the North Carolina Library Association, and the Georgia International Conference on Information Literacy.

Derek Mosley is the archivist and assistant director of the Ernest J. Gaines Center at the University of Louisiana at Lafayette. He attended Morehouse College in Atlanta, Georgia, and graduated with a bachelor of arts degree in history and a minor in African American studies. Choosing to continue his education, Mosley attended Simmons College Graduate School of Library and Information Science in Boston and earned a master of science degree with a concentration in archives management. While at Simmons he interned at Tufts University Digital Collections and Archives and the Harvard University Arnold Arboretum.

Joyce Nutta is an associate professor at the University of Central Florida School of Teaching, Learning, and Leadership in Orlando, Florida. She specialized in second language acquisition at the University of South Florida and has been teaching ESL in Florida since 1988. Her PhD is in second language acquisition/instructional technology. She has published many works in the field and is currently working with a PhD candidate who runs the new ESL program at the Orange County Library System.

Maria A. Pacino, EdD, is director and professor of school library programs at Azusa Pacific University in Azusa, California. Prior to that, she was also the chair of the Department of Advanced Studies in Education. She teaches other courses in the School of Education at the master's and doctoral levels. Her research includes diversity, literacy, and technology. She has presented at national and international conferences and has several publications, including the book *Reflections on Equity, Diversity, and Schooling* (2008). Pacino is also a commissioner at the Azusa City Library.

Rebecca Marcum Parker earned her bachelor's in library science education and MA in literature from the University of Central Missouri. Her experience includes three years as a rural bookmobile librarian and fourteen years as inner-city school librarian with the Kansas City (Missouri) School District. She is a member of the Midwest Center for Holocaust Education's Isak Federman Teaching Cadre, the Missouri Association for School Librarians, and the Greater Kansas City Association of School Librarians. She is a contributing author in *Library Management Tips That Work* (2011) and *How to Thrive as a Solo Librarian* (2012).

Padma Polepeddi is the supervisor of Eloise May Library at the Arapahoe Library District in Arapahoe County, Colorado. She handles the day-to-day operations of this high-volume library branch, which serves a widely diverse population. She was named a 2008 *Library Journal* Mover and Shaker for her passion for diversity. She earned her MA in English from the University of Hyderabad, India, and is currently pursuing her doctoral studies in library and information management at Emporia State University, Emporia, Kansas.

Heather Ross is a librarian supervisor with the Pima County Public Library in Tucson, Arizona, and has worked in both adult and children's services. A member of the library's "Welcome to America" work group, Ross advocates for multicultural and refugee populations. Her joint presentation at the Arizona Library Association's 2010 conference was awarded the President's Program Award. Ross is also a member of the 2012 Leadership Team for the Refugee Integration Service Provider Network of Tucson.

Amauri Serrano is the humanities collections librarian at Appalachian State University in Boone, North Carolina, where she is responsible for selection and management of all library materials for English, history, art and design, and theatre and dance. Serrano has taught English as a Second Language in Italy and the Italian language at the college level. She is a member of the American Library Association, the Association of College and Research Libraries, and the Modern Language Association. She holds an MS in library and information science, an MA in Italian literature, and BAs in history and Italian from the University of Illinois, Urbana-Champaign.

Xiaorong Shao, PhD, is an information literacy librarian in Belk Library and Information Commons at Appalachian State University in Boone, North Carolina. Her primary responsibilities are conducting library instruction, individual research consultations, reference services, and library outreach to diverse and international patrons. Shao has published ten articles during the last five years in the areas of international librarianship, library services for international users, and other areas of academic interests. She has collaborated with scholars and students from universities in the United States and abroad.

Fantasia Thorne has been employed at Syracuse University Bird Library, in Syracuse, New York, since 2009 as a Learning Commons librarian, and also at the Onondaga County Public Library as a substitute part-time librarian. She holds a BA in English from Southern Connecticut State University and an MLIS from Simmons College. She is a member of the American Library Association, as well as the Black Caucus of the American Library Association. She serves as the liaison between Bird Library and the office of multicultural affairs.

Carissa Tsosie, MLS, is a Navajo woman from Arizona. Tsosie earned degrees in anthropology and history at Northern Arizona University before graduating with her MLS from the University of Arizona. She is currently a graduate student in history at Northern Arizona University and is a library specialist at Cline Library. As library specialist, her responsibilities include aiding Native American students in reaching success in higher education through partnerships with the Native American Student Services office and the Commission for Native Americans, and through the Native American and Indigenous Film Series.

Julie Ventura received her MLS from Emporia State University in Kansas and is now branch manager of the South Creek Library, part of the Orange County Library System in Orlando, Florida. She has been with the library system since 2002. She is project director for the Congressionally Directed Grant, a three-year, $500,000 project aimed at improving books and media offerings to the Hispanic population in Orlando, as well as increasing patron awareness and designing new products and services. This is her first published work.

Donna Walker is the manager of neighborhood libraries at the Arapahoe Library District in Arapahoe County, Colorado. She oversees five facilities and enterprise-wide services in Child and Family Library Services and Outreach. She was named a 2011 *Library Journal* Mover and Shaker for advocacy to underserved populations. Recently, Walker presented at the ABOS/ARSL conference in 2010 and at PLA in 2012 on innovations in mobile library services. She earned her MLIS at the University of Washington and her MA in English at the University of Denver.

Kimberly Williams, associate director in the office of multicultural affairs, Syracuse University, Syracuse, New York, since 2005, obtained her master's in human resource management from the University of Charleston in Charleston, West Virginia, in 2005 and a second master's degree in 2011 in communications and rhetorical studies from Syracuse University in Syracuse, New York. She liaisons with Bird Library at Syracuse University frequently on many initiatives, including those directly related to issues of privilege and disenfranchisement.

Wendy G. Wu has served as public services librarian at Shiffman Medical Library, Wayne State University, Detroit, Michigan, since 1996. Wu is a member of the Medical Library Association (MLA) and Metropolitan Detroit Medical Library Group. She has published articles in *Bulletin of the Medical Library Association, Medical Reference Services Quarterly, Informed Librarian Online, Journal of Electronic Resources in Medical Libraries, Internet Reference Services Quarterly*, and *Health Care on the Internet* and presented at professional organization conferences. Wu received a 1999 MLA Career Development grant and WHO Scholarship in 1989.

Made in the USA
Middletown, DE
31 May 2018